MILLER'S YEAR BOOK—A YEAR'S DAILY READINGS
J.R. Miller

A verse of Scripture in the morning, may become a blessing for all the day. It may sing in the heart as a *sweet song,* from morning until evening. It may become a *liturgy of prayer* in which the soul shall voice its deepest needs and hungers—amid toils, struggles, and cares. It may be a guide through perplexing tangles, 'God's voice' whispering cheer, a *comforter* breathing peace in sorrow.

JANUARY

January 1.

"May the Lord bless you and protect you.
May the Lord smile on you and be gracious to you.
May the Lord show you his favor and give you his peace."
   Numbers 6:24-26

In the first days of a new year, we all say to our friends and neighbors, "Happy New Year!" Our hearts are full of generous feelings and wishes for all we meet. But what can we do to *give* them a happy new year? We cannot compel their circumstances into fortunate adjustments, so as to produce happiness. Besides, we cannot know what would be the truest and best blessings for our friends.

After all, the only really safe thing is to pray that God may be with them through the year, and may bless them in his own best and truest way. He knows better than we do—what is the best blessing.

January 2.

"You have made your way around this hill country long enough; now *turn north.*" Deuteronomy 2:3

We ought never to be willing to live any year—just as we lived the last one. No one is striving after the best things—who is not intent on an *upward* and a *forward* movement continually. The circular movement is essential too, the going around and around in the old grooves, routine work, daily tasks; yet, even in this *treadmill round*, there should be *constant progress*. We ought to do the same things, better each day. Then in the midst of the outward routine—our inner life ought to be growing in earnestness, in force, in strength, in depth.

Yet there are some people whose life year by year is only a going around and around in the old beaten paths, with no *onward* movement. They are like men who walk in a circular course for a prize, covering a thousand miles, perhaps, but ending just where they began. Rather, our daily walk should be like one whose path goes around a mountain, but climbs a little *higher* with each circuit, until at last he gains the clear summit, and looks into the face of God. While we must do in a measure the same things every day—we should do them a little better with each repetition.

January 3.

"The jar of flour was not used up—and the jug of oil did not run dry." 1 Kings 17:16

There was always just a *little* flour and a little oil—but the supply never grew any less. After each day's food had been taken out—there was another day's left. There was never a *month's* supply ahead, nor even *two days'* supply. The added provision came—only as there was need. Thus there was in that household, a continuous lesson in faith. But the food of no day failed.

The lesson is, that God wants us to *live by the day*. The same truth is taught us in the prayer Christ gave: "Give us this day, our daily bread." Enough for the day is all we are to ask. God does not promise supplies in advance. If we have only bread for today, and are doing our duty faithfully, we may trust him until tomorrow, for tomorrow's food. And it will surely come, for God's Word fails not.

It is well that we get this lesson fixed in our heart at the beginning of the year. As the *days* come, each one will bring with it its own little basket, carrying a day's supplies—but no more!

January 4.

"If you *continue* in My Word, then you really are My disciples." John 8:31

It is not enough to *begin*; *continuance* is necessary. Mere *enrollment* will not make one a scholar; the pupil must *continue* in the school through all the long course, until he has mastered every branch. One who has observed the course of men for many years, says that success in life depends upon *staying power*. The reason for failure in most cases—is lack of perseverance. Men get tired and give up. There are thousands who *begin* to follow Christ—but who, when discouragements come, faint and drop out.

To *continue* in Christ's word—is to *obey* him. We must do it continuously too; not today only—but tomorrow as well, and tomorrow, and tomorrow, unto the end.

There is another way of abiding in the word of Christ. Many of his words are *promises*. The forests in summer days are full of bird-nests. They are hidden among the leaves. The little birds know where they are; and when a storm arises, or when night draws on, they fly each to his own nest. So the promises of God are hidden in the Bible, like nests in the great forests; and there we should fly in any danger or alarm, hiding there in *our soul's nest* until the storm be over and past. There are no castles in this world so impregnable, as the words of Christ.

January 5.

"We must do the works of Him who sent Me while it is *day*. Night is coming when no one can work." John 9:4

We are all in this world on divine missions, are all sent from God to take some specific part in blessing the world. To do this—we have just a day of time. A *day* is a brief time. It is a fixed time. When the sun comes to his going down, no power in the universe can prolong his stay for one minute.

Yet the *day* is long enough for God's plan. The sun never sets too soon for his purpose. Each life is long enough for the little part of the world's work allotted to it. This is true even of the infant that lives only an hour, merely coming into this world, smiling its blessing, and flying away. It is true of the child, of the young man or young woman, of him who dies in the maturity of his powers with his hands yet full of unfinished tasks. No one can ever offer as an excuse for an unfinished life-work, that the time given to him was too short. It is always long enough, if only every moment of it is filled with simple faithfulness.

To have our work completed at the end, we must do it while the *day* lasts, for there will be no opportunity afterward. If we are living earnestly, we shall live all the time under the pressure of the consciousness, that *the time is short*. We must not waste nor lose a moment. Soon it will be night—when we cannot work!

January 6.

"The *pillar of cloud* moved from in front of them and stood behind them." Exodus 14:19

It is not always *guidance* that we most need. Sometimes we must *stand still*, with danger all around us, and then God goes behind us to shelter us. He always suits himself to our need. When we require guidance—he leads us. But when we need protection—he puts himself between us and the danger.

There is something very striking in this picture the *divine presence* moving from before, and becoming a wall between Israel and their enemies. There are some mother-birds, storks for instance,

which cover their young with their own body in time of peril, to shield them, receiving the dart themselves. Human love often interposes itself as a shield to protect its own. *On the cross, Jesus bared his bosom to receive the storm of wrath—* that on his people no blast of the awful tempest might strike!

But not only does Christ put himself between us and our *sins*; he puts himself also between us and *danger*. The Lord God is our shield. Many of our dangers come upon us *from behind*. They are stealthy, insidious, assaulting us when we are unaware of their nearness. The tempter is cunning and shrewd. He does not meet us full-front. It is a comfort to know that Christ comes behind us—when it is there we need the protection.

January 7.

"But store up for yourselves treasures in heaven, where moth and rust do not destroy, and where thieves do not break in and steal." Matthew 6:20

Saving, in order to "lay up for a rainy day", is universally commended. By just so much more as the object is higher, is it commendable to *economize* in order to "lay up treasures in heaven." We really have—only what we have used well for Christ. When one has learned this secret of *banking in heaven*, one has the true *philosopher's stone* which turns everything to gold. The simplest possessions, are transformed into eternal treasures. A threadbare coat becomes a robe of righteousness, a last year's bonnet a crown of glory, when worn in self-denying economy for Christ's sake. We should live always for the *highest* and *best* things!

January 8.

"You are my friends—if you do whatever I command you." John 15:14

There is something very sweet in the thought, that we may be Christ's friends, and that he opens all his heart to us. "The secret of the Lord is with those who fear him." This means that if we are Christ's friends—he takes us into the closest intimacy. Not many of us realize all that is possible, in the way of companionship with Christ. If we are on terms of unhindered friendship with him—we can indeed talk with him freely, intimately, as friend with friend.

"How does he talk with us?" some one asks. A heathen convert said, *"When I pray—I talk to Christ! When I read my* **Bible**—*Christ speaks to me!"* If we live close to Christ—the words of Scripture are very plain to us; Christ himself indeed speaks to us in them.

There was a godly man in Germany, named Bengel, who was noted for his intimacy with Christ. A friend desired to watch the saintly man at his devotions. So he concealed himself one night in his room. Bengel sat long at his table reading his New Testament. The hours passed. At length the clock struck midnight, and the old man spread out his hands, and said with great joy, "Dear Lord Jesus, we are on the same old terms." Then closing his book he was soon in bed and asleep. He had learned the secret of friendship with Christ.

January 9.

"So he called ten of his servants and gave them ten *pounds*. 'Put this money to work,' he said, 'until I come back.'" Luke 19:13

We are *doing business* in this world for Christ. Each one of us has something of His—a *pound* which He has entrusted to us to trade with as his agent. Our *life* itself, with all its powers, its endowments, its opportunities, its privileges, its blessings, its possibilities—is our pound. Our *life* is not our own. We are not in this world merely to have a good time for a few years. Life is a *trust*. We are not done with it either, when we have lived it through to its last day. We must render an *account* of it to him who gave it to us. Our business is to gather gains through our trading with our Lord's money. We are required to make the *most* that is possible of our life!

People often speak of the *solemnity of dying*. It is a grave and serious matter—but it is a great deal more solemn thing to *live*. Dying is but giving back into God's hand his own gift—life. If we have *lived well*, dying is victory, glory, the trampling of life's fragile vanities to fragments, as our soul bursts into real and full life and blessedness.

It is *living* then, which is serious and solemn. Life to its last particle is our Lord's property, entrusted to us to be used so that it shall grow. Then comes the judgment. We shall have to look up into our Lord's face, and tell him what we have done with his *pound*. We shall be expected to return our trust, not , only kept safe—but enhanced in value!

January 10.

"The first came forward and said—*Master, your pound has earned **ten** more pounds!"* Luke 19:16

We always find these *ten-pound servants* among the followers of Christ. They are those Christians who, from the very beginning, strive to reach the *best* things attainable in life—through divine grace. They are not content with being merely saved from sin's guilt, with being mere members of the church. They make their *consecration* to Christ complete, keeping nothing back. They set their ideal of obedience to their Lord at the mark of *perfectness*, and are not slack in their striving, until they reach the mark in heaven. They seek to follow Christ wholly, fully, with their whole heart. They accept every duty—without regard to its cost. They seek to be like Christ, imitating him in all the elements of his character. They give their whole energy to the work and service of Christ. They lie, like John, on the

Master's bosom, and their souls are struck through, as it were, with the Master's loving spirit.

So these men and women grow at last into a saintliness, a spiritual beauty, and a power of *usefulness* and *influence*, by which they are set apart among Christians, shining with *brighter luster*than other stars in the *galaxy of the church*. Their one *pound* has made *ten* pounds more! Their *high spiritual attainment* has been won by their diligent and wise use of the pound with which they began!

January 11.

"The second came and said—*Master, your pound has earned five pounds!"* Luke 19:18

Christ gives into no man's hand at the beginning of his life—a finely trained, fully developed mind. The great poets and writers of the world, began with only *one pound*. There was *capacity* for growth—but that was all. Christ gives to no one at the start a noble, full-statured, rich, transfigured Christian character, with spiritual graces all blossoming out. The most saintly Christians began with very little saintliness, very little spiritual power. The most useful men in the church, began with a very small and imperfect sort of usefulness.

Those whose *influence* for good now touches thousands of lives, and extends over whole communities, or fills an entire country—had nothing to begin with—but *one little pound of capacity* which the Master entrusted to them. This is the principle on which all our Lord's gifts are distributed. He puts into our hands a *little* at first; and as we *use* what we have, and gain experience, and show ability, and prove faithful to our trust—he adds more and more, giving us all we can use well, and as fast as we can use it!

January 12.

"Those who hope in the LORD will renew their strength. They will soar on wings like eagles; they will run and not grow weary, they will walk and not be faint!" Isaiah 40:31

The source of strength in any life—must be God. It is only when we are co-workers with him—that we are unconquerable. If we would be strong, therefore, able to resist sin, able to do valiant battle for the truth, able to touch other lives with healing, uplifting influences—we must *abide in Christ*. Then *his strength* shall be in our heart and in our arm.

It is told of General Gordon, that each morning, during his journey in the Soudan country, for half an hour there lay outside his *tent a white handkerchief.* The whole camp knew well what it meant, and looked upon the little signal with the utmost respect; no foot dared cross the threshold of that tent while the little guard lay there. No message, however pressing, was to be delivered. Matters of life and death must wait until the *white signal* was taken away. Everybody in the camp knew that God and Gordon were communing together. Sweet is the communion of the spirit—which obtains nearness to its God. Powerful is the influence of the soul that hourly longs to draw near to its God and drink in the inspiring draughts of his presence.

January 13.

"Whoever is fearful and trembling—let him return!" Judges 7:3

Through God wanted only a *few* men—he wanted the *best*. So the first thing was to *weed out the incompetent*. The army would be stronger with all these sent home—rather than with them all straggling along. There were twenty thousand cowards; and the ten thousand brave men would be stronger alone than the thirty thousand, having the timid thousands among them.

Timidity is infectious. Many a church would be stronger if it were weeded out—just as Gideon's army was. Its weakness lies in its great numbers, not because numbers necessarily weaken—but because there are so many half-hearted people on the church roll. They have lost their interest, if they ever had any, and are indifferent, without thorough consecration. They add no strength—but only *hinder* the other members and dampen their zeal.

January 14.

"I now establish my covenant with you and with your descendants after you and with *every living creature* that was with you—the birds, the livestock and all the wild animals, all those that came out of the ark with you—every living creature on earth." Genesis 9:9-10

It is strange how God's care extends even to animals. This covenant was not with *man* only—but with all the *animal* creation as well. Think of God making a covenant with the *cattle* that roam in the valleys, the *sheep* that graze in the meadows, the *birds* that fly in the air, and even with the *insects* that chirp in the fields. Yet that is what he did! We know, too, that this *divine care* is real. There are other promises which contain the same assurances.

"He feeds the wild animals, and the young ravens cry to him for food." Psalm 147:9. Our Lord said, "Look at the birds. They don't need to plant or harvest or put food in barns—because your heavenly Father feeds them!" Matthew 6:26. God cares for birds. There is a promise, too, for the flowers, "Look at the lilies and how they grow. They don't work or make their clothing, yet Solomon in all his glory was not dressed as beautifully as they are!" Jesus says.

Of course the lesson for us from all this, is the one which Jesus taught. If God cares for the birds and flowers—how much more will he care for his own children! Therefore we ought to trust him without fear!

January 15.

"I have set my *rainbow* in the clouds, and it will be the sign of the covenant between me and the earth." Genesis 9:13

There can be no *rainbow*—unless it is *raining*. So we cannot see the brightest glory of God's grace, without entering into the experiences of trial. We can learn the full preciousness of the divine promises, only in the circumstances of *need* for which they were given.

A young friend told me that she had seen richer revealings of the love of Christ in the weeks she had been in her sick-room, than in all the former years of her life. *Words of God* which she had known from childhood, had flashed out then for the first time in the rich splendor of their meaning! There had been no clouds in her life before—all was health and happiness, and she had not seen the *rainbow hues*.

The same is true of all the divine comforts; we never can know the best of their meaning—until the sorrow comes in which they are meant to give strength. A beatitude reads: "Blessed are those who *mourn*—for they shall be *comforted*." We cannot receive the comfort—until we mourn. Every Christian who has passed through sorrow understands this. In the deepening darkness—the lights in the heavenly promises flashed out bright and clear, showing him for the first time—the fullness of their blessed comfort.

January 16

"I am God Almighty; walk before Me and *be perfect*." Genesis 17:1

"Perfection is impossible!" we are in the habit of saying; and therefore we do not try to reach perfection. It is better for us always to keep our aim high, although we cannot hope to reach it. If we have low ideals and aims—our attainments will be low. We cannot look with approval upon anything lower than the perfect beauty of God Himself, and not have the beauty of our own life dimmed thereby. We should always keep perfection before us—as our aim. We should keep our eyes ever fixed upon the perfect model, Jesus Christ!

Jesus taught, "Be perfect, therefore, as your heavenly Father is perfect." Matthew 5:48. We are always to seek to model our life upon the divine pattern. Of course we cannot reach this lofty standard in a day—but the way to Christlikeness, is to strive toward it.

When a child begins to write, his scrawling lines fall far short of the beauty of the original at the top of the page. Book after book he fills with his scribbling—but if he is diligent, each new page shows a little improvement, and by and by his writing rivals the original. We can learn to live holy and sweetly, only in the same way. Begin where you can, no matter how imperfect or faulty your life—but strive always toward perfection, and at last you shall be like Christ! That is the hope which shines before us—when we shall see Him as He is—and shall be like Him!

January 17

"Praise the LORD, O my soul, and forget not all his benefits—who *forgives* all your sins and *heals* all your diseases, who *redeems* your life from the pit and crowns you with love and compassion, who satisfies your desires with good things!" Psalm 103:2-5

What an enumeration of divine blessings this is! Any one of them is worth more than all earth's treasures combined!

If we are not forgiven—we must rest forever under the burden of sin, a weight greater than all the Alps! But God forgives—and forgives all our sins—and forgives freely, fully and forever!

If we are not healed—we must be sick forever, sick with the plague and leprosy of sin! But God heals—and heals all our evils, and heals completely!

If we are not saved from the dangers of this ensnaring world—we never can reach heaven! But God keeps, rescues, and saves our life from all impending destructions!

Earth's crowns are made of thorns, and at the best are only what the children call, 'play-crowns', for they are but of leaves that wither, or of gold and gems that will not last. But God crowns His people with crowns of love and compassion, which are real and radiant, which shall never fade—but shall shine forever, becoming crowns of eternal life and glory in heaven!

This world cannot satisfy a heart's deepest cravings. Its possessions only make the hunger more intense! But God satisfies the souls of His people, and meets all their cravings and hungers with truly good and eternal realities!

January 18.

"Cast your burden upon the Lord—and He shall *sustain* you!" Psalm 45:22

There are some mistaken notions current concerning the ways in which God would help us. People think that whenever they have a little trouble, a bit of hard path to go over, a load to carry, a sorrow to endure—all they have to do is to call upon God, and He will at once take away their sorrow, or free them from the trouble. But this is not the way God helps us! His purpose of love concerning us is—not to make all things easy for us—but to make something of us!

When we ask God to save us from our trouble, to take the struggles out of our life, to make the paths mossy, to lift off every heavy load—He will not do it! It would be most unloving in Him to accommodate us. We must carry the burden ourselves! All God promises is, to sustain us—as we carry it! He wants us to learn life's lessons, and to do this—we must be left to work out the problems for ourselves.

There are rich blessings which can be gotten, only in sorrow. It would be short-sighted love indeed—which would heed our cries, and spare us from sorrow—and thus deprive us of the wonderful blessings which can be gotten only in sorrow! God is too good to us to answer our prayers—which would save us from pain, cost, and sacrifice today—at the price of holier, better, truer life in the end. He would not rob us of the blessing that is in the burden—which we can get only by carrying it!

January 19.

"He knows our frame; He remembers that we are but dust!" Psalm 103:14

God does not treat us as if we were strong, holy, and unfallen angels! He does not forget that we are weak, that it is hard for us to live right, that we are easily tempted and overcome. He is very patient and gentle with us when we have sinned—binding up our wounds, restoring our soul. He does not lay upon us loads too great for us—for He knows how weak we are! He gives us help, too, with our burdens—that we need not faint under them.

We ought to get a great deal of comfort out of these words.

You say you are so *weak* that you cannot resist temptation. Does not God know it? Will He not help you to overcome?

You are *weary* through trouble or burden-bearing—but God knows all about it! You find your work hard, and cannot see how you are ever to get through with it; but God understands. He knows how *frail* you are; He remembers that you are only dust. He is pitiful, and gives always *needed* help!

January 20.

"Take My yoke upon you and learn from Me, because I am gentle and humble in heart—and you will find rest for your souls!" Matthew 11:29

We have to learn to live—if ever we are to live worthily. No one becomes a fine musician, without much learning. Nor can anyone take a piece of canvas, with palette, paints, and brushes—and at once paint a masterpiece.

Learning to live beautifully—is harder than learning music or art. We must learn to live—and the lessons are hard, requiring long years of patience and practice. But we ought to learn the art of living, whatever the cost may be!

Life is a sacred trust. We are accountable for it to God, who gave it to us. We are required to make the most of our abilities, training them to their best capacity. By self-discipline, we are to get the perfect mastery of our being—and then do the things which we were made to do.

Yet many people never seriously try to learn to live! This is unworthy a being endowed with immortality, and sent forth on a divine errand. We should live in a way, which will not shame us when we come to the end.

January 21.

"Whoever wants to become great among you—must be your servant; and whoever wants to be first—must be your slave." Matthew 20:26-27

There are some people with a little measure of "position" who seem to accept all favors shown to them, and all services rendered to them by others, as *due* to them because of their exalted rank, or their exceeding importance among men. They stand upon their dignity, and in effect *demand* attention, and a degree of subserviency from their plain, ordinary fellow-men. They complain, if by any accident they appear not to receive their due quota of honor. They seem to feel that their high place among men—entitles them to a great deal of consideration; and they are offended if they do not get it!

It would seem, however, in the light of our Lord's teaching, that the truly *greatest* among men—are those who are most ready to *serve*. The haughty spirit described above, is scarcely, therefore, a mark of real greatness in Christ's eye—but really, a mark of littleness. All self-seeking is littleness. The *law of service* is taken from the very heart of God; nothing else is truly great.

January 22.

"The Son of Man did not come to be served—but to serve, and to give his life as a ransom for many!" Matthew 20:28

The art of photography is now so perfect, that the whole picture of a large newspaper can be taken in miniature so small, as to be carried in a little pendant—and yet every letter and point be perfect.

Just so, the whole life of Christ is photographed in one little phrase, "not to be served—but to serve." He came not to be served; if this had been His aim—He would never have left heaven's glory, where He lacked nothing, where angels praised Him and ministered unto Him. He came to serve. He went about doing good. He altogether forgot Himself. He served all he met—who would receive His service. At last He gave His life in uttermost service giving it as a sin-atoning ransom for others. He came not to be served—but to serve.

You say you want to be like Christ. You ask Him to print His own image on your heart. Here, then is the image! It is no vague dream of perfection that we are to think of—when we ask to be made like Christ. The Catholic monks thought that they were becoming like Christ—when they went into the wilderness, away from men, to live in cold cells. But that is not the what this picture suggests. "To serve"—that is the Christlike thing! Instead of fleeing away from the world—we are to live among men, to serve them, to seek to bless them, to do them good, to give our life for them!

January 23.

"No longer do I call you *servants* . . . I have called you *friends*." John 15:15.

If we *ask*, "What is the best that *Christ's friendship* can be to any soul?" We may *answer*, "It is shelter, comfort, rest, inmost refreshment, guidance, and far more. Christ is an atmosphere about us—an atmosphere of love, warm with all tender influences, all healthful inspirations, all holy impulses. Christ comes into all our life—as our *friend*—so really, so fully, that he becomes "an unconscious part of every true beat of our heart." As the *summer sunbeams* enter into the flowers, and reappear in their lovely hues and sweet fragrance—so does Christ enter into the lives of his people, and permeate and transform them, until they become like him in spirit, in character, in disposition, in every feature. "Christ, who is our life." Colossians 3:4. "Christ in you, the hope of glory." Colossians 1:27. "Until Christ is formed in you." Galatians 4:19

We know what *Christ's friendship* was to his disciples. He found them crude—and left them refined. He found Matthew a publican, unjust, grasping, an outcast—and made him an apostle, then a writer of a Gospel. He found Peter profane, rough in manner, impetuous—and made him an eloquent preacher, a man of marvelous power, whose influence lives today wherever the Christian church has gone. He found John *a son of thunder*, with a strong, fiery temper—and made him the apostle of love, the human embodiment of all the sweet, gentle, tender graces of his own life. The friendship of Christ, can do the same for us!

January 24.

"You have answered correctly," Jesus replied. "Do this and you will live." Luke 10:28

That is just the trouble with a great many people—they can answer correctly. They know all about their duty. They can repeat with glib tongue, text after text of Scripture. They can recite catechism and creed without missing a word, and like to boast of their thorough familiarity with these sacred formularies. But it is the doing that they fall short in.

They know the commandments—but they fail to keep them. They can quote any number of Bible texts about honesty and truthfulness—yet they are neither honest nor truthful. They like to talk about the love of Christ, which is meek, gentle, patient, and compassionate—but they do not think of getting any of this spirit into their own life!

They recite texts about sending the gospel to the heathen, and make speeches about saving the lost—but neither give money nor make any personal effort to save others!

If doing were as easy as knowing—how blessed we would all be! Would it not be a beautiful thing for us—to try to live all the duty we know?

"Now that you know these things—you will be blessed if you do them!" John 13:17

January 25.

"I no longer call you servants, because a servant does not know his master's business. Instead, I have called you *friends*, for everything that I learned from my Father—I have made known to you." John 15:15

One of the marks of a noble nature, is *open-heartedness*. Jesus gave it as the chief privilege of friendship with him that he would make known to his friends—all that his Father had taught him. That is, full, trusting confidence is the deepest, truest thing—in the highest and best possible friendship. Soul and soul should be thoroughly united in two friends.

Two gentlemen lived in houses adjoining each other. Their back yards were separated by a fence. A warm friendship grew up between the two families; and soon that fence came down, and the children played together alike in both yards. True friendship *pulls down the fences* between lives.

Therefore a *secretive* man can never be a friend—nor have a friend at more than a few points. He is afraid to let his friend know what he knows, what he has been doing, what he is intending to do. *Secretiveness* is narrow, hindering, cramping. It is like living in a closed cell. It robs one's own life of sweet blessings which it might get from others—and it robs others of pleasures and benefits which it might give to them. The *secretive man* has not yet learned the meaning of the sweet word about the *open-heartedness* of the Master toward his friends, which he would have them repeat toward other Christians.

January 26.

"Unto Him who is able to do exceeding abundantly above all that we ask or think!" Ephesians 3:20

God often does better for us—than we ask.

We go to Him—with our little requests.

We are in need—and ask for temporal relief.

We are suffering—and ask that our pain may cease.

We are poor—and ask Him for more money.

We are just like the beggar, holding out our hands for paltry alms to eke out the day's need. Then God looks down upon us and says, "My child, are these little trifles all you want Me to give to you—daily bread, clothing, fuel for your fire, medicine for your sickness, comfort for your grief? The small things to supply your common needs—are these the only gifts and blessings you want and ask from the hand of your heavenly Father, who has infinite treasures to give to you?"

Yet thousands never get beyond just such requests in their praying! Bowing daily before a God of infinite power and love, in whose hands are unsearchable riches—they never ask for anything, but fleeting earthly comforts and worldly trinkets! They ask only for things for their bodies, or to beautify their homes—making no requests for the heavenly and spiritual gifts God has for their souls! We should learn to ask for the best things in all God's treasure house!

"Since, then, you have been raised with Christ, set your hearts on things above, where Christ is seated at the right hand of God. Set your minds on things above, not on earthly things!" Colossians 3:1-2

January 27.

"Happy is the man who finds wisdom!" Proverbs 3:13

It is worth our while to study what the Bible says about happiness, and how to get it. All people want to be happy—but most miss the mark.

Yet those who follow the Bible rules for happiness, will never be disappointed. "Happy is the man who finds wisdom."

WISDOM is a large word. It is not merely knowledge. A man may know so much, that he is a walking encyclopedia, and yet not be happy. He may pursue knowledge into all its nooks and hiding-places, dig it out of the rocks, extract it from the minerals, gather it from flower and plant, draw it down from among the stars—and yet not find happiness. Knowing a great many things—does not make one wise!

Wisdom is knowledge applied to life. He has found wisdom—who has learned to live well. To live well—is to live according to God's laws, which are summed up in one word, love—love to God and love to man. No one is happy who does not recognize God and do His will. "The fear of the Lord is the beginning of wisdom."

Likewise, no one can be really happy who does not love his fellow-men. Happiness never is found in selfishness. Those who seek happiness in thinking, toiling, and striving only for themselves—will have a vain quest! It never lies that way. He only has found wisdom—who has found rest in Christ.

January 28.

"The angel of God . . . went before the camp of Israel." Exodus 14:19.

This *angel* was revealed in the form of *cloud* and *fire*. It was wonderful guidance which God gave to his people in their marches. By *day* the pillar of cloud sheltered them—and then by *night* the same cloud was light. By day it was shelter—by night it was light. And always it was *guidance*. When they were to move, it lifted and went in advance, to lead them. When they were to halt and rest, it settled down, thus giving them the signal to pitch their tents.

This was *miraculous guidance*; but *we* have God's presence just as really, though without a visible 'pillar' to lead us. *God guides his people by his Word, by his providence, by his Spirit.* If we are willing to follow unquestioningly, we shall never be left long in perplexity, as to the way we should take. Our guidance is given to us only as we will accept it and shape our course by it.

Nor is the guidance given in maps and charts, showing us miles and miles of the road; it is given *only step by step* as we go on.

January 29.

"And as soon as the priests who carry the ark of the Lord, set foot in the Jordan, its waters flowing downstream will be cut off, and stand up in a heap." Joshua 3:13

There must be *faith* first. The priests must take up the ark and walk with it down into the flowing stream—before the waters would be cut off. They did not see a path across the river before they started. They broke up their camps and began their march while there was no sign of any crossing-place. If they had walked down to the edge, and then stopped to wait for the path to be opened, it would not have been opened. If they had lifted their feet and held them over the water, waiting for its flow to cease, they would have waited in vain. They must take one step into the water—before the current would be cut off. They must move on as if the way were open, believing that it would be open.

Likewise, we must learn to take God at his Word and go forward in duty, though we see no way by which we can go forward. The reason we are so often balked by *difficulties*, is because we expect to see them *removed* before we venture to pass through them. If we would move right on in faith, as soon as our feet touch the brim, the waters would flow away and leave a path. A great many people stand on the edge of the Christian life, waiting for feelings, before they will begin to follow Christ. If they would but begin to follow him, the way would open before them.

January 30.

"All things were created through Him, and apart from Him not one thing was created that has been created." John 1:3

We like to look at a beautiful piece of workmanship, and remember that some beloved friend of ours fashioned it. This makes it more precious and sacred.

Some orphan children had been received into an institution, and were exchanging their old garments for new ones. One poor boy was seen picking up the wretched cap he had been wearing, and tearing out of it a piece of faded silk that had been sewed into it. He was asked why he wanted to keep the patch; and he said, his eyes full of tears, that his mother had sewed it into his old cap with her thin frail fingers when she was on her death-bed, and he wanted to keep it in remembrance of her.

Men prize old paintings, and pay large prices for them, because they were painted by some famous master. All the works of nature would be sacred to us—if we but remembered that our Savior made them. The sweet flowers in the field would be all the sweeter—if we only thought as we look upon them, "The hands of Christ painted these!"

January 31.

"In him was life; and the life was the light of men." John 1:4

Life is a mystery. We can note its *manifestations*—but we cannot find its *source.* We see that a man lives—we see it in his actions; but we cannot tell what it is, that keeps the heart beating, beating, beating, without pause, for sixty, seventy, years. We can read the poet's lines, and look at the artist's pictures, and hear the musician's songs; but what do we know of the inner mental life that produced the poem, the pictures, the songs? It is *hidden* life.

So spiritual life is hidden. We see one supported in quiet peace, amid great trial; another comforted into sweet acquiescence in a bitter sorrow; another living purely and nobly amid sore temptations; another lifted up out of degradation, and transformed. We cannot understand the *processes*; we see only the *effects.* So all life is mysterious.

But we know that it all comes from Christ. He is the fountain of all life. No human genius, skill, or power has ever been able to produce life of any kind, even a living blade of grass or a little violet. Still less can any human power give new life to a dead soul. Only Christ can do this. We must get our life from him.

FEBRUARY

February 1.

"I establish my covenant with you: Never again will all life be cut off by the waters of a flood; never again will there be a flood to destroy the earth." Genesis 9:11

Science now explains so many things, which devout people in the past loved to look upon as the very *acts of God*, that some have begun to wonder whether after all our Father really has anything to do with nature. But what is nature? It is God's handiwork. The powers that work so mightily in earth and air—God put there. Can these powers be greater than he who lodged them in his works? We need never fear that any scientific discovery shall show us a universe without a God. We know, too, that the God who controls all the forces and energies of nature, holding all in his hands—is our Father!

During a great flood, when houses, barns, outbuildings, and fences were swept away in the wild current, some men in a skiff saw a baby's cradle borne along in the stream. Rowing to it, they found in it, sleeping as quietly and sweetly as it had ever slept in its mother's bosom, a little baby. So, in the wildest floods of earth, God cares for his little ones. He is Lord of all the forces of nature. Not a drop of water, even in angriest billows, ever breaks away from the control of God! Natural law!

Yes—but natural law is only the *leash of divine control* which is held firmly in the hand of God. No wild tempest ever sweeps beyond the "Hitherto" of our Father!

February 2.

"When I send *clouds* over the earth, the *rainbow* will be seen in the clouds" Genesis 9:14

So always, too, in spiritual life, whenever a cloud is in the sky—the rainbow appears on the cloud, the rainbow of divine promise, of God's love and grace. We are accustomed to say that *every cloud has a silver lining*, and the saying is true. In other words, every dark providence has a bright, shining side. As God sees it, there is a blessing in it. It is not always true that we can see the rainbow on the cloud; sometimes we can see only gloom and shadow. But faith can always be sure of good in every trial, in every sorrow, in every loss, even when the natural eye cannot see it. "We know that all things work together for good—to those who love God."

Someday we shall know that many of our best blessings have come to us out of our *sorrows*. In the Book of Revelation we are told that there is a *rainbow* about the throne of God and the Lamb in heaven, which would seem to be a suggestion that God's covenant is not for earth only—but also reaches forward into the blessed life beyond. *Perhaps our richest blessings in heaven—will be from earth's sorrows!*

February 3.

"O the depth of the riches both of the wisdom and the knowledge of God! How unsearchable are his judgments, and his ways past tracing out!" Romans 11:33

Our knowledge is *limited*. We see only little *fragments* of truth. We are like children on the shore of the sea, gathering a few pebbles and shells—while the ocean's depths are hidden from us. Says Zophar: "Can you fathom the mysteries of God? Can you probe the limits of the Almighty? They are higher than the heavens—what can you do? They are deeper than the depths of the grave—what can you know?" Job 11:7-8

Job himself, speaking of God's works in nature and in providence, adds: "And these are but the outer *fringe* of his works; how faint the whisper we hear of him! Who then can understand the thunder of his power?" Job 26:14

We ought to learn the lesson. God is not a man—not one of ourselves. If we could understand him, he would not be God. His *greatness* puts him beyond our comprehension. We cannot hope to know the *reasons for his acts*. Some of his ways with us are mysterious. We are perplexed; we say, "God cannot love me—or he would not do these things." We should learn to trust God even in the deepest mysteries, not expecting to understand—but sure of his *love* and *goodness*—even when it is darkest and when his face is veiled in most impenetrable mists. We should be silent unto God, when we cannot fathom Him. That is the truest faith.

February 4.

"Do not be afraid," the prophet answered. "Those who are with us are more than those who are with them!" 2 Kings 6:16

It is not enough just to put on a bold face and compel ourselves to be brave or appear brave. It will not do merely to try to make ourselves *think* there is no danger—when we know very well that there is danger. We cannot play tricks on ourselves. The true secret of confidence and fearlessness in danger—is faith in the *divine keeping*, not in thinking there is no peril. "I have told you these things so that in Me you may have peace. You will have suffering in this world. Be courageous! I have conquered the world." John 16:33

The great truth to be learned by all who would acquire true moral courage—is the reality of *God's care for his people in all their dangers*. The ninetieth and the one hundred and twenty-first Psalms describe this care. "The Lord is your keeper." "The Lord shall keep you from all evil." "He who keeps you will not slumber." I have slept in a camp with armed enemies on all sides; but I was not afraid, for I knew that waking sentinels formed a complete circle all around the camp. Likewise in any danger we may feel safe—because God wakes and watches!

February 5.

"Go and see how your brothers and the flocks are getting along," Jacob said. "Then come back and bring me word." So Jacob sent him on his way, and Joseph traveled to Shechem from his home in the valley of Hebron. Genesis 37:14

Joseph left his home in good spirits. We can imagine his *good-by* as he set out. The family would see him off, expecting him to fare well and to return again in good time. Not one of them dreamed that it would be *twenty years* before they should see his face again! If they had imagined this, then their parting that morning would have been very tender.

We never know when we say *farewell* at our door to the friends we love, as they or we go out for a time, that we shall ever see them again. We should always say good-by, even for the briefest parting, with thoughtfulness and with love's warmth, for we may never clasp hands with them any more.

February 6.

"For everyone who exalts himself will be humbled, and the one who humbles himself will be exalted." Luke 14:11

HUMILITY is an excellent grace. It is the *empty hand* which God fills. Self-conceit is weakness. We are strongest, when we distrust ourselves, and are thus led to lean upon God. Emptiness is the cup into which God puts blessing. Pride leaves no room for the divine strength. But there is a danger also in *self-distrust*. It sometimes makes a person shrink from duty. It almost wrecked the mission of Moses. A little more excusing of himself, and God probably would have left him with his sheep in the wilderness, seeking some other man to bring Israel out of Egypt. No doubt many people have failed altogether of the mission for which they were sent into this world, through a like feeling of *unfitness for the work*. When God clearly calls us to undertake any task, we should never raise the question of *ability*. He would not call us to it—if He did not equip us for the task.

February 7.

"You will have tribulation in this world." John 16:33

The word *tribulation* is very suggestive. It comes from a root which means 'a flail'. The thresher uses the flail to beat the wheat sheaves, that he may separate the golden wheat from the chaff and straw.

Tribulation is *God's threshing*—not to destroy us, but to get what is good, heavenly, and spiritual in us—separated from what is wrong, earthly, and fleshly. Nothing less than blows of pain will do this. The evil so strongly clings to the good; the golden wheat of goodness in us is so closely wrapped up in the strong chaff of sin, that only the heavy flail of suffering can produce the separation!

Suffering is like John the Baptist, wearing grim garments, with stern visage and rough hands and a baptism of bitter tears, uttering sharp, harsh words, going before Christ to prepare us for his gentle coming and his message of love. Many of us would never enter the gates of pearl—were it not for this unwelcome messenger, pain.

February 8

"Therefore, brothers, by the mercies of God, I urge you to present your bodies as a living sacrifice, holy and pleasing to God . . . " Romans 12:1

A Christian man had quoted this verse, urging those whom he had addressed to present their bodies to God as a living sacrifice. When he closed, a good friend who sat beside him said, "John, the next time you quote that verse, you would better quote all of it."

"Didn't I quote it all? "

"No; you left off the last words, *which is your reasonable service.'* That is very important."

The old Quaker was right. We had better quote the whole verse. It is not an *unreasonable* thing that God asks us to do when he beseeches us to present ourselves to him as a living sacrifice.

He is our *Father*, and we are his children; is it unreasonable that a child shall be asked to do a father's will?

We may think of our redemption, and remember at what tremendous cost Christ bought us, and then of all the blessings and hopes that are ours through his sacrifice for us. Is it unreasonable that we should be asked to consecrate our lives to God when he has done such things for us?

We may think, too, of what will be the result if we do not yield ourselves to God—that our lives will be lost in sin's darkness; and of the good that will come to us through devoting ourselves to him eternal life and blessedness. Is it, then, unreasonable that we should be called to make this presentation of ourselves to God?

February 9.

"If only we had died by the Lord's hand in the land of Egypt, when we sat by pots of meat and ate all the bread we wanted. Instead, you brought us into this wilderness to make this whole assembly die of hunger!" Exodus 16:3

It is a sad thing when we allow life's disappointments to make us despondent! The problem of Christian living in this troublesome world, is not to escape experiences of hardship—but to retain sweetness of spirit in all such experiences.

You must have hardships, losses, sorrows. But see to it that you retain through all these—a gentle heart, full of trust and hope. Then when the harsh adversity is past—you will emerge unharmed, with even richer life, tenderer beauty, and deeper joy! The secret of such victorious living—is a trust in God which never fails.

February 10

"She has done what she could!" Mark 14:8

A child offered her teacher a *handful of weeds and grass*, wilted and soiled, and said, "Here is a bouquet for you!" The teacher saw the love in the child's eyes, and accepted the gift with sincere gratitude. Just so, Christ accepts our smallest gifts or services—if He sees love in our heart.

This is the spirit with which Christ receives the gifts and services of those who love him. The gifts may be worthless, and the services may avail nothing—but for the *love* that prompts them, he accepts them with real gladness, and richly rewards them.

February 11.

"Every skilled woman spun with her hands and *brought what she had spun*—blue, purple or scarlet yarn or fine linen." Exodus 35:25

Many young ladies make beautiful things—but do not bring them to Christ. They keep them for their own adornment. But these women brought their fine handiwork to the Lord. They spun beautiful threads to be woven into the curtains and embroideries of the tabernacle. Christian girls and women may help in many ways in preparing dwelling-places for God. They can make a place for him in their own heart. They can put touches of beauty into the lives of others. It needs not *great* things—but only service of truth filled with love, to please God. The threads may be coarse—but in God's eye they will be beautiful—if *love* spins them.

February 12.

"I will test them and see whether they will follow my instructions." Exodus 16:4

Everything God gives or sends to us—tests us in some way.

Trials test us, whether we will submit with humility and patience to the experiences that are sore and painful, and learn the lesson set for us in them.

But none the less do the ***blessings*** of life test us. They test our *gratitude*. Do we remember God all the time—as the Giver of each new blessing? They test our *faith*. Do we still lean on him while we have plenty? Oftentimes the trust that turns to him when help is needed—fails to look to him when the hand is full. They also test our *obedience*. Sometimes when our needs are all supplied, we forget our obligation to serve God. Thus every day is a probation. We are always on trial.

February 13.

"*Stand still* before the LORD as I remind you of all the great things the LORD has done for you." 1 Samuel 12:7

It is good to *stand still* sometimes, and look back over the way by which God has led us. Of one thing we may always be sure—all God's dealings with us are right. Some of them may seem hard. We all have our trials, disappointments, sorrows, sufferings, our cups of bitterness. There is no way in which we can see *goodness* in all these experiences, except by faith in the unfailing righteousness of God. Yet a firm conviction of this truth brings peace in the darkest hour. God cannot be unloving. He is our Father.

It does us good to stand still before God at times, and look back over our life—and see all our experiences in the light of the love that streams from his face. We cannot understand all seems mysterious and dark; yet we know God is righteous, and righteousness is goodness. If we firmly believe this all through life, whatever may come, faith will live, and its light will shine as a bright star in the blackest midnight.

February 14.

"You are my hiding place." Psalm 32:7

God is a hiding-place from all sorts of dangers. He is a hiding-place from **sin**. His mercy is an eternal refuge. "There is therefore now no condemnation to those who are in Christ Jesus."

God is a refuge from **trouble**. "God had one Son without *sin*—but he has none without *sorrow*." Where shall we go to get away from sorrow? There is no place on earth into which it never enters, no Eden bower, no Paradise, where grief never comes. But there is a hiding-place to which sorrowing ones can flee, and where they will find comfort that shall give them peace. "In the world you shall have troubles; in Me you shall have peace," said Jesus. The sorrow may not be shut out—but the divine peace comes into the heart and calms it. Sorrow is seen then, as *God's messenger of love*, sent by him on some good errand, and is accepted in faith. So in the pain and loss—there is no more fear. The sufferer has found a hiding-place in God.

God is a hiding-place from **danger**. In the wildest terrors and alarms—we can run to Him, and, lying down in his bosom, be safe. A Christian sailor said that even if his ship went down into the sea—he would be safe; for God holds the waters in the hollow of his hand, and he would only fall into his Father's hand.

February 15.

"The unfailing love of the Lord never ends! Great is His faithfulness; His mercies begin afresh each day!" Lamentations 3:22-23

It is the glory of God's love, that it is always fresh and new. It is never the same in its expression in any two days. We have to patch up our old things and keep them, using them again and again; but God never does. He never gives us the old leaves a second time; each spring, every tree gets new foliage, new garments of beauty. He does not revive last year's withered flowers, and give them to us again for this year; he gives us new flowers for each summer.

So he does with his messages of love; they are not repeated over and over again, always the same old ones. Every time the reverent heart reads the Bible, its words come fresh from the lips of God, always new. They never get old. They are like the water that bubbles up in living streams from the depths in the wayside spring— always fresh, sweet, and new.

So it is with the blessings of prayer. Morning by morning we kneel before God, seeking his blessing and favor. He does not give us always the same blessing—but has a new one ready for each new day. Our needs are not the same any two mornings when we bow before him, and he always suits the blessing to the need. We are taught to live day by day. God's goodness comes to us new every morning.

February 16.

"The king and his men marched to Jerusalem, to fight against *the Jebusites* who inhabited the land." 2 Samuel 5:6

The Jebusites still held a *stronghold* in the heart of the country, never having been dislodged. There are 'Jebusites' in every Christian community, and also in every Christian heart. For example, there is worldliness, which has its Jebusites everywhere.

In the midst of a **community** containing its beautiful Christian homes, sanctuaries, and refinements, one finds a licensed *drinking-saloon*. It is so entrenched there, too, that it seems impossible to dislodge it. There are many other such citadels of evil, which rear their proud towers and defy conquest.

In every **heart**, there are little 'Jebusite strongholds', which it seems impossible for us to conquer. Sometimes it is a secret sin which lives on, unconquered, amid the general holiness of a life. Sometimes it is a remnant of the old nature—such as pride, worldliness, selfishness, lust, or bitterness.

"We all have our faults!" we say, and under this 'cloak'—we manage to tuck away a large number of dear idols that we do not want to give up!

We ought to give attention to these unsubdued parts of our life—that every thought, feeling, and temper may be brought into subjection to Christ. It is perilous to leave even one such unconquered stronghold in our heart. "We take captive every thought to make it obedient to Christ!" 2 Corinthians 10:5

February 17.

"He asked this to *test* him, for He Himself knew what He was going to do." John 6:6

Jesus is continually testing his disciples, putting them to the test to draw out their faith. He is constantly bringing before us cases of need, sorrow, and trial—to test us. He wants to draw out our love, our sympathy, our tenderness, and train us to do the works of love which he leaves us in this world to do.

The disciples thought they could not feed the multitude before them—yet Jesus meant that they should do it. Their 'little', blessed and then used, proved quite enough. We think we cannot answer the needs, sorrows, and hungers that appeal to us; but we can if we will. Christ wants us to go forth to minister in his name to all whom he sends to us. We do not appear to be able to do much. But even our few *words* spoken kindly, our *tears* of sympathy, our *expressions* of love—Christ can use to do great good to the faint and the weary hearts before us. We must never say of any appeals that come to us, "We cannot do anything!" To our word of powerlessness, when we have a bidding of duty, Jesus only answers, "Give them something to eat!" and we must go out to feed them, though we seem to have only a crumb or a crust to give.

February 18.

"Gather the *fragments* that are left over. Let nothing be wasted!" John 6:12

It seems remarkable, that he who so easily could multiply the five loaves into an abundant meal for thousands, should be so particular about 'saving the fragments'. But Jesus would teach us economy. No matter how great our abundance, we should take care of the 'fragments'. After we have eaten at our tables, there are hungry people who would be glad for the pieces that are left over.

This applies also to the fragments of time. Many busy people waste whole years of time in their life—in the minutes which they lose every day! If at the end of a year they could gather up all these 'fragments', they would have many basketfuls of golden time in which they might do much good.

Likewise, we should not waste our strength. Many people waste their bodily energy, using it in play, or useless amusements, when it belongs to God—and ought to be employed to its last particle for His glory!

Likewise, we should not waste our affections by allowing them to be given to unworthy objects, or people.

There is no limit to the application of this principle. We must give account of everything we have, even the minutes of time, the little fractions of strength, and the smallest bits of bread on our tables!

February 19.

"Jesus took the loaves; and when he had given thanks, he distributed to the *disciples*, and the disciples to those who were seated—so also with the fish." John 6:11

Jesus himself wrought the miracle—but he did it *through his disciples*. That is his usual way. When he wants to take care of a little baby, and train it for a worthy mission, he puts a portion of his own love and gentleness into a mother's heart, and commissions her to train the child for him.

When he wanted to give his Word to the world, he did not speak directly from heaven—but put His thoughts into the lips of holy men to speak them for him. When he wants now to send his grace to a sinner, he does not command an angel from his throne, nor come himself in form of majesty—but sends the message through a saved one.

The disciples that day stood *between Christ and the multitude*, and so Christ's disciples always do. If they had merely eaten of the bread themselves, and had not passed it to the hungry multitude, the people would have starved, though provision was in the disciples' hands, enough to feed them all. If we who have the *gospel bread* only feed ourselves with it, and do not carry it to perishing sinners, they will die in their sins, because we have not taken the salvation to them.

February 20.

"Lord, give us this bread always!" John 6:34

That was a good prayer. It is just the prayer for each one of *us*—every day! But the people who made it first, did not know what they were asking.

It is often so in our praying. We have a dim, glimmering vision of something very beautiful—but it is only a shadowy vision to us. The thing we think we want, is not the thing at all that God had in mind in his promise. He meant something most worthy—but we have in our mind the thought of something *material* and *earthly*. It is well that we have an Intercessor into whose hands all our requests must pass, who will take our poor, mistaken prayers—and interpret them aright for us, giving us, not what we thought we would get—but something better, diviner!

Abraham sought all his life, for a *country* which he never received. But he got something *better* in his unavailing search—his faith was growing all the while; his thoughts and hopes were turned to spiritual things, of which the earthly possessions he sought were only shadows. So it is in the *disappointments* of our praying: what we seek—we find not—but meanwhile we are getting blessings a thousand times better. On weary paths of earth where we toil in search of supposed blessings, we are really rising step by step on invisible stairs, and reaching blessings of which the *earthly illusions* were only pictures.

February 21.

"Then the Lord said to Satan, Have you considered My servant Job? No one else on earth is like him, a man of perfect integrity, who fears God and turns away from evil. *He still retains his integrity, even though you incited Me against him*, to destroy him without just cause." Job 2:3

It is a noble thing, when a man stands steadfast and faithful to God in the midst of trials and adversities. Such a man is like a *mighty rock* under the beatings of the angry waves of the sea.

Thus Job stood. Trial after trial came. His *property* was swept away by marauders and by fire, and his *children* were crushed by falling walls, until in a little while he was stripped of all he had, and left a childless man! His heart was broken with *sorrow*—but his *faith* failed not. The Lord kept his eye upon his servant, and was pleased to see how trustingly he endured his losses and sorrows.

The affliction of Job, as described here from the divine side, suggests to us, what may ofttimes be the reason for trouble in the lives of God's children. Job suffered in order to prove to a scoffing adversary, the *genuineness of his religion*. Job did not know *why* these sore losses came upon him. Likewise, we do not know, when we are in trouble, why God sends or permits the affliction. But we should always bear ourselves so as to honor God, and prove the reality and sincerity of our faith. We are set to witness to the *power of divine grace in trial*, and should not fail God nor disappoint him. No duty of ours is more sacred—than being true to God in pain and trouble. To murmur or complain—is to sin.

February 22.

"What? Should we accept only *good* things from the hand of God—and never anything *bad*?" Job 2:10

So often *weak faith* is moved from its steadfastness, by trials. People say, "God cannot love me—or he would not send this affliction upon me!" Job's answer, however, shows nobler faith. We take good, earthly good, from God's hands. We believe that God loves us—so long as he showers upon us favors, and gives us pleasant things, joys and prosperities. Very well. But when he changes the form of his providence, and gives us *troubles* instead of favors, should we conclude that he no longer loves us?

In the case of the change in his treatment of Job—*we are permitted to look within the heart of God*, to learn what his feelings were, and we see that he had never loved his servant more than when he was allowing him to suffer so sorely!

At the close of the first trial, Job said, "The Lord *gave*—and the Lord has *taken away*." The same Lord who gave—took away! Yes, and the same love! God knows best, what we need any particular day, and what will most advance the kingdom of Christ; and we ought to trust him so implicitly, so unquestioningly, that whether he gives a new favor—or takes one away; whether he grants us our request—or withholds it; whether he bestows upon us earthly good—or causes us to suffer loss and adversity—we shall still believe and say, "God loves me, and he is blessing me!"

"Naked came I out of my mother's womb, and naked shall I return! The Lord gave—and the Lord has taken away; blessed be the name of the Lord!" Job 1:21

February 23.

"Behold, happy is the man whom God corrects!" Job 5:17

He is not happy at the time! No one enjoys having troubles, sufferings, sorrows. Therefore this verse appears very strange to some people. They cannot understand it. It is contrary to all their thoughts of happiness. Of course, the word *happy* is not used here in the world's sense. In the world's estimation, "happiness is the pleasure that comes from the things that happen. It depends on personal comfort, on prosperous circumstances, on kindly and congenial conditions. When these are taken away the happiness is destroyed."

But the word here means *blessed*; and the statement is, that blessing comes to him who receives God's correction. To *correct* is to *set right* that which has been wrong. Surely if a man is going in the wrong way, and God turns his feet back and sets him in the right way, a blessing has come to him. *Afflictions* are **God's corrections**. They come with a purpose of love in them. They are hard to accept—but afterward the blessing is revealed. "No discipline seems pleasant at the time, but painful. Later on, however, it produces a harvest of righteousness and peace for those who have been trained by it." Hebrews 12:11

February 24.

"I know that You can do all things; no plan of Yours can be thwarted!" Job 42:2

We cannot do what we desire to do. Many of our purposes are thwarted. We desire to do good and beautiful things, and we try—but our achievements fall far below our thought. Our clumsy hands cannot fashion the loveliness which our hearts dream of. Our faltering weakness cannot do the brave things our souls aspire to do. No artist ever paints on his canvas—all the beauty of his ideal. No singer ever expresses—all the music which burns within him as he sings. No eloquent orator ever utters—all that he feels as he pleads for truth or for justice.

So in all our life—we do only a little of what we strive to do. We set out in the morning with purposes of usefulness, of true living, of gentle-heartedness, of patience, of victoriousness; but in the evening we find only little fragments of these good intentions actually wrought out.

But God's plans and intentions are all carried out! No power can withstand Him—or frustrate His will. It was in this thought, that Job found peace in his long, sore trial. All things were in God's hands, and nothing could hinder His designs of love. Our God is infinitely strong. In all earthly confusions, strifes, and troubles—His hand moves, bringing good out of evil for those who trust in Him. He executes all His purposes of good. He is never hindered in blessing His children.

February 25.

"I would state my case before Him and fill my mouth with arguments!" Job 23:4

Job had confidence that God was his Friend, and that if he could stand before Him and tell Him all about his life—it would be well with him. Every Christian may have the same confidence. This does not mean that we have no sins, and that we can appear in God's presence and explain our acts to Him and show Him that we have done nothing wrong. We are sinners, and we can come before Him only with penitence and confession. But when we come thus, and cast ourselves on His love and mercy—we may state our case before him without fear—not pleading innocence, but pleading the grace of Christ. We know that God is pitiful toward our infirmities. Knowing all about us—He yet loves us with a love that is infinitely gracious! "Like a father pities his children—so the Lord pities those who fear Him. For He knows our frame—He remembers that we are but dust!"

A still sweeter truth than that which is uttered here—is that we have One who can order our cause before God, and who will always find acceptance for us. "If anyone sins," said the beloved disciple, "we have an Advocate with the Father, Jesus Christ, the righteous." We may go to God always in His name, sure that in His hands all our interests will be safe, for He ever lives to make intercession for us! Our cause will never suffer—in the hands of Him who died for us!

February 26.

"Would he oppose me with great power? No, he would not press charges against me!" Job 23:6

Job was sure that if he could only get to God, that he would find in him a friend. He had been learning more and more of God's real nature, and had at least some thought of the true character of the mighty God. Especially does he seem to have gotten some glimpses of the divine Redeemer, who was his Friend. Thus a few chapters back he says: "But as for me, I know that my Redeemer lives, and that he will stand upon the earth at last. And after my body has decayed, yet in my body I will see God! I will see him for myself. Yes, I will see him with my own eyes. I am overwhelmed at the thought!" Job 19:25-27

Just how much *Job* really did know of the character of God—we cannot tell. He certainly believed now that if he could come before God, that he would meet a friend.

But *we* live in full gospel light, and we know that God is our truest and best friend; that he is our Father; that we need never fear to make an appeal to him. He is not against us. His almighty power is not used to oppose us, to break us and crush us. He gives heed unto our cry. He loves us. All his omnipotence is on our side. No mother's heart was ever so full of love for her child—as is the heart of God for us, his children. We know that God's thoughts toward us are kindly thoughts of peace.

February 27.

"He hides Himself—that I cannot see Him. Yet He knows the way I take; when He has tested me, I will emerge as pure gold!" Job 23:9-10

God is invisible—and we cannot see Him. We know that He is working here and there, and we turn quickly to find Him—but our eyes get no glimpse of Him. We cannot lay our hand upon Him. We cannot see His face. Yet we know that while He is not visible to our sight—that He sees us always and knows our way where we are, what we are doing, what our circumstances and experiences are. "He knows!"

One evening Jesus sent his disciples out upon the sea in the boat, to go to the other side—but He did not go with them. In the night a great storm arose, and the disciples were alone. They were in sore distress—but they could not find their Master. Meanwhile, however, though unseen by them—He was looking down upon them in tender love from the mountain-top. He knew the way that they took, in the darkness on the sea.

In our experience, it may often be that we cannot find God; that we cannot see Him; that He shall elude our search, not answer to our cry, and not come when we call for Him. Yet it is a precious comfort that in all such cases—He knows the way that we take, where we are, and what we are suffering. We are never out of His sight! Always, "He knows!" and that is enough!

February 28.

"After Job had prayed for his friends, the Lord restored his prosperity and doubled his previous possessions." Job 42:10

A great many people who try to be comforters, only lay *thorns* under aching heads. No art needs a more delicate touch, than the comforter's. The hands of most of us are *too rough* to be laid on throbbing hearts. No wonder Job felt that his friends were *miserable comforters*, or that he was not at first in a mood to pray for them. But until he could pray for them—blessing could not come to him.

The lesson is for us. Others may have injured or grieved us in some way, and we may not be ready to *forgive* them. But while we feel so, we are shutting out divine blessing from ourselves. Job's praying at length for his friends, showed that his heart was now softened toward them, that he had forgiven them.
Then *blessing* came to him. When we can pray for one who has wronged us, misjudged us, or said unkind things of us or to us, hurting us in some way—we are in a condition to receive blessing from God.

Job was also ready now to come out of his own sorrow—to try to help others. We do not find comfort by staying in the darkness of our own grief, by thinking only of it; we must forget ourselves, and begin to serve others and seek their good, before we can find the light of God's comfort. Selfishness in sorrow is selfishness, and selfishness in any form misses God's blessing.

February 29.

"I admit that I worship the God of our fathers as a follower of the Way, which they call a sect." Acts 24:14

It is easy enough when we are in meetings of *Christians*—to be known as one of them. But Christ wants us to confess him just as distinctly when we are among his *enemies*. If anyone sneers at us as Christians, we should not blush and hang our head, and stammer out an apology, or, far worse, a denial. We should be ready, without bravado, modestly and humbly—yet boldly, to admit that we are Christians, and to do it in such a way as to show that we rejoice in our relation to Christ, and in confessing it.

Miss Havergal tells of going into a boarding-school as a pupil just after she had united with the church. She was startled to find that in a school family of a hundred, that she was the only Christian. Her first feeling was that she could not avow her love for Christ, with all that company of worldly girls around her. But her second thought was that she could not but avow it, since she was the only one Christ had there to represent him. This thought was most strengthening, and from that hour she quietly took her place as a *friend of Christ*. It ought to help us, whenever we stand amid enemies of Christ, to remember that he has put us there to *represent* him, and that if we are ashamed or afraid—we shall be sadly failing and disappointing him.

MARCH

March 1.

"Be men of courage; be strong." 1 Corinthians 16:13

Gentleness and *good temper* are not all. One may have these qualities, and yet be lacking in the completeness of well-rounded Christian character. There must be *strength* as well as *beauty*. Love is the fulfilling of the law; all the commandments being summed up in one, "You shall love." But love is a large word. It is like one of those composite pictures, into which many pictures are blended. All the elements of duty to God and to our fellows—are wrapped up in the divine conception of loving.

It will not do, therefore, for us to take merely the things that belong to the gentle side, and think of these as the *whole* of Christian character. Christ was infinitely gentle. The warmth of his heart made a tropical summer all about him. But behind the gentleness, was also infinite strength. We must be like him, not only in gentle warmth—but also in truth and strength and righteousness. We must be to others, not only tenderness—but also strength to lean upon, and stability in which they may find refuge.

March 2.

"You are light in the Lord; *walk* as children of light." Ephesians 5:8.

The tendency to *morbidness* which shows itself in some people, is most unhealthy. In some it is *habitual*; a disposition to gloom has been permitted to have its way so long—that now the feelings run, even unimpeded, in melancholy grooves. In others it is *incidental*, caused by loss or trial, the life requiring some time to react after its shock of grief, and rebound to its wonted cheerfulness. The latter experience is not so unwholesome, because it is transient; but the former, wherever it exists, should be treated as a mental disease, and subjected to the wisest processes of cure. It is destructive of the life's beauty. It mars one's usefulness. It grieves God, for it is *practical unbelief.*

Why should one persist in refusing the blessing of God's bounteous sunshine, and walk only in gloomy paths? Why should one close windows and doors and live in darkness—when God's glory of light flows everywhere? The morbid person should heroically set himself the task of getting rid of his miserable gloom! It may take time; for when darkness has become *ingrained* in the soul—it can yield but slowly to the influence of light. Yet the task should be achieved. To stay in the *shades of melancholy* is most unchristian.

March 3.

"May the Lord direct your hearts into God's love and Christ's patience." 2 Thessalonians 3:5

We need the *patience of Christ* to keep us from *over-helping* others. No peril is greater than this *too eager love*, when brought close to those who are in need. We would help too *much*—or too *soon*. We would lift away burdens—that God would have the person carry longer for his own good. We would make the way easy—that would better be left hard. We would hasten the *learning of the lesson*—that could far better be learned slowly. We would force the bursting of the flower—before the time God has appointed, thus spoiling his perfect work.

We want to hurry the spiritual development of lives, not content to wait until the development comes naturally. There are hundreds of lives hurt by the *impatience* of good people, who desire to do them good.

If we would be truly helpful to others, we must never try too hard to help. It is hard for us, in our eagerness to help, just to do *our little*—and then stand aside and let God work. We feel we ought to be doing something; but in truth our doing is only *hurtful intermeddling*, and we would far better keep our hands off!

March 4.

"Jesus did not answer a word!" Matthew 15:23

Who has not come to Christ with a burden, crying out for help or for relief—only to find him silent? To many of our earnest supplications, he seems not to answer a word. We are told to ask—and we shall receive, to seek—and we shall find, to knock—and it shall be opened unto us. Yet there come times when we ask imploringly, and do not seem to receive; when, though we seek with intense eagerness, we do not seem to find what we seek; when we knock at the door of prayer until our hands are bruised and bleeding, and there is no opening of the door.

Sometimes the heavens seem to be *brass* above us; and we ask, "Is there anywhere, an ear to hear our pleadings? Is there anywhere, a heart to feel sympathy with us in our overwhelming need?" Sometimes God seems to be far off—so far that our cries cannot reach him. Nothing is so awful as this *silence of God*—the feeling that communication is cut off. Few prayers in the Bible are more pathetic than that in the psalm: "Be not silent to me, lest I become like those who go down into the pit!" Anything from God, any punishment, is better than his silence!

Oh, it would be a dreary world, if the *atheist's creed* were true, that there is no God, no ear to hear prayer; that no voice of answering help, or love, or comfort, ever comes out of the heavens.

March 5.

"He will not break a bruised reed, and He will not put out a smoldering wick." Matthew 12:20

It is a high honor that is conferred upon us—when God sends to us human hearts to be comforted, or human souls to be helped. Yet every thoughtful person must tremble as he accepts the responsibility of such *delicate* and *holy* work. It is a serious moment when there is brought to a surgeon a case, on the skillful treatment of which, a life depends; or when a physician stands by a bedside to administer remedies at critical illness. But it is a far more serious moment, when a human life is put into one's hands to be cured of its *faults*—or comforted in its *sorrow*—or to have its heart's *wounds* healed. We need divine skill and wisdom, and great delicacy, for such sacred work! Only Christ can teach us how to deal with human lives, in their need and sorrow. He has a most gentle touch. He binds up with infinite skill the wounds that sin or grief have made. He never breaks a bruised reed. He will give us skill in dealing with hurt lives.

March 6.

"I long to see you—so that I may impart to you some spiritual gift, to make you strong." Romans 1:11

We ought always to desire to be a blessing to those we love. God sends many of his best spiritual gifts, through human hearts and hands. There could be no fitter morning prayer, as we go out for the day, than that we may be permitted to carry some help, comfort, instruction, inspiration, courage, or cheer—to every life that our life touches. There are always those who need such help. No aim in life is nobler—than to be a help to others in all gentle, quiet ways.

We should make sure, too, that it is the best we have, that we impart to others. There are times when the best thing we can do for a man is to make him laugh. But there are other gifts which we should seek to impart. Sometimes it is *cheer* to a disheartened spirit. Sometimes it is *comfort* for sorrow. Sometimes it is the *inspiration* of a fresh thought which we have found. We should make sure at least that to everyone we meet—we are ready to impart some gift which will do him good.

March 7.

"When he has brought out all his own, he goes on ahead of them, and his sheep follow him because they know his voice. But they will never follow a stranger; in fact, they will run away from him because they do not recognize a stranger's voice." John 10:4-5

It is true of sheep in the East, that while they quickly respond to their names when their own shepherd calls them, because they know his voice—yet if a stranger comes to the door of the fold and calls them by the same names, they will be alarmed and will turn and run. It ought to be so with Christ's sheep. They should be quick to hear and know their own Shepherd's voice whenever he calls. They should never be afraid when they recognize his call, though it be in the darkness of sorrow or of trial. But they should also be quick to detect any voice that is not their own Shepherd's.

Such voices do fall continually upon the ears of Christ's friends. There are *temptations* which would lure them away from the truth—into paths of wandering, which lead to sin and end in death! There are *false guides* who profess to be true, and to be very much wiser than the old-fashioned, true guides whom Christ has set to be under shepherds; and they want to turn the sheep away from the old paths. Everywhere the "voice of strangers" is heard. The true sheep flee from the voice of strangers, knowing it is not their shepherd's. Every voice which is not known to be Christ's, should alarm the Christian, causing him to run quickly to his own Shepherd for shelter and protection.

March 8.

"So Abram departed as the Lord had instructed him. Abram was seventy-five years old when he left Haran." Genesis 12:4

That was faith. Obedience proved it. Abram did not know *where* he was going; he had simply the call of God and a promise. But he asked no questions. He did not insist on knowing how his journey would come out, how profitable it would be, just what he would get in exchange for the land he was leaving and the sacrifice he was making. Quietly, without question or hesitation, he arose, cut the ties that bound him to his old home, and departed.

That is the kind of faith all of us should have, whenever God gives us a call and a promise. Some people want to see where they are going before they will begin to follow Christ; but that is not walking by faith at all.

We should not trouble ourselves to know *where* we are to be led, if only we know that God is leading us. His guidance is safe; and we should be willing to trust him, do precisely what he says, and go just where he leads, without asking any questions. Abraham's life is a picture of a true "walk with God."

March 9.

But Jesus told them—"You don't know what you are asking! Are you able to drink from the bitter cup of sorrow I am about to drink?" "Oh yes," they replied, "we are able!" Matthew 20:22

It was an *ignorant prayer* which the two brothers had offered. They did not know what they were asking for. We know that one dark day two malefactors had the places on the Lord's right and left hand. We all ask many a time for things which we would not dare to seek—if we knew what they would *cost*.

There is a *heathen story* which tells us that once a man asked for the *gift not to die*; and it was granted him by *the Fates*. He was to live on forever. But he had forgotten to ask that his youth and health and strength also might last forever, and so he lived on until age and its infirmities and weaknesses were weighing him down, and his life grew to be a weariness and a burden to him. *Existence,* for it could hardly be called *life,* was one long torment to him; and then he wished to die—and could not. He had asked for a thing which he was totally unfit to enjoy—but he had to take the consequences of it when it was once given.

In our prayers we seek things which we might shrink from seeking, if we knew that they must come to us through pain, tears, and loss. The better way to pray, however, is to let *God choose* for us, and to give *what* he sees best for us, and in the *way* that he knows to be the best.

March 10.

"When Solomon was old, his wives seduced him to follow other gods. *His heart was not perfect* with the Lord his God." 1 Kings 11:4

The Arabs have a tradition that for a long time a little worm was gnawing in the staff on which Solomon leaned, until at last the staff broke and the great king fell. It was at the king's heart—that the worm was really gnawing.

A *perfect* heart does not mean a *sinless* heart—but a heart wholly devoted in its aim and motive to God. Solomon had a corner in his heart for the Lord, and then other corners for the gods of other nations. The Savior's words come in here: "You cannot serve both God and Money."

We need to be on our guard against this *Solomonian religion*. There is plenty of it. It is very *broad* church. It abhors the preaching of the stern truths of God's Word about sin and holiness. It sends well-near everybody to heaven, and regards hell as a mediaeval fable. It calls strict Christians, intolerant and narrow-minded. It calls great sins 'escapades', and finds no use for such psalms as the fifty-first. It is not hard to see in the story of David and Solomon, however, which of the two kinds of religion pleases God the better, and which leads to the nobler end. If what his religion did for Solomon is a fair sample of the outcome of that sort, it does not appear to be quite satisfactory.

March 11.

"As for the other events of Solomon's reign—all he did . . . are they not *written* in the book of the annals of Solomon?" 1 Kings 11:41

They are all *written!* They are not all written in the Bible—but they all went down in the chronicles of the kings. Nor was that all. When their ancient paper was used, the *impression* of the writing goes through and is traced on underlying sheets.

Just so, our life makes its records in the chronicles of the times; but the writing also goes through, and every line and word goes down on pages invisible to our eyes the pages of *God's book*. We read in the Bible, that the books will be opened for final judgment; and Solomon himself tells us that "God shall bring every work into judgment, with every hidden thing, whether it be good, or whether it be evil."

Solomon is gone, and his record cannot now be changed; but we are concerned with our own lives. The *young* have the chief portion of their life yet before them. It is important that they remember that all their acts are written; that things which are hidden from the eyes of the world—are yet written down on the Book within the veil; and that some day—all secret things shall be manifested, brought fully to the light, before all the universe. It is important, therefore, that they do, along the common days, only the things which they will be glad to see revealed when all secret things shall be uncovered. When the day of judgment comes, we shall be asked how holy were our lives—and not how fine our words!

March 12.

"The *sweet psalmist* of Israel." 2 Samuel 23:1

Think of the influence of David's psalms. Take one for example, the twenty-third. Who can count up the blessings it has left, in its wanderings through the world? How many *children* have learned to say it almost with their first efforts at speech! How many *sick* people have listened to its sweet, musical accents, as it has been read in softened tones in the hushed chamber! How many *dying* ones have lisped the beautiful sentences as the gloom gathered about them, especially lingering on the words: "Yes, though I walk through the valley of the shadow of death, I will fear no evil: for you are with me; your rod and your staff they comfort me." This precious psalm has been like a beautiful angel, flying up and down through the world, bearing its joy and gladness to hearts of young and old, of rich and poor.

I would rather have written the twenty-third psalm—than have been the greatest emperor this world ever saw! Yet this is only one of many. The psalms contain the records of men's heart-life, and heart-life is the same in all ages; hence people will always find here words which will interpret their own feelings. There never can be another such a prayer-book as the Psalms.

"He leads me beside the still waters. He restores my soul; He guides me in the paths of righteousness."

March 13.

"Just then a woman who had been subject to bleeding for twelve years came up behind him and touched the hem of his cloak. She said to herself—If I only touch his cloak, I will be healed." Matthew 9:20-21

The 'cloak of Christ' still trails nearby us. It is by us, when we open the Bible and read His words. It is by us, when we feel the presence of the Holy Spirit with us. It is by our beds of pain, when we are sick. It is by us, when it grows dark around us with the gloom of sorrow. It is by us in our busiest days, amid the tasks and toils and cares of our life. We never get anywhere but 'that mystic cloak' trails close to us—so that we can reach out and touch it with our hand, and have the feeling of our heart's cry conveyed to the very soul of Christ. If there is in us only a sense of our need, and a turning, with even feeblest faith, to Christ—our touch is instantly felt in heaven, and a voice of love calls, "Who touched Me?"

March 14.

"It is the Lord who judges me!" 1 Corinthians 4:4

There is a story of a young composer whose music was being performed. The audience was enthusiastic, applauding wildly as the composition was played. But the young man seemed utterly indifferent to all this applause. He kept his eye fixed intently on one man in the audience, watching every expression that played upon his features. It was his *teacher*. He cared more for the slightest mark of favor on his face—than for all the applause of the great company.

Likewise, in all our life we should watch the face of Christ, caring only that he should be pleased. It matters far more what he thinks of our performance, than what all the world besides thinks. If we live to win his approval, we shall not be afraid to have all our deeds laid bare at the last, before the judgment throne.

You who see my soul within,
You who know my unknown sin,
Through your holy eyes let me
Learn what sin is unto Thee.

Make me, Pure One, as you art,
Pure in mind and soul and heart;
Never satisfied with less
Than your perfect holiness.

March 15.

"Do not let the sun go down while you are still angry" Ephesians 4:26

The only way to make our life continuously beautiful, and to keep it ever sweet with love—is to insist on *judging ourselves day by day*. Old accounts are hard to settle. Each setting of the sun, should be a signal to us to apply the law of Christ to all our life for the day. The hour of evening prayer, should always be a time for getting right all that may have gone wrong in us during the day. Then every *feeling* of bitterness against another should be cast out of our heart. Life is too critical for us to venture into any night's darkness, nourishing anger or envy. "Do not let the sun go down while you are still angry" is a wise counsel.

The anger left in the heart tonight—will be harder to overcome tomorrow, than it is today; for bitter feelings grow more bitter as they are cherished and nursed, and who knows what the end may be? They may grow into *crimes*—unless quickly put out of the heart. Evening prayer should bring *love's flood* into all the life.

March 16.

"I have glorified You on the earth by completing the work You gave Me to do." John 17:4

Jesus is the only man who has ever lived—so as to be able to say this!

The best lives are but fragments, leaving many things unfinished. Yet we ought to take a lesson from Christ's finishing of His work. He did it, simply by doing each day—the will of His Father for the day.

He was a young man when He died—only thirty-three. We think of those who die young—as dying before their work is completed. We learn, however, that even a young man, dying, may leave a finished work.

The truth is, enough years are given to each one—in which to do our 'allotted work'. Even a baby that lives only a day, merely looking into the mother's eyes and then going away, does the work that was given it to do. The young man who dies at thirty-three, with his hands full of tasks—if only he has lived faithfully, has finished the work which God gave him to do. Not years—but faithfulness, counts with God!

March 17.

"Moses was shepherding the flock of his father-in-law Jethro. He went deep into the wilderness" Exodus 3:1

For forty years Moses had been *shepherding sheep* in the wilderness. It appears to us as if all those years were *lost*. We can see how profitably the first forty were spent. Those earlier years under his *mother's influence*—he carried their lessons and impress to the end. Then those years in the *schools of Egypt* and in the *palace* he learned much there which was essential to his mission. But what did that long period in the *desert* do toward fitting him to be a leader, a lawgiver, the builder of a nation? Far more, no doubt, than we can tell. All that while, his *character* was knitting itself into strength. He was learning *self-discipline*. In the wilderness, he was taught many a lesson which made him more fit for his work—lessons he could never have learned in the busy life of Pharaoh's palace.

Nowadays, boys can scarcely wait until they are out of their teens to begin their life-work. Some of them think it a waste of time to take a regular college course before they enter a profession. They think they must get at once into the ministry, or into the medical or legal profession. They cannot afford the time to study through all the long course. No wonder such *boys* fail as *men.* When God trains a man for any great work—he always takes plenty of time. No boy acts wisely who is in such a hurry to get to work that he cannot wait to prepare well.

March 18.

Now the Lord had said to Aaron, "Go out into the *wilderness* to meet Moses." Exodus 4:27

God always knows where to find the man he wants. Indeed, he trains men while they know it not—for the work he means them to do by and by. For *eighty* years Moses had been in special preparation for his great mission as leader. Aaron also had been in training for the particular part of the work he was to do. He did not know what he was being prepared for—but God knew. Probably Aaron had naturally a fine voice. Then we may suppose that while in Egypt he was led to give much attention to elocution and oratory. He did not know what special use was to be made of his power—but God knew. Then when the time came for him to enter upon his work, he was ready.

The young man does not know what work God may have waiting for him to do. But he possesses certain talents and gifts. These he should train to the very highest degree of efficiency. Then when God wants him—he will be ready.

It was the daily prayer of a young Christian girl, that God would prepare her for whatever he was preparing for her. Many lives are failures, because when God wants them they are not ready. Many a young man enters a profession without qualification, having squandered his opportunities. Is it any wonder he makes a failure? We should train ourselves to *proficiency* in something, and God will want us by and by, and we shall be ready.

March 19.

"And Aaron spoke all the words which the Lord had spoken unto Moses." Exodus 4:30

One of the excuses Moses offered when God bade him go to be the deliverer of his people—was that *he was not a good speaker*. God met his difficulty by telling him that he would provide a speaker. Aaron would be his mouthpiece. So all along the history, Moses is a *silent* man, and Aaron's is the voice we hear. Each did his own part.

It is just in this way that God's work is always to be done. No one person has *universal* gifts. One man is a poor talker—but has *brains* and *heart*, and can make plans, and impart energy and inspiration. Another is an eloquent speaker—but lacks in the very points in which the first excels. Put the two together, and they can achieve great results.

In a church, some can sing well; some cannot sing—but can teach; some can do neither—but can carry comfort to the sick; some can manage business affairs; some can make money—and give it. There is a *diversity* of gifts, no two having the same; but if all work together, each doing his own part, the church is not only a power— but there is no *necessary work* which is not done. Never worry because you have not the gift some other one has; you have some gift, and that is the one God wants you to use!

March 20.

"Moses made an end of speaking." Deuteronomy 32:45

So we all shall do some day. Moses knew it was the end for him; we may not know when our end is at hand. Any word of ours, spoken amid glee and merriment, may be our last!! If we always thought of this—would it not make us more careful? Would we ever say an unkind word to a friend, if we felt that we may never have an opportunity to unsay it or repent of it? Would we ever utter an angry, untrue, or unclean word—if we only remembered that it may be the *last* utterance our lips shall give forth?

We want to have *beautiful endings* to our life, to leave sweet memories behind us in the hearts of those who love us. We want our names to be fragrant in the homes on whose thresholds our footfalls are accustomed to be heard. We want the *memory* of our last words in our friends' ears—to live as a tender joy with them as the days pass away. We can be sure of all this—only by making *every* word we speak beautiful enough to be a last word. For with any sentence—we may come to the end of our speaking.

March 21.

"On that same day the Lord spoke to Moses—Go up Mount Nebo . . . You must die there on the mountain" Deuteronomy 32:48-50

To each of us the *summons* will sometime come: "Go away from your farm, your store, your desk, your books, your pleasure, into the silence of your own room—and die." We may not hear the voice, when we lay down our work at nightfall, nor be conscious that we are going away to die; but this will not alter the fact. We will come to our last hour—when *the voice none can resist* will call us from earth.

Moses was to die **alone**. None of the people accompanied him. Every one of us really has to die alone. Our friends may gather around us; they may hold our hand; they may sing or pray with us; they may drop their tears on our cold cheek, and print hot kisses of farewell on our lips—yet we must die alone. No one can accompany us *beyond the foot of the mountain*. This is a point at which the tenderest affection can give no help. It is like one going out on the sea in a ship. Friends come to the shore and wave their farewells as we go out—but not one of them goes with us. We must die alone!

"So Moses, the servant of the Lord, *died* there . . . just as the Lord had said." Deuteronomy 34:5

March 22.

"After the death of Moses the LORD's servant, the LORD spoke to Joshua son of Nun, Moses' assistant. He said—Now that my servant Moses is dead—*you* must lead my people across the Jordan River into the land I am giving them." Joshua 1:1-2

Sorrow came to you yesterday—and emptied your home. Your first impulse now is to give up and sit down in despair amid the wrecks of your hopes. But you dare not do it. You are in the line of battle, and the crisis is at hand. To falter a moment, would be to imperil some holy interest. Other lives would be harmed by your pausing. Holy interests would suffer—should your hands be folded. You must not linger even to indulge your grief. Sorrows are but incidents in life, and must not interrupt us. We must leave them behind, while we press on to the things that are before.

Then God has so ordered, too, that in pressing on in duty—we shall find the truest, richest comfort for ourselves. Sitting down to brood over our sorrows, the darkness deepens about us and creeps into our heart, and our strength changes to weakness. But if we turn away from the gloom, and take up the tasks and duties to which God calls us—the light will come again and we shall grow stronger!

March 23.

"My prayer is not that you take them out of the world but that you protect them from the evil one." John 17:15

Christ does not wish that we shall be kept from suffering—but that in our suffering, we shall not sin. He does not wish that we may never have sickness—but that in our sickness, we may not fail of patience, sweetness, and trust. He does not wish that we may have no trials or struggles—but that in our trials and struggles, we may not be overcome and our lives hurt or marred.

There is only one evil in the world—SIN, and it lurks everywhere! It comes even in our purest joys; we may forget God in them. The happiest home may become a place of peril to us, leading us to self-indulgence, love of ease, forgetfulness of the world's need and sorrow, neglect of duties, even to forgetfulness of God.

There is no sin in our being hated by the world, in our being wronged or injured by others; but if we endure the hatred and the wrong resentfully, if we grow angry and seek to avenge ourselves—we have sinned. There is no sin in our being assailed by temptations, we cannot live a day without being tempted—but the moment we yield to the temptation, we have sinned. There is no sin in our suffering adversity, disappointment, loss, need; but the moment that in any such experience we repine, doubt God, or rebel against his will—we have done evil and sinned.

March 24.

"Dear friends, we are God's children now, and what we will be has not yet been revealed. We know that when He appears, we will be like Him, because we will see Him as He is!" 1 John 3:2

Think of the possibilities of man, in the light of the revealings of Christianity. You know what the Christ says of the future of everyone who believes in him—but have you ever thought deeply about it?

Have you ever thought seriously about the word 'eternity', as a definition of the duration of your own life? Jesus tells us we shall have eternal life, and that means not *endless existence* only—but endless growth, development, progress. The New Testament tells us that we know now only in part, only little fragments of any knowledge—but that some day we shall know perfectly. It tells us also that there will be the most wondrous moral development in these lives of ours.

There is a glory in the Christian's soul, which is not yet revealed. The Bible lifts the veil, and shows us a glimpse of our eternal stat, "We shall be like Him!" I cannot explain that. It is too high for any human thought to comprehend it. But surely it tells of marvelous possibilities in men. That is the future of every one who will link his life to the life of Christ.

March 25.

"For we do not preach ourselves, but Jesus Christ as Lord, and *ourselves as your servants* for Jesus' sake." 2 Corinthians 4:5

It is said of a great artist, that when painting his immortal pictures on the ceiling of St. Peter's Cathedral, he carried a little lamp fastened to his cap on his forehead, so that no *shadow of himself* should fall on his work. It would be well if we should learn always so to carry the light by which we work, that *SELF* shall never in any way come between our lamp and our work. We should so relate our own personality to our serving—that it shall never cast a *shadow* on the things we are doing for Christ.

It is not easy so to move through life that no mood or feeling of our own, shall ever affect our spirit or temper as we go on with our duty. Ofttimes the temptation is strong. Things do not go altogether to our mind. Other people do not accord to us the honor or respect we think we deserve. The tendency is to feel hurt, and then to allow our hurt consciousness to affect our interest in the work or our relations with our fellow-workers. But this is not the Christian way—not the way Jesus would act. No *apparent* or *real* slighting of us—should make us less faithful. *Touchiness*is not among the fruits of the Spirit.

March 26.

"You wicked servant! I canceled all that debt of yours because you begged me to. Should not you have had mercy on your fellow servant just as I had on you?" Matthew 18:32-33

Though the servant had been forgiven all his *vast* debt, he had not been willing to forgive a fellow servant a mere *trifle* of debt.

No Christian precept is urged more repeatedly and more earnestly than this. In the form of prayer which our Lord taught his disciples, he linked together divine and human forgiveness: "Forgive us our debts—as we forgive our debtors." Then he added a clear and unmistakable word, emphasizing the lesson: "For if you forgive men their trespasses, your heavenly Father will also forgive you; but if you forgive not men their trespasses, neither will your Father forgive your trespasses."

Paul enjoins, "Be kind one to another, tender-hearted, forgiving one another, even as God for Christ's sake has forgiven you." This is but one of many repetitions of the solemn lesson. If we are not ready to forgive those who do us *little injuries*—it is proof that we ourselves are not forgiven of God. If there be not in the heart the spirit of forgiveness, evidently it has not yet experienced the mercy of God.

It was said of one: "His heart was as great as the world—but there was no room in it to hold the memory of a wrong."

March 27.

"I am the light of the world. Whoever follows me will never walk in darkness, but will have the light of life." John 8:12

We are always coming to points we have never passed before. Every new *temptation* is such a point. We cannot get through it unless we have a guide.

Some of you know how dark and strange it seemed to you, the first time you had to enter the *valley of sorrow*. A godly man says: "I shall never forget, while memory lasts, the strangeness of the experience through which I passed, when first the *reaper* whose name is *Death* came into my home, and with his sickle keen cut down at one thrust, two of my children! The stroke blinded me for the moment; but when at length I opened my eyes, I saw the *ark* in the river, and that instantly steadied me. I knew then where I was."

Every new *duty* brings us also to a way we know not. Every fresh *responsibility* calls us to walk in an unfamiliar road. All of life is untrodden, and we cannot find the way ourselves.

Then there is that last walk on earth—into the *valley of shadows*. We never can get any experience in dying; for no feet ever walk twice on that way, nor has any friend ever come back to tell us what it is like. When we come to die, we shall find ourselves in an experience we have never known before. If we have not Christ in the strange, unfamiliar path, we shall not find the way.

March 28.

His disciples asked him, "Rabbi, who sinned, this man or his parents, that he was born blind?" "Neither this man nor his parents sinned," said Jesus, "but this happened so that the work of God might be displayed in his life." John 9:2-3

Are troubles sent to *punish* us for our sins? The people in Christ's day thought so. But Jesus gave a different explanation. He said the man was blind—that the works of God should be displayed in his life. His blindness led him into contact with Jesus—and thus brought him a double blessing, the opening of his *natural* eyes, and the opening of his *soul's* eyes. Probably he would never have met Jesus—but for his misfortune of blindness. If he had not been blind, this miracle of his healing would never have been wrought!

A great many revealings and blessings come through troubles. Jesus said the *sickness of Lazarus* was for the glory of God, that the Son of God might be glorified thereby. No doubt every sickness is an opportunity for a blessing of some kind, both to the person who is sick and to his friends. Every *loss* we have, is meant to be the revealing to us of a gain which would more than make compensation. Every *disappointment* in our life, is intended to give us a better thing than that which we have failed to get.

March 29.

"Be imitators of me—even as I also am of Christ." 1 Corinthians 11:1

You may think you have no influence over any other lives—but you have. There are those who will *do* what you do, and *be* what you are. If you are reverent, they will be reverent; if you are false, they are false. Your influence touches many other lives, and leaves either blessing or curse.

A gentleman told the story of his conversion to Christ: "If I had been going to damnation alone," he said, "I would have gone on. But one night I came in from the wine-table, and looked at my sleeping babes as they lay in their holy innocence amid the snowy pillows. I held the lamp so that its beams fell full upon their sweet faces. As I stood there in the awful silence, unbroken, save by the ticking of the clock on the mantel, and the soft breathing of my little ones, there arose a terrifying vision before my eyes. I saw myself sweeping down toward perdition, and these, my precious children, clinging to my garments. I could not stand that. I could go to ruin myself—but to drag my *angel babes* there with me oh, I could not do that! So right there beside the crib, I fell on my knees before God, and asked him to save me for my children's sake."

Few motives in life could be stronger than the consciousness that the career and destiny of *other lives* will depend on what we do with our own life! We should be able always to say, "Imitate me—and you will live nobly!"

March 30.

"And if anyone gives even a cup of cold water to one of these little ones because he is my disciple, I tell you the truth, he will certainly not lose his reward." Matthew 10:42

We never can know what the full outcome of our simplest kindnesses will be. We speak a cheerful word to one who is discouraged. We pass on, scarcely giving another thought to the matter. Yet perhaps our word has saved a life from despair, helped a fainting robin back unto its nest again, or changed a destiny from darkness to light.

Nor can we know how far the influence of our word shall extend. A pebble dropped into the sea, starts wavelets which go around and around the world. A word spoken into the air, goes pulsating in the atmosphere forever. So it is with the things we do for Christ. We cannot follow them, to trace their story; but their blessing shall never cease from the world's life. There will be many surprises in heaven, when we learn the *effects* of our words and deeds of love.

March 31.

"Having loved *His own* who were in the world—He loved them to the end." John 13:1

Follower of Jesus—you may write your own name into this verse, and it will be as true as it was of the company at the table that night! Having loved you—Jesus loves you unto the end!

It was the night before Jesus died. He was with His disciples at the Passover. Holy memories filled His mind. But amid these, His love for His own people lost none of its warmth. His "hour" of sorrow and shame was come. But with all this before Him, He did not forget "His own." He gathered them about Him, and spent the last evening with them. He had no thought for Himself; He thought only of "His own." His personal grief and bitterness were kept in His own heart, while He gave them joy. His love over-mastered His sorrow.

Then there was something else. The words read: "His hour had come to leave this world and return to His Father." So there was glory for him beyond His cross! There were a few hours of darkness, woe, and anguish—and then He would leave this world and be at home again! His heart must have been full of rapture and expectancy as He looked forward, knowing that He would shortly be home with His Father. Yet even this blessed consciousness did not make him forget His friends. "Having loved His own who were in the world—He loved them to the end."

APRIL

April 1.

"She did what she could. She poured perfume on my body beforehand to prepare for my burial." Mark 14:8

Many people would have kept the jar of perfume until Jesus was dead, and would then have broken it to anoint his cold body. At least, that is the way too many of us do in these days. We wait until our friend dies—and then send our flowers and speak our words of appreciation. Should we not learn a lesson from Mary? The *kind words* we mean to speak when our friends are dead—let us speak while they can hear them! The *flowers* we mean to send for their coffin—let us send to brighten the rough paths for their feet. The epitaphs we mean to put upon white marble—let us carve in deeds of gentle love while our friends are with us. Words of cheer today— are what people crave.

"Withhold all eulogies when I am dead,
All noisy sorrow;
Give me the tender word *today*
Instead of tears tomorrow."

April 2.

"Surely he has borne our griefs, and carried our sorrows." Isaiah 53:4

Whatever the cause of grief may be, there is rich comfort in the remembrance of the *sorrows of Christ*. It assures us that Christ understands our pain. In the garden he went a stone's cast farther than any of his disciples went. The picture is a parable to us. It is always so. Wherever you bow in the *deep* shadows of grief, you have but to lift up your eyes, and you will see Jesus in still *deeper* shadows—a stone's cast beyond you. His sorrow was sorer than yours.

There is comfort also in the remembrance that *blessing* comes out of *suffering patiently endured*. All the world's peace and hope, and all heaven's joy and glory—

are fruits of a great sorrow—the sorrow of Christ. Blessing will come always out of sorrow, if we but accept it submissively and reverently.

While we think of the sufferings of Christ, we must remember also that he came from them all *unharmed*, his life shining in divine radiance, lifted to glory, too, as a fruit of his suffering. This reminds sorrowing believers, that they too shall pass through their time of tribulation, that no scars and no manner of hurt shall be upon their *souls* because of their sufferings—but that they shall shine in fairer beauty and diviner glory, and shall be lifted up to higher honor, because of what they have suffered with Christ.

April 3.

"Christ died for our sins, according to the Scriptures." I Corinthians 15:3

There have been great days in the history of the human race, days of triumph whose victories have enriched the world; days of honor whose brightness has made the world lighter; days of great deeds which have lifted man to loftier, diviner heights; days of heroic, self-forgetful love which has made the air sweeter with its odorous perfumes. But the *day of all days* in fruit of blessing and good in the world's story, was that holy Friday when the Son of man gave his life on the cross to save men!

There could have been no rising again, without the dying on the cross. Christ must die—before he could offer deathless life to every man. The *touch of the cross* is on every hope of Christian faith. The light that shines in soft luster throughout all the world—streams from the cross. The sorrow of Calvary is that which is softening all human hearts, and making all life gentler and sweeter. The power that is drawing all men upward—is the Christ lifted up.

April 4.

"My God, My God, why have You forsaken Me!" Matthew 27:46

There is a picture which represents the after-scenes on that day of the crucifixion. It is all over. The crowds have gone away. The evening sun is shining out again on Calvary. The body of the Savior has been borne to the sepulcher. The cross has been taken down, and lies on the ground. A company of little children, bright with the glow of childhood's innocence, led to the place by accident or curiosity, are seen bending over the signs of the day's terrible work. One of the children holds in his hand a nail which a little time before, had pierced a hand or a foot of the patient Sufferer, and stands spellbound with horror as he gazes at it. His gentle heart is shocked at sin's dreadful work! On all the children's faces, the same expression of horror is depicted.

No one with pure and gentle heart, can ever look at the death of Christ on the cross—with any but feelings of amazement and horror at sin's awfulness!

It was sin that nailed Jesus on the cross!

It was sin that wreathed the circlet of thorns for his brow!

We say the Jews crucified Christ; yes—but WE helped to do it!

Our sins drove the nails!

Would you see what sin is? Stand by the cross and ponder its terrible work, there in the death of the Redeemer. See what it cost the Lamb of God, to take away sin!

April 5.

"He was *raised* on the third day according to the Scriptures" 1 Corinthians 15:4

If your faith stops at the cross—it misses the blessing of the fullest revealing of Christ!

You need a Savior who not merely two thousand years ago went to death to redeem you—but one who also is alive to walk by your side in loving companionship.

You need a Savior who can hear your prayers, to whose feet you can creep in penitence when you have sinned, to whom you can call for help when the battle is going against you.

You need a Savior who is interested in all the affairs of your common life, and who can assist you in every time of need.

You need a Christ who can be a real friend—loving you, keeping close beside you, able to sympathize with your weaknesses.

You need a Savior who will come into your life, and will save you, not by one great act of centuries past—but by a life warm and throbbing with love today, and living again in you.

It is for love that our hearts hunger. The bread that will satisfy us, is not the bread of memorial merely—the memory of a great devotion of love long, long since—but the bread of love—living, present, warm and throbbing! Nothing less than a LIVING Christ will do for us!

And that is the Christ the gospel brings to us: one who was dead—and is now alive for evermore!

"I am the *Living* One; I was dead, and behold I am *alive* for ever and ever!" Revelation 1:18

April 6.

"Why do you seek the living—among the dead?" Luke 24:5

A DYING Christ alone, will not satisfy your heart. While you praise the love that was crucified for you—you crave love from a Savior who lives. Memories of a friend who has died, may be very sweet. The fragrance of 'departed love' stays in a home, like the perfume of sweet flowers, when the flowers have been borne away. But how unsatisfying are the mere memories of your friend—when your heart hungers for love's real presence, and touch and tenderness! No more will the mere memories of the Love that died on the cross for you—satisfy your cravings for Christ. You must have the living One for your friend!

"My soul thirsts for God, for the living God!" cried the psalmist, and cries every redeemed soul. It is only as we realize the truth of a living Christ—that our hearts are satisfied. We crave love—a bosom to lean upon, a hand to touch ours, a heart whose beatings we can feel, a personal friendship that will come into our life with its sympathy, its inspiration, its companionship, its shelter, its life, its comfort. All this, the living Christ is to us, if we but learn the blessed truth of his resurrection. "I am the Living One; I was dead, and behold I am alive for ever and ever!" Revelation 1:18

April 7.

"Very early on the first day of the week, just after sunrise, they were on their way to the tomb" Mark 16:2

The women did not find the body of Jesus in the grave. Suppose they had found it there, still held in the power of death; suppose that Jesus had never risen; what would have been the consequences? It would have been as if the sun and moon and stars were all to be blotted from the sky, or as if they had all set one day and never risen again.

Paul tells us in his immortal chapter on the resurrection, what our loss would be, should it be found that Christ did not rise. "If Christ has not been raised, then is our preaching vain; your faith also is vain. ... You are yet in your sins!" Paul had preached of a Savior who *died* for men's sins—and then *rose* for their justification; but if Christ yet lay in the power of death, his sacrifice for sin had not availed.

If you were imprisoned in some great fortress, and one who loved you went forth to try to rescue you, and fell and died fighting upon the walls, you would cherish the memory of your friend's valiant effort on your behalf—but you would still remain *undelivered*. So would it have been with those whom Christ came to save, if he had perished in death and had not risen. He would have been defeated in his great effort, and those for whom he died would have remained without deliverance!

April 8.

"But go, tell his disciples *and Peter*" Mark 16:7

The joyful news must not be kept—but must be carried to the other sorrowing friends of Jesus, and must be carried 'quickly'. There must not be a moment lost. The happy women must not sit down together in mere personal enjoyment of the blessed news; there were others in the darkness of sorrow—and to these they must hasten with the gladness. We must not forget in our joy of Christian faith, that there are others who have none of this joy; our mission is to carry the good news, and to rejoice as we go on our way.

"Tell his disciples *and Peter*." Why was Peter specially named? It was because he was the saddest of all, the one who most needed the comfort. He had sinned, and was weeping in penitence. This showed the tenderness of the heart of Christ toward all penitents. It must have given Peter unspeakable joy to get this message. Jesus then had not cast him off. He would now have an opportunity to weep on his Lord's bosom, confess his sin, and crave and obtain pardon.

"And Peter" has its gracious message for every penitent soul. Have you grieved Christ by sin, by denial, by any unfaithfulness, and are you weeping in sorrow over your sin? Those who have fallen are the very ones that lie most heavily on the heart of Jesus, just because they have fallen. "It is not the healthy who need a doctor, but the sick. I have not come to call the righteous, but sinners to repentance." Luke 5:31-32

April 9.

"Then their eyes were opened, and they recognized Him, but He disappeared from their sight!" Luke 24:31

Anniversary days always bring back the memories of those who have died. Out of what home, has not some beloved face vanished? You are thinking of these departed ones. If they died in Christ—the gospel of these *Easter days* lifts the veil, and shows them to you away beyond death, unhurt by death, living still, the same gentle friends they were when you knew them here and clasped them in your arms.

I had a letter the other day from Rome, written by a dear friend who is journeying abroad in search of health. The letter was full of bright words which reminded me of my friend's beautiful life. There was the same old warmth, the same eager interest in things and people, the same kindly thoughtfulness. "Just like my friend!" I said, as I read the letter. Being in Rome has made no change in his gentle spirit.

It is just so with our friends in heaven. My father and mother are there. If I were to go to my 'long home' today, I know I would see them unchanged. Of course the marks of care are gone, or have become transfigured, and are now marks of beauty. They have not their earthly bodies—but then, those *worn and weary bodies* were not my *real* father and mother. Death ended nothing beautiful in them. I would see them living in new and richer life, engaged, as they used to be on earth, in loving ministries.

April 10.

"Very early on the first day of the week, just after sunrise, they were on their way to the tomb and they asked each other, *'Who will roll the stone away from the entrance of the tomb?'* But when they looked up, they saw that the stone, which was very large, had been rolled away!" Mark 16:2-4

This stone had worried the women, as they hurried toward the grave. They knew it was there, that it was too heavy for them with their frail hands to roll away, and they wondered how they could get it removed. But now, when they came in sight of the tomb—they looked up and saw that the stone was rolled away!

This incident illustrates many experiences in our common life. We worry about difficulties and obstacles which lie in our path—and seem to block our progress. But when we move on obediently, and come to the place of the supposed hindrance or obstacle—it is gone, or it was never there, except in our imagination! We all know that very many of our anxieties prove to be really groundless in the end.

Here, we ought to learn the lesson once for all—when God sends us anywhere, that He also makes it possible for us to go. Duty's paths always open for us, as we go on—not before we start—but as we obey and move forward. Yet we must not expect there will never be any difficulties to meet, or obstacles to surmount. God never has promised that! Too easy a path is often a bane in life—not a blessing! The difficulties and obstacles that remain, may be made stepping-stones by which we shall rise to nobler and higher Christian character!

April 11.

"Then the eleven disciples went to Galilee, to the mountain where Jesus had told them to go." Matthew 28:16

We should always keep the *appointments* Jesus makes with us. If we fail—we shall surely be the losers. Suppose some of our Lord's disciples had stayed away, for some cause, from this meeting in Galilee. Think what they would have missed! They might have said: "It is such a long distance;" or, "The mountain is steep, and I will have difficulty climbing it;" or, "I fear it will rain or be stormy;" or, "Perhaps Jesus will not be there; I cannot understand how he can be risen from the dead."

For any of these, or for other similar reasons, some might have been absent that wonderful day. But they would have missed *a glorious sight of the risen Jesus*, and would not have heard his words of commission and promise. To the end of their life, they would have regretted that they had not kept *their Lord's appointment* that day.

Christ makes many appointments for us. Sometimes we do not think them very important, and are easily hindered from keeping them. But we never can know what we lose by these neglects. Jesus always comes where he asks us to meet him, and gives blessings there to those who have been faithful in gathering to wait for him. We do not know what we may miss, any common Sunday—by staying away from the services appointed by Christ.

April 12.

"I have the same *hope* in God as these men—that there will be a *resurrection* of both the righteous and the wicked!" Acts 24:15

A *hope of resurrection* to a believer in Christ—ought to be a wonderful inspiration in the earthly life. The *grave* is not the *end*; we shall come again from it in new beauty, and shall live on forever. Not only did Christ teach that the dead shall rise again—but he himself went down into the grave and then came out again, after three days, alive! Thus he showed the reality of resurrection; *one* man died and rose again, and may not all? But his resurrection meant more than that. He was the head of his people, and as such—his victory was for *them*. He met and conquered death *for them*.

Now death is a vanquished foe. Paul puts it very strongly, and says that *Christ abolished death*. Jesus himself put it no less strongly when he said, "I am the resurrection and the life . . . whoever lives and believes in me—shall never die!" There is no break, no interruption, in a Christian's life, in what we call *dying*. The spirit lives more really, fully, gloriously, a moment after death—than ever it lived before. Then the body which goes down into the grave, 'sleeps'—that is the Christian word—sleeps in Jesus, until the resurrection, when Christ will come and call it up; not the old earthly, worn-out, sin-corrupted, mortal flesh and blood—but a new, strong, glorious, incorruptible, immortal, spiritual body, to live with Christ forever!

April 13.

"I do not practice what I want to do—but I do what I hate!" Romans 7:15

Think of the brokenness, the incompleteness, the littleness, of these lives of ours! We get glimpses of beauty in character, which we are not able to attain! We have longings which seem to us too great ever to come true. We dream of things we want to do; but when we try to work them out, our clumsy hands cannot put them into realizations! We have glimmerings of a love that is very rich and tender, without a trace of selfishness, without envy or jealousy, without resentment—a love that seeks not its own, is not provoked, and bears all things. We get the vision from the life of Christ Himself. We say, "I will learn that lesson of love; I will be like that!" But we fail.

We strive to be sweet-spirited, unselfish, thoughtful, kind—but we must wet our pillow with tears at the close of our marred days, because we cannot be what we strive to be! We have glimpses of a peace which is very beautiful. We strive after it strive with intense effort—but do not reach it!

So it is in all our living. Life is ever something too large for us. We attain only fragments of living. Yet take heart, "The *desire* of the righteous shall be granted!" Proverbs 10:24

"We know that when He appears—we shall be like Him!" 1 John 3:2

April 14.

"Therefore, my dear brothers, be steadfast, immovable, always excelling in the Lord's work, knowing that your labor in the Lord is not in vain!" 1 Corinthians 15:58

Jesus walks no more among men, doing his deeds of love—but he sends his followers forth to do the works in his name. We ought to abound in all *loving ministry* just as he did. It is not enough to be good, gentle, sweet, amiable, kindly, patient. It is beautiful to live such a life; and its influence is far-reaching, like the fragrance of Mary's ointment. But we must also be full of good works. We must be winners of souls. We must live to do good to men, to comfort sorrow, to feed hunger, to relieve distress, to cheer the disheartened, to break chains and liberate sin's captives, to stand up for the truth, to do battle for the right. We are to be like Christ, and we begin to be like Christ—only when we begin to be useful.

It ought to be a wondrous inspiration to us, in our work for Christ—to read that our labor for God is not in vain. No word of truth spoken in this world is ever lost. On the *rocks* we find the impressions left ages since by leaves that fell on the soft clay and seemed to perish. So somewhere every word we speak for God, and every smallest deed we do for the love of Christ, leave their immortal record.

April 15.

"Then the disciple whom Jesus loved said to Peter—It is the Lord!" John 21:7

One compares the character of John, in its mellow ripeness, to an ancient, extinct volcano. Where once the crater yawned—there is now a verdurous, cup-like hollow on the mountain summit. Where once the fierce fires burned—lies a still, clear pool of water, looking up like an eye to the beautiful heavens above, its banks covered with sweet flowers. "It is an apt parable," he says, "of the apostle John. Naturally and originally volcanic, capable of profoundest passion and daring—he is new-made by grace, until in his old age he stands out in calm grandeur of character, and depth and largeness of soul, with all the gentlenesses and graces of Christ adorning him a man; as I imagine him to myself, with a face so *noble* that kings might do him homage, and so *sweet*that little children would run to him for his blessing." This is a true and striking portrait of this *disciple of love*.

What was it that wrought this transformation in John, that changed the "son of thunder" into the *apostle of Christly affectionateness?* It was *leaning upon the Master's bosom* that did it. The lump of *common clay* lay upon the *perfumed rose*, and the sweetness of the rose entered into it. John lay on Jesus' bosom, on the bosom of the all-loving One, and the love of Jesus passed into John's soul and transformed it. That was the secret of John's sanctification.

April 16.

Again Jesus said, "Simon son of John, do you truly love Me?"

He answered, "Yes, Lord, you know that I love You." John 21:16

We are striving to follow Christ—but we are weak. We intend to be loving—but we mar our days with unhappy tempers and selfish strivings. We intend to be strong in faith—but many times our trust fails us. We bow our heads to take the Master's blessing, "Peace be unto you;" but again and again—the peace is broken. We intend to show the world a pattern of Christlikeness, but the temptations about us are so sore, that every day we are conscious of having failed to be true. We set out in the morning brave and confident; but alas! how often does the evening find us defeated!

What shall we do? There stands the Master, patient, unwearied in His love, asking, "Do you truly love Me?" Dare we say, "Yes, Lord, you know that I love You." If He were but a man like ourselves, we could not; for our failures would seem to disprove our word, and He could not read the love in our secret heart, under all our inconsistency. But He knows all the truth about us. He knows we are sincere and loyal in heart, though so unworthy. He sees the love—amid the broken vows and the failures. Therefore, we can look up out of our deep humiliation, and say with inexpressible comfort, "Yes, Lord, you know that I love You!"

April 17.

The third time He said to him, "Simon son of John, do you love Me?" Peter replied, "Lord, You know all things; You know that I love You!" John 21:17

You look into your life today and what do you see there? Failures, broken purposes, promises not kept, commandments violated, purity stained, everything sullied! Jesus comes and looks into your face, with that calm, holy, searching gaze of His, and says, "Do you love Me?" As you are about to answer, you think of all you have done that has been dishonorable and sinful. You are speechless before Him. Yet you are conscious that you do love Him; that in your heart, beneath all your sins, failures, and faults—there is love for Him. What a comfort it is to cast yourself on His knowledge of what is in you! Perhaps men sneer, and say that one who has stumbled as you have done—surely cannot love Christ. But Christ knows the love, even amid the sins and failures.

I am glad that perfection is not the test of discipleship. We may be full of faults. We go on stumbling every day. We do nothing beautifully. We misrepresent the Christ whose name we bear. We hurt the friends we want to help.

Christ knows all these sad failures. He looks at the stained scroll we fold up at the close of the day—with the blots on it. But while He sees the worst, He sees also the best; and He loves on loves unto the uttermost! "Lord, You know all things; You know that I love You!"

April 18.

Jesus said to her, "Your brother will rise again!" John 11:23

There is wondrous music in these words, as they are spoken in the ears of sorrowing ones beside the coffin and by the new-made grave. It was a dim teaching in Martha's time—but soon afterward that occurred which made it bright and clear as day. Jesus himself lay in the grave, and then rose from death, walking forth in the light and radiancy of immortal youth.

Christ was the first fruits of resurrection; that is, his resurrection was a *pledge* as well as an *example* of the coming resurrection of all who believe on him.

We have a right to lay flowers on the coffins of our *Christian dead*. They will come forth in the beauty of new life. We open our New Testament and see Jesus, after he had risen, away beyond death. He has not been *harmed* by dying. No beam of the beauty of his life is quenched. The threads of the earthly life are not severed. He has not forgotten his friends—but takes up again the old companionships and friendships. So will it be with our beloved ones who sleep in Jesus. They will rise—and they will be the same people we have known here, only they will be cleansed of their *earthliness, mortality* and *sinfulness*. And they will not have forgotten us. Love never fails. We shall resume friendship's story on the other side!

April 19.

"Take away the stone," Jesus said. John 11:39

We find in all our Lord's life, an *economy of miracle*. He never put forth supernatural power, unless it was necessary. Could not Jesus have taken away the stone himself? Certainly he could. The power that could call the dead to life, could easily have lifted back the piece of rock from the door of the tomb. But there is always something left for *human hands* to do.

God honors us by making us co-workers with himself, both in providence and grace. He feeds us—but ordinarily we must toil to earn and gather our own food. He saves people's souls; but he uses men to speak the message, and then to help in winning the lost. He makes his work dependent, too, upon our fidelity in doing our part. He still wants us to *take away the stones* that shut our friends in their prison.

This command also exercised the faith of the friends. If they had refused to do what he bade them do, the miracle could not have been wrought. "Did I not tell you that if you *believed*, you would see the glory of God?" Had not the unbelief given away to faith, Lazarus would not have been raised. May it not be that many times, in our own days, and in the experiences of our own lives, great works of divine power which Christ stands ready to perform, are not wrought because we do not believe?

April 20.

"As the Father has sent Me, I also send you." John 20:21

The Son of God came down and lived in human form on the earth—that men might see *God in the flesh*. He said, "He who has seen me, has seen the Father." All the love, the gentleness, the patience, the compassion, the purity, the truth, the righteousness, which people saw in the life of Jesus—was simply a revealing of God. That is what God is like.

Now the Christ sends *us* out to reveal God to men. We are to show to them in our character, disposition, spirit, and temper—the qualities of God. If anyone asks us to tell him what God is like, we ought to be able to say humbly and yet truthfully, "I am trying to be like God. He lives in me, and his qualities shine out in my life. Look at me—and you will see what God is like."

I know how dimly the beauty of God shines in us, even at the best; but we cannot get away from the truth that if we are indeed Christ's, he lives in us. Paul said more than once: "Be imitators of me—even as I am of Christ." We must be able to say the same.

April 21.

"For I know the plans I have for you," declares the LORD, "plans to prosper you and not to harm you, plans to give you hope and a future." Jeremiah 29:11

It is better that *we* should not know our future. If we did, we would often spoil God's plan for our life. If we could see into tomorrow, and know the troubles it will bring, we might be tempted to seek some way of avoiding them, while really they are God's way to new honor and blessing. God's thoughts for us—are always thoughts of love, good, promotion, but sometimes the *path to the hilltop* lies through *dark valleys* or *up rough paths*. Yet to miss the *hard bit* of road is to fail of gaining the lofty height. It is better, therefore, to walk with God, not knowing the path ourselves, than it would be to see the way and choose for ourselves. God's way for us—is always better than our own.

April 22.

"I will lead the blind by ways they have not known, along unfamiliar paths I will guide them; I will turn the darkness into light before them and make the rough places smooth. These are the things I will do; I will not forsake them." Isaiah 42:16

God leads often to good ends—through ways which to us seem dark. He can make crooked things, straight for us. Perhaps we shall find at the last, that many of the best things of our life, are things over which we grieve now as *blunders*. We do the best we can, and yet we fail, or *seem* to fail; but in God's eyes, the effort tells of love and of desire to please him, and thus wins from him warmer commendation than does many a piece of elaborate work, wrought in most intricate way.

God can use our poorest efforts ofttimes to greater purpose, than our finest and most polished endeavors, because they are less spoiled by human pride. Self-consciousness always mars human work. The things we do which satisfy *us*—are not likely to satisfy *our Master*. Many times the piece of work which we think very fine, which pleases us well, turns put to be of little use. God cannot use it because we have left no place in it for him. Then, ofttimes something which we think of no account—God uses to accomplish great results. The less of *SELF* there is in our service—the more is the service worth. There is room then in it for more of God, and it is the *divine* in what we do—that alone gives it efficiency and value.

April 23.

"As the rain and the snow come down from heaven, and do not return to it without watering the earth and making it bud and flourish, so that it yields seed for the sower and bread for the eater, so is my word that goes out from my mouth: It will not return to me empty, but will accomplish what I desire and achieve the purpose for which I sent it!" Isaiah 55:10-11

Everyone knows the effect of the rain, especially when it falls on a field that has been parched and withered. Its drops go down to the *roots* of the dying grass, the fading flowers, and the drooping trees—and soon new life appears everywhere. The grass is greener. The flowers revive and pour out fragrance. All vegetation is renewed. So it is when God's Word comes to a fainting, failing human life.

Sometimes rain comes in storms, with black clouds and fierce lightnings and thunders. People tremble and are afraid as they look on. But the storm passes, pouring out rich blessings of rain, which make all the fields rejoice. God sometimes sends his Word to us in dark, portentous forms—sickness, loss, disappointment, sorrow, trial. At first we are terrified; but in the end, when the storms have cleared away, we find that the *dark clouds* we so dreaded—were but *God's messengers* to bring to us rich blessings of grace.

April 24.

"As he was scattering the seed, some fell along the **path**, and the birds came and ate it up.

Some fell on **rocky places**, where it did not have much soil. It sprang up quickly, because the soil was shallow. But when the sun came up, the plants were scorched, and they withered because they had no root.

Other seed fell **among thorns**, which grew up and choked the plants." Matthew 13:4-7

From the heart trodden down by passing feet of pleasure, business, or care—the birds carry off the seeds the moment they are cast from the sower's hand.

On the heart with a thin, emotional stratum on its surface, the seed seems for a time to make a deep impression. The hearer weeps under the sermon. He is amazed at the coldness of ordinary Christians. But in a little time, it is all over. He has no depth of conviction, and the quick growths of his first faith, are soon withered in the heat of life's trials.

In the heart filled with the briers and thorns of earthly care, ambition, and pleasure, the seed has little chance to grow. All around the feeble stalks, grow the hardier briers and thorns, whose hungry roots and stems absorb the soil's nourishment, leaving the wheat robbed and starved. There is much of such Christian life as this.

Its possibilities are withered, stunted, choked to death by worldliness or by care. No fruit comes to anything beautiful in such lives.

It is discouraging to think that so much of the *good seed sown* comes to naught, fails through *unfavorable conditions*. Yet we should never falter in our sowing, praying for God to watch over his own holy seed.

April 25.

"Consider carefully how you *listen*." Luke 8:18

We hear a great deal about the "fearful responsibility" of those who preach and teach the Word of God. No doubt it is a solemn thing to *speak for God to men*. Those who are called to this duty, should be very faithful. But there is also a "fearful responsibility" attached to *hearing* the Word. One of our Lord's most earnest words was: "Consider carefully how you *listen*."

When the preacher's work is done in the right way, his responsibility ceases, and that of the *hearer* begins. He has heard the truth; what will he do with it? Will he believe it and accept it? Or will he reject it? He cannot be again—as if he had never heard it. It must be either a savor of life, or a savor of death, to him. Not only must he account for the opportunity of hearing—but he is also affected in his own spirit by the hearing. If he listens and yields to the influences of the truth, his heart grows softer; but if he rejects it, he is hardened by it.

No sermon or other message of truth, heard or read—leaves a man as it finds him. It makes some *impression*, that is determined by what the hearer does with it. We need to think a little of this side of the responsibility. We are hearing much that is good these passing days; it would be sad if nothing came of it all.

April 26.

"Throughout the night the cloud brought *darkness* to the one side—and *light* to the other side." Exodus 14:20

God appears different to his friends and to his enemies. To his own people he is light, comfort, joy, protection, and gladness; but to those who reject him—he is darkness, dreadful terror, and stern judgment. The thought of God's presence, fills the Christian with confidence and peace, with the warmth of love; but the same thought makes the unreconciled sinner tremble! "I thought upon God, and was troubled."

The *providence* of God, too, has this same double aspect. The Christian sees God's love everywhere. He sees his Father's hand ordering all things with loving wisdom.

When he cannot understand, he can trust and wait in confidence. But to the unreconciled man, the same providence is a dark mystery, full of dread and alarm. He has no sense of safety anywhere he may go. There is no assurance of protection, no consciousness of God's love, anywhere in the universe for him.

Death to the ungodly is a heavy cloud, charged with lightnings and thunders; but to the Christian it is a glorious blaze of divine love pouring brightness and peace all about his bed.

It will be the same on the day of *judgment*. To his own people, Christ on his throne will be all glorious, and his appearance will give unspeakable joy; but to the ungodly, his presence will be an appearance of the most appalling terror!

April 27.

"Will not the Judge of all the earth do right?" Genesis 18:25

Some people worry about the *fate of the heathen*, and ask if God can is just and do so and so. A great deal better solution of such perplexities is Abraham's: "Will not the Judge of all the earth do right?" Surely we can trust him with all such things, and leave them in his hands.

Others have perplexity concerning the apparent lack of justness in the allotments of earth. Some good people have nothing but trouble here in this world, and some wicked people have very much worldly blessings. We have the same truth on which to rest all such seeming inequities. God will surely do right. What we call *trouble* may have more real *blessing* in it—than what we call *prosperity*. Then, the end of life is not here. God has eternity in which to *adjust the equities*.

There are other people who think that their own lot is very hard. They complain about their trials and disappointments, and are discontented with what God does for them and gives them. They say God is good; yet they imply by their complaining, that he is not good. This word of Abraham's should rebuke all such complaints. Sooner might the heavens fall—than that in any smallest thing, God could do anything but what is absolutely right and just.

April 28.

"Now the Jordan is at flood stage all during harvest. Yet as soon as the priests who carried the ark reached the Jordan and their feet touched the water's edge, the water from upstream stopped flowing. So the people crossed over." Joshua 3:15-16

God does not open paths for us—in *advance* of our coming. He does not promise to help—*before* help is needed. He does not remove obstacles out of our way—before we reach them. Yet when we are on the edge of our need—God's hand is stretched out to help us.

Many people forget this, and are forever worrying about *difficulties* which they foresee in the future. They expect that God is going to make the way plain and open before them, *miles and miles*ahead; whereas he has promised to do it only *step by step* as they move on.

There is a Scripture promise which reads: "When you go through deep waters and great trouble—I will be with you." You must get into the deep waters—before you can claim this promise. Many people dread death, and lament that they have not "dying grace." Of course they will not have dying grace—when they are in good health, in the midst of life's duties, with death far in advance. Why should they have it then? Grace for *duty* is what they need *then*—living grace; then dying grace—when they come to die. When their feet are dipped in the brim of Jordan, the torrent will sink away!

April 29.

Joshua replied, "*If* the hill country of Ephraim is not large enough for you— *then* clear out land for yourselves in the forest where the Perizzites and Rephaites live." Joshua 17:15

It is the part of true wisdom—to live our life in its *actual conditions*, not calculating what we could do or could be—IF we had certain other circumstances; but rather accepting the conditions in which we must live, and making them serve us with opportunities for being noble and doing worthy things.

The learning of this bit of practical wisdom, will be worth more to many of us than any change of circumstances or conditions could be.

April 30.

"One of them, the disciple whom Jesus loved, was leaning on Jesus' bosom." John 13:23

I like the word *leaning*. John leaned his weight on Jesus, on his bosom, near his heart. We need to learn better our privilege of leaning, nestling, in the bosom of divine love. We think of giving a few of our burdens to Christ; but he wants to carry both *us* and all our load!

A gentleman was moving his library, and his boy was helping him. The child had gathered his arms full of books, and had gone off proudly with his load. Presently, however, the father heard a call for help. The little fellow had gotten half-way up the stairs when the load proved too heavy, and he sank down. The father heard the call, and, coming up the stairs, lifted and carried both the boy and his load.

That is like what Jesus will do for us. He takes our sins—and forgives them. He takes our wicked heart—and changes it. He takes our ruined life—and restores it. He takes all our mistakes and faults—and corrects them. He takes into his hands the ordering of our steps, the shaping of our circumstances, the ruling and overruling of the events of our days, our deliverance in temptation. We really have nothing whatever to do with our own life—but *our simple duty* day by day, hour by hour.

MAY

May 1.

"Do this in remembrance of me." Luke 22:19

A young man came to me one morning, holding a letter in his hand. Opening it, he showed me some pressed flowers and leaves. "My sister gathered these from my mother's grave," he said, with a voice soft and tender. Then he told me about his mother, her beautiful life, her deeds of self-denial, her loving counsels, her prayers, lingering especially on her long illness, when she faded like a flower.

"It was ten years ago," he said, "ten years ago, this very day, that she died; but it seems as if it were only yesterday." The faded flowers and leaves from her grave, had brought back the *memories* in all their vividness.

Perhaps you have in your home, some memento of a departed friend. Every time you see it—it recalls your friend. This suggests why Jesus gave us the *Last Supper*. He would keep his love and death always fresh in our mind. "My people will forget me, and what I have suffered for them. The memory of my sacrifice will fade out as the years pass. I will give them this *memorial*, so that each time they take the bread and the cup, they may freshly *remember me.* " So all these centuries, the Lord's Supper has kept the *memory* of the love and sacrifice of Christ fresh in the hearts of his people, and this memory has made all the world sweeter and gentler.

May 2.

The Lord had said to Abram, "Leave your country, your people and your father's household—and go to the land I will show you." Genesis 12:1

All noble life begins with *sacrifice*. To gain the higher—the lower must be given up. We must leave our own country—before we can get into God's country. We can have the better—only by giving up the less valuable. God calls us all to leave the old—in order to enter the new. It may not be literally to leave country, kindred, and home—and go out into a strange land; but in a spiritual sense it always is just this. If we would follow Christ—we must cut loose from the world, and go out with him.

Perhaps there is too great a tendency in these days—to try to follow Christ without cutting loose from the world. Too many people imagine that they can take the pilgrimage to Canaan—without leaving Ur! But this is quite impossible. We can get to our land of promise—only by leaving all, and following where Christ leads. This means that we must give up this world as our portion, and take the heavenly inheritance instead; we cannot keep both. The rich man who came to Christ could not sacrifice his earthly possessions, and therefore could not get the heavenly riches.

May 3.

"I will bless you; and you will be a blessing." Genesis 12:2

This God's offer and message to all of us. He wants to bless us, and then he wants us in turn to be a blessing to others. God's way is to send very many of his good things, through human mediators. When he would bless a little child, he puts a gift of wondrous love into a mother's heart. When he would bless a class of young people or children, he sends a teacher with a heart full of warm sympathy and earnest interest in life. When he would bless a community, he raises up a good man, and touches his heart, that he may scatter benefits among the people.

When God enriches us with gifts of whatever kind, he wants them to be blessings to others. Nothing that we have, is ours for ourselves alone; we *receive*—that we may *dispense*. When God gives a man *money*—he intends him to use it so as to make it a blessing to the world. When God bestows upon anyone the gift of *song*, of eloquence, of the artist's power—he desires these gifts to be used to make men better and happier. We should never live for ourselves. We should seek always to live—so as to make the world purer, truer, holier, sweeter.

May 4.

"So Jacob was left alone, and a man wrestled with him until daybreak." Genesis 32:24

We are all having our Jabboks continually. We are coming face to face with *wrestlers in the darkness*. We go away from our wrestling, too, many a time, carrying the marks of wounding; and yet in the experience, we have gotten blessing.

That touch on the hollow of Jacob's thigh—was the touch that withered the old boasted strength. You say Jacob was victorious. Yes; but when? Not while he wrestled—but after his thigh was out of joint and he could wrestle no more. He clasped his sinewy arms about the neck of his antagonist, and clung, saying, "I will not let you go—unless you bless me." That was the way he prevailed; not in the old way of cunning—but by having the old man crippled, defeated, and then by the new way of trust and clinging.

May 5.

"This is how my heavenly Father will treat each of you—unless you forgive your brother from your heart." Matthew 18:35

If we have truly received divine forgiveness—we will be forgiving toward others. As one says, "If you get pardon from God, you will give it to a brother; if you withhold it from your brother, you thereby make it manifest that you have not gotten it from God."

So we are brought face to face with a most solemn practical teaching which we dare not ignore. Have we the *forgiving spirit?* Can we sincerely pray, "Forgive us our sins—as we forgive those who sin against us"? No doubt the lesson is hard, for it is so against nature; yet we all know by experience that the cherishing of resentment never brings peace to our hearts. People say, "Revenge is *sweet;*" but it is not true. It really makes *bitterness* for him who cherishes it. The gratification of a moment, becomes pain afterward.

May 6.

"Some of those present were saying indignantly to one another, "Why this *waste* of perfume?" Mark 14:4

There are some who think that every sacrifice for Christ's sake, is a waste. They think that money which is given to build churches, or to send missionaries to the heathen, is wasted. They think that lives are wasted which are devoted to Christ and sacrificed in his service. But is it so? Is it really the money that is spent in advancing Christ's kingdom, which is wasted? Are they the wasted lives, that are emptied out in love for Christ?

There is *money* that is wasted; but it is that which is used for selfish and sinful purposes, or squandered in the mere extravagances of worldliness. There are *lives* that are wasted; but they are those which are thrown away in evil courses, sacrificed in pleasure, in dissipation, in lust, in passion's fires.

Indeed, all lives are wasted—which are not lost for Christ's sake; for did he not say, "He who saves his life—shall lose it"? To withhold one's life from Christ—is therefore to waste it. It has been noted as very suggestive, that our Lord uses the self-same word for "wasted" when he describes Judas as a "son of perdition." Judas had wasted that which was more precious than the ointment of spikenard, even the gift of eternal life which once had been within his reach. What we give to Christ—is indeed all that we do not waste of our life and of our substance.

May 7.

"Rejoice in the Lord always! I will say it again: Rejoice!" Philippians 4:4

The Bible insists upon JOY as an element of Christian life. Christ spoke of his desire that the disciples should have *his joy* fulfilled in themselves. Paul exhorts Christians to rejoice always, and speaks of joy as one of the fruits of the Spirit.

Christian joy is *not* hilarity. One maybe sorrowful, and yet have the joy of the Lord in the heart. It is an inner joy—a fountain in the heart, supplied from heaven. Every Christian should have this joy. It belongs to the ideal of the complete Christian character. It is very evident, however, that there are many Christians who do not have it. Their spirits go up and down like the mercury in the thermometer, varying with the atmosphere. When things are pleasant—they have joy. When circumstances are hard or painful—they have no joy.

We ought to know how to get the joy of Christ. One secret is absolute devotion to the will of God. Another is serving others. Only as we learn to live the life of love, "Not to be ministered unto—but to minister" can we find true, deep joy. Every self-denial or sacrifice of love for another's sake, adds to the Christian's joy. We reach the ideal life—only as joy lives in our heart, and shines out in our life.

May 8.

"See how the lilies of the field grow." Matthew 6:28

God looks up at us—from every sweet flower that blooms. The beauty that fills our earth—is a pledge to us of God's thought and love for us. We all know the familiar story of the great traveler who was saved from perishing on the desert where he had fallen, faint and famishing for water, by seeing a little speck of green moss peeping up out of the hot sand. This gleam of life assured him that God must be near, thus putting new hope into his heart, and giving him strength to rise and struggle on until he found water. Every plant or flower should remind us of God, and make us reverent.

May 9.

"Comfort, comfort my people, says your God." Isaiah 40:1

Comfort is a very sweet word. It has music in it—for those who are in trouble. And most people have some trouble. This verse was spoken first to *captives*. There are a great many captives—people carried away from home into a strange land. Many people are in bondage of *sorrow*; it is hard to find a home without its grief. Many are in bondage of *circumstances*; life is too hard for them. There is a great deal of poverty in the world.

But here is God's gospel: "Comfort my people." Few words are more misunderstood, however, than the Bible word 'comfort'. Many people think it means mere condolence to sit down with sufferers and weep with them, pitying them—but doing nothing to *lift* them up. But God's comfort is no such weak, sentimental thing as this. He never merely sits down with us, in passive yielding to trouble. He comes to deliver us, to lead us out of our bondage, to make us victorious over trial or sorrow. There is always in *Bible comfort*, the thought of *strength*. No bondage is hopeless, under the skies of divine love. The stars shine into the deepest dungeon. There is not in any prison in this world, a captive to whom the gospel does not come with its "Speak comfortably."

May 10.

"For My thoughts are not your thoughts, and your ways are not My ways. For as heaven is higher than earth, so My ways are higher than your ways, and My thoughts than your thoughts!" Isaiah 55:8-9

It is well indeed, that God's ways *differ* from ours. For example, if God's *forgiveness* were like ours—it would do us little good. We hold our petty grudges and resentments; we remember men's smallest unkindnesses to us, allowing them to embitter our love, and stop the flow of our affections. We profess to forgive—but retain the *grudge* in our heart.

But God's ways of forgiving are not as our ways. He forgives the worst of sinners, the greatest of sins, and the largest number of transgressions. In the parable, it was God who forgave the ten thousand talents; and it was a man who would not forgive his fellow, a miserable pittance. The most wonderful thing in this universe, is God's forgiveness. We ought to be thankful for it; for if it were less—we could not be saved. Then, when we have received it, we ought to let its spirit work in our heart, to change us into its own image. We pray, "Forgive us—as we forgive others." If we mean this, we should look well to the kind of forgiveness we show to others.

May 11.

"For I was hungry—and you gave Me nothing to eat;
I was thirsty—and you gave Me nothing to drink;

I was a stranger—and you did not take Me in;
I was naked—and you did not clothe Me, sick and in prison and you did not take
care of Me." Matthew 25:42-43

The *'not doing'* of things they ought to have done—here determines the doom of the
unrighteous. They had not been cruel or unkind to any of Christ's little ones—no
such charge is made. They had not wronged anyone. Only *neglects* are mentioned.
They had seen "little ones" hungry, and had not fed them; thirsty, and had not given
them drink; naked, and had not clothed them; sick, and had not visited them. They
had merely "passed by on the other side" when they saw human need and misery
which they might have relieved. Yet their *omissions* and *neglects*, count as *actual
sins*.

Many of us are apt to neglect opportunities of helping others, and of relieving
distress, never thinking that we are sinning against Christ; that is, are
leaving *him* unhelped and unrelieved in distress, when we might have given him
comfort. The result of the teaching should be to make us more thoughtful of others,
and more alert to embrace every opportunity of ministry to others in Christ's name.
It is because we do not think—that we fail so often in *love's duty*.

May 12.

"Therefore let us stop passing judgment on one another. Instead, make up your
mind not to put any stumbling block or obstacle in your brother's way." Romans
14:13

Instead of keeping our eye ever on *others*, looking for faults and mistakes in them—
we are to look to our own example, lest something we do may hurt others' lives, or
cause them to do wrong. If everyone would do this, it would go far toward making a
paradise of *this world of thorns and briers*. We easily get in the habit of overlooking
our own faults, or imagining that we are well-near perfect, while in reality our life is
full of inconsistencies. We poke at our neighbor's eye, to pull out some *little
mote* we imagine we see in it, while at the same time we have a great beam in our
own eye which sadly disfigures us, and is a reproach to us in the sight of others!
"Why do you look at the speck of sawdust in your brother's eye and pay no attention
to the plank in your own eye?" Matthew 7:3

The habit of judging and condemning others—is usually a great deal more serious
blemish, than are the things we so glibly point out as flaws or faults. The first duty
of every Christian is to make sure that he lays no stumbling-block in others' way. It
is said that Rutherford Hayes did not carry a watch. When he was a young man his
watch was twice stolen, and the thief each time was arrested and imprisoned. Mr.
Hayes then resolved never to wear a watch, because twice his carrying one had
made a temptation for another. We may call this excessive conscientiousness—but
we can scarcely overdo in this duty.

May 13.

"An inheritance that can never perish, spoil or fade—***kept*** in heaven for you, who through faith are shielded by God's power until the coming of the salvation that is ready to be revealed in the last time." 1 Peter 1:4-5

It is related of a saintly man, that by his own request his only epitaph was "Kept!" All Christians are *kept* by the power of God unto final salvation. Only those who overcome at last get home to glory. Only Christ can help us to be conquerors. And important as was his *death* for us, his real work in saving us is that which he does with us, one by one, in keeping us, guiding us, giving us grace for living, lifting us up when we have fallen, bringing us back when we have wandered away. Were it not for the patient, watchful, never-wearying love of Christ—not one of us would ever get home. We are kept!

This *divine keeping* comes to us in many ways. We believe in *angel* guardianship. Then there is *human* guardianship. The mother is her child's first keeper. The old rabbis used to say that God could not be everywhere present, and therefore he made mothers. All through life God gives human guardians who become helpers of our faith. Then we have ever the real divine presence in which we find perfect keeping. "The Lord is your keeper." Psalm 121:5

May 14.

"I have come down to rescue them from the power of the Egyptians and to bring them from that land to a good and spacious land, a land flowing with milk and honey." Exodus 3:8

"Weeping may endure for a night—but joy comes in the morning." The night may grow very dark—but the morning will break. "We must through much tribulation enter the kingdom of God;" but notice the word "through." "The valley of the shadow of death" lies in the path; but we are to pass through it, and beyond comes, "I will dwell in the house of the Lord forever!" After Egypt and its bondage—comes the "good and spacious land, a land flowing with milk and honey." So it is always. After *winter*, with its death and desolation, comes *spring* with its flowers, fruits, harvests, and life. After earth with its sorrows, comes heaven, where joy shall be eternal!

May 15.

"Take them down to the water, and I will *test* them for you there." Judges 7:4

The way the men drank water from the brook, was the test of their fitness for the work of conquering the Midianites. It seemed to make the smallest difference in the world whether a soldier drank by bowing down with his face in the water, or by lapping up the water with his hand as he knelt; yet it was a difference that settled the question of fitness or unfitness for the great work before the army.

It is in just such little ways, and in such matters of everyday and commonplace action, conduct, and manner—that God is always testing us and deciding whether we are fit or unfit for the greater work for which he is seeking men. By the way a boy lives at home, by the way he treats his parents, by the way he performs his duties at school, by the spirit he shows on the play-ground, by the diligence which he displays in the store or office in which he is first employed—by the way he acts in all these relations and duties, the question is being settled to what *greater responsibilities* the Lord will call him in after-days. Every young girl, by the way she deports herself in her girlhood, at home, at school, at play, and in all the days of youth—is settling the place in life she shall fill in full womanhood and strength. We cannot know what future honor, may depend on the way we do the simplest, most commonplace thing today.

May 16.

"Therefore the children of Israel cannot stand before their enemies." Joshua 7:12

This is the only record in the Book of Joshua, of a lost battle. The word "therefore" tells us that it was a *sin* that caused this defeat, a secret sin, and the sin, too, of but one individual. How little do we know of the real causes of the failures we see about us!

All of us have our Ais, too, our defeats in battle; and very often they come just after our Jericho, our victories. It was only a little town, too, at which this disaster occurred, so small that it was thought unnecessary to send more than a handful of soldiers to take it.

Is it not often just so in our spiritual warfare? One writes, "Our *greatest failures* often happen in the *little things* of life. We miscalculate the strength of the foe; we fail to spy out the reserved forces. Indeed, we mistake, when we think it an easy matter to subdue any enemy. How often has it happened that he who has won his most signal victory in some great crisis of the church, who has rescued the truth from the teachers of false doctrine, or stormed the entrenchments of vice—has forthwith failed in some petty domestic disturbance, in some social duty, or in a trifling claim of common charity? If there is a time in life when we need more than ever to watch and pray lest we enter into temptation, it is in the hour of success."

May 17.

"The Lord has heard all your grumblings against Him!" Exodus 16:8

Does God really hear every discontented word which I ever speak?

Does He hear *when I grumble about the weather* . . .
about the hard winter,
about the late spring,
about the dry summer,
about the wet harvest?

Does He hear when I grumble . . .
about the frosts,
about the drought,
about the high winds,
about the storms?

Does He hear when I grumble . . .
about my circumstances,
about the hardness of my lot,
about my losses and disappointments?

If we could get into our heart, and keep there continually, the consciousness that God hears every word we speak—would we murmur and complain so much as we now do?

We are careful never to speak words which would give pain to the hearts of those we love. Are we as careful not to say anything that will grieve our heavenly Father?

"I tell you this—that you must give an account on judgment day of every idle word you speak!" Matthew 12:36

"He who complains of the weather—complains of the God who ordains the weather!" William Law

May 18.

"Every skilled woman spun with her hands—and brought what she had spun—blue, purple or scarlet yarn or fine linen." Exodus 35:25

It didn't harm their hands a bit either! Some dainty women are like the lilies, "They do not labor or spin!" They keep their hands soft and white. They think any kind of work would mar the delicate beauty of their fingers. But they make a great mistake. The hands that are beautiful in heaven's sight—are not the dainty ones that are never roughened or hardened by toil. Anything is beautiful, just in the measure in which it fulfills the mission for which it was made. Hands were made to work; and an idle, useless hand, no matter how delicate and fair, is not a lovely hand!

These ancient women had learned to spin, and now they spun for God. Here we see how everyday talents and occupations, may be turned over into God's service. The young women of today do not spin much; many of them never saw a spinning-wheel; but they have other common talents and abilities which they may consecrate to Christ.

"Even while we were with you, we gave you this rule: Whoever does not work—should not eat!" 2 Thessalonians 3:10

May 19.

"All who were willing, men and women alike, came and brought gold jewelry of all kinds: medallions, earrings, rings from their fingers, and necklaces. They presented gold objects of every kind to the LORD." Exodus 35:22

When the ancient Hebrews were preparing to make a tabernacle for God, they brought the richest and best things they had. They looked on their heirlooms and their most prized possessions, and brought the things which were dearest and most sacred, to God.

WE should follow the same rule when we are giving to God. When we make presents to those whom we love tenderly, we are at great pains to get the best and loveliest gifts we can find.

But do we always bring Christ the best?

Do we give Him the best of our heart's affections?

Do we bring Him the best of our life, our time, our energy?

Do we do our best work in His service?

Are our gifts for Him—the most precious things we possess?

These Israelites brought their gold jewelry of all kinds: medallions, earrings, rings from their fingers, and necklaces. They had nothing that was too good or too precious to be offered to God.

Is it thus with, us? Do we not sometimes bring to God—the very smallest gifts we can find? We keep the bright gold and the large bills for ourselves—and give Him the dimes and nickels!

Just so of our time, of our thoughts, our skills, our energies. We put Him off too often with what is left over—after we have served ourselves!

May 20.

"Clothe Aaron with the holy garments, anoint him, and consecrate him, so that he can serve Me as a priest." Exodus 40:13

One feature of the high priest's dress was very suggestive. On each shoulder, in the golden clasp that fastened together the two parts of the ephod, was an onyx stone, on which were engraved the names of six of the tribes of Israel. Thus, in an emblematic way, the high priest bore the people on his shoulder, the place of strength. He was a type of Christ; who thus Christ carries His people on His shoulder—bearing them and their burdens.

Another feature of this dress, was the breastplate which was worn by the high priest. It had in it twelve precious stones, with the names of the twelve tribes engraved on them. This the priest wore over his heart. When he went in before God, he thus represented all the people. He not only carried them on his shoulder, for support and upholding—but near his heart, for affection.

Just so does Christ carries His people in His heart—in deep, tender, unchanging love. Thus we are sure of both the strength and the love of Christ, are engaged for His people!

May 21.

"As dead flies give perfume a bad smell—so a little folly outweighs wisdom and honor." Ecclesiastes 10:1

It is sad to see how some holy and noble characters are marred by little—yet grievous, faults and blemishes!

One man is generous—but he desires always to have his charity praised.

Another is disposed to be kind and helpful—but by his manner, he hurts or humiliates the one he befriends.

Another is unselfish and devout—but is careless of promises and engagements. He makes appointments, and never thinks of them again. He borrows money, and does not repay it. His friends say, "He is so forgetful!" Yes; but how his forgetfulness mars his character and hurts his influence! Forgetfulness is worse than an acceptable weakness; it is a sin!

Untruthfulness is a blot in all eyes.

Whenever SELF leaks out in conduct or disposition—it is a dead fly in the perfume!

It makes little difference, that a person is not intentionally at fault in the things which so mar his life. Carelessness and thoughtlessness are themselves such serious moral blemishes—that they make impossible, any excuse for delinquencies resulting from them. We need to look to "the littles" which either make or mar godly character. No fault is too small to be worth curing, and no fragment of beauty is too small to be worth setting in the mosaic of character.

May 22.

"He heals the brokenhearted—and binds up their wounds!" Psalm 147:3

It is said that when one branch of a tree is bruised, the whole tree begins to pour of its life toward the wounded place, to restore it. It is in this manner, that Christ heals His people when bruised by sorrow. "Blessed are those who mourn—for they shall be comforted."

There are **fields** where once fierce battles raged, great armies contended, and blood flowed—but where now the birds sing sweet songs, in summer days flowers bloom, meadows are green with waving grass, and ripening harvests bend. So there are **homes** where once sorrow's dark clouds hung, tears flowed, and cries of grief were heard—but where now joyous songs ring out, and glad faces smile. God's comfort has healed the brokenhearted home.

There are many ways in which God restores sorrow's devastation. He sends new blessings instead of the old ones, which he took away, as new flowers come in place of those that fade. He hides a blessing, too, in the very *heart of the sorrow* itself!

Grief is like the cloud which comes with its dark portents, into the blue summer sky. It blots out the blue, and fills the air with terrors. The lightnings flash, the thunders roll; but out of the bosom of the blackness—pours the *soft rain*. So sorrow's cloud comes with dark, portentous aspect; but it empties blessings upon the life, thus carrying in itself—its own power of restoration.

May 23.

Then the *righteous* will answer Him, "Lord, when did we see You hungry and feed You, or thirsty and give You something to drink? When did we see You a stranger and take You in, or without clothes and clothe You? When did we see You sick, or in prison, and visit You?" Matthew 25:37-39

True goodness is not conscious of itself. Moses did not know that his face shined. The noblest Christians put the lowest value on their own good works. No doubt many of the commendations and rewards of the righteous in the judgment, will be surprises to them. They keep no record of their own good deeds. Their own sense of personal unworthiness, hinders their seeing anything worthy in their humble services.

Besides, we do not see Christ in the lowly and the suffering ones who come before us needing our love and help; we see only poor, sick, unfortunate people, with no outshining of glory, no hints of nobility, no marks of heavenly beauty.

There is a picture which, seen in ordinary light—shows only a very poor man dying in a miserable, garret, with tokens of abject poverty on all sides; but seen in another light—it shows a throng of angels waiting to bear a child of God up to glory!

Just so, we do not see things as they are! Jesus Himself is ever before us in lowly disguise! We are unconsciously serving the Master Himself, whenever we do any humble service of love in His name. Every true Christian is preparing for himself many a blessed surprise of reward and glory—when he enters the fuller, richer life of heaven, where all the results of service, and all the fruits of kindness—shall be revealed!

Then the King will say to those on His right, "Come, you who are blessed by My Father, inherit the kingdom prepared for you from the foundation of the world!" Matthew 25:34

May 24.

"Whatever is born of the flesh—is flesh; and

whatever is born of the Spirit—is spirit." John 3:6

Like produces like. To be born of the Spirit—is to have a new life imparted by the Spirit. This new life will be like that which produces it. Everyone who is born of God—will have some features of God's likeness. He will love the things that God loves, and hate the things that God hates. In some measure, he will be like God . . .
in holiness,
in unselfishness,
in gentleness,
in patience,
in forgiveness,
in truthfulness,
in love.

If we would know what God is like—we have only to look at Jesus Christ, for He was the image of God; and if we are born again, we shall have the same features in our lives! They will be dim at first; but they will come out clearer and clearer each day, as we grow in grace.

We can tell whether or not we are born again—by looking closely at ourselves to see if we have the marks of the Spirit in our life. Do we hate sin? Do we love holiness? Do we love the Bible and prayer, and fellowship with the Lord's true people?

We have the same thought presented by Paul under the figure of the seal of the Holy Spirit. All Christians are sealed by the Spirit. The seal impresses its own features on the wax. So the Holy Spirit seals believers—by stamping His own image on their hearts. Those who have received the Spirit—will bear the marks of His beauty in their lives!

May 25.

"The fruit of the Spirit, is love." Galatians 5:22

The sum of all practical religion is love. "Love is the fulfilling of the law." All Christian growth is to be toward the likeness of Christ, and all His character is summed up in LOVE. Whatever is unloving in us—is unlike Jesus; and we should seek to overcome the evil with good.

Perhaps the ordinary Christian conscience has not been sufficiently exacting on this line of character and duty. Scripture demands truthfulness, justice, honesty, purity; but it does not tolerate bad temper, resentment, unkindness or other phases of unamiableness, in those who profess to follow Jesus!

May 26.

"I was in the Spirit on the Lord's day." Revelation 1:10

We should all seek to be *in the Spirit* on the Lord's day. During the week we have our cares of business, and our hands are full of work that must be done. The world is apt to get into our heart during the week-days; and if there is no break in this secular life, we are apt to become secularized in spirit, losing interest in spiritual things. The trouble is not that we are *in* the world—but that the world too often gets into us. It is a proper enough thing for a ship to be in the sea; but *when the sea gets into the ship*—that is an end of sailing, and the ship sinks into the waters! Christ wants us to be in the world—but he does not want the world to get into us!

On the Lord's day, therefore, we should run our ship just as completely as possible out of the world's troubled waters into the peaceful bay of spiritual rest and enjoyment. We should think on spiritual things, and seek to have our heart thoroughly cleansed of worldliness and filled with God. One who thus faithfully uses the Lord's day each week—will be safe amid the world's unspiritual influences. A well-spent Sunday, will keep up the *spiritual tone* of the life amid the most intense pressure of week-day duty. But there is no other antidote to worldliness; and no Christian who desires to be faithful, dare lose the Sundays out of his week.

"I am not praying that You take them out of the world—but that You protect them from the evil one. They are not of the world, as I am not of the world." John 17:15-16

"You adulterous people, don't you know that friendship with the world is hatred toward God? Anyone who chooses to be a friend of the world becomes an enemy of God!" James 4:4

"Do not love the world or anything in the world. If anyone loves the world, the love of the Father is not in him!" 1 John 2:15

May 27.

"Learn this parable from the fig tree." Mark 13:28

The parable of the fig-tree, teaches that we should not shut our eyes to the foreshadowings of future things. We are taught not to be anxious about tomorrow. But there is also a duty of looking ahead—as well as not looking ahead. The good *sailor* watches the skies, and he would be criminally foolish—were he to pay no heed to the foretokens of storm. The prudent *farmer* watches the forerunners of winter, and gathers in his fruits, houses his cattle, puts wood and coal in his bins, when he can do so easily—and is ready before the snows and the bitter cold come. So in all our life we should watch the "signs of the times," and shape our course accordingly.

Young people, as they feel the impulses of life in their souls, and hear the calls of God sounding in their ears, should be reminded of the *duties and responsibilities of life*, toward which they are moving, and should diligently prepare themselves for filling well their place. Each period of life brings its own special work; and there are always *forecasts* which, if heeded, will enable us to prepare ourselves for what God is preparing for us. If we are faithful, one day will prepare us for the next, and we shall never be found by any event, however sudden, unprepared to meet it.

May 28.

Samuel did what the Lord said. When he arrived at Bethlehem, the elders of the town trembled when they met him. They asked, "Do you come in peace?" Samuel replied, "Yes, in peace!" 1 Samuel 16:4-5

God's messengers do not all wear *gentle faces*; ofttimes they come in a *garb of sternness*. Yet they come always with a blessing. **Sickness** is one of these dark-visaged prophets. We cannot welcome it. Yet if we ask this messenger, "Do you come in peace?" the answer is, "Yes, in peace." Sickness always brings messages of peace, of good—if only we have grace to receive them.

The same is true of all the **hard trials** of life. We would rather have *easy times*. Boys and young men who are poor, think ofttimes that they have scarcely a *fair chance in life*, when they see the sons of rich fathers reveling in luxury, with plenty of money. Yet really the *stern prophet of poverty* brings ofttimes a holier message and a richer, truer blessing—than the smiling-faced, silken-robed messenger brings to the youth in the fine mansion.

The **best** things in life, can be developed only by work and discipline. Hence, whatever compels a boy or a young man to toil, to deny himself, to make strenuous efforts—is a blessing to him. The 'prophet of necessity' therefore comes to him peaceably. We should never turn from our doors any prophets which God sends, however stern they may appear. They all come with a good message.

May 29.

The LORD said to Samuel, "Fill your horn with oil and be on your way; I am sending you to Jesse of Bethlehem. I have chosen one of his sons to be king." 1 Samuel 16:1

The Lord is never at loss for a man. When one fails—he has another ready. His plans and purposes go on—in spite of human failure, and through all seeming disaster.

Here was a boy, keeping the sheep in the fields, probably not dreaming of greatness, and yet God had him marked out to be king! The boys do hot know what God has in mind for them. They may be sure, however, that for every one of them—God has some plan. It may be a great place or a small one, as the world rates greatness or smallness; but every boy should feel that to be just what God made him to be—is the grandest, noblest, best thing possible for him. If God made him to be a carpenter, and by his own restless strivings he gets to be a member of Congress or Parliament, or President of the United States, his place is not half so high and great in the angels' sight—as if he had been the carpenter he was meant to be.

The greatest place anyone can attain—is the place God intended him to fill. How can we know what God wants us to do and to be? By doing his will, day by day, with quiet fidelity, wherever we find ourselves. God's will for each day—is God's plan for us for that day. Thus God will lead us continually to that which he has for us to do. Failure in the lowlier duties—will hinder our promotion to the higher.

May 30.

"Since he had no sword, he ran over and pulled Goliath's sword from its sheath. David used it to kill the giant and cut off his head!" 1 Samuel 17:50-51

If he had not cut off the giant's head—the old Philistine champion would have gotten up by and by, and walked away; for he was only stunned, not killed, by the stone. David made sure work of his victory!

A great many of our attacks upon sin in our own hearts, and in the world—only stun, and do not kill the evil. We walk away, thinking we have done a fine thing. But shortly, we meet the 'old giant' again, stalking abroad as before! He soon recovers from our blow, and we have to fight the battle over; and perhaps we fight it again in the same half-hearted way—and thus on and on, to the end of life!

Most of us have had just such experience as this, with our own evil lusts and passions. We overcome them very often, and think each time that we are through with them—but soon again they are as active as ever.

We need to learn a lesson from David—and finish our victories by cutting off the head of every giant we strike down!

There is no other way of killing sins!

The life is in the head—and the head must be struck off—or the enemy will be facing us again in a day or two, with but a scar on his forehead!

The only way to get a real victory over vices—is to decapitate them! Bruises and wounds are not enough. There must be thorough work done, in the name of the Lord. Half-way measures will not avail.

"Put to death, therefore, whatever belongs to your earthly nature: sexual immorality, impurity, lust, evil desires and greed, which is idolatry." Colossians 3:5

"Samuel hewed *Agag* to pieces before the Lord." 1 Samuel 15:33. Like Samuel, we must hew our *Agags* to pieces!

May 31.

"Then David went to Jonathan and asked—What have I done? What is my crime? How have I wronged your father, that he is trying to kill me?" 1 Samuel 20:1

A true friend is a refuge. We all have troubles at some time. For many years we may get along quietly, and without sore trial; but the day will come to all of us—when we shall be in sorrow or danger. It may be in such an experience as David's, when people shall misjudge us, or become our enemies without cause, and may seek to harm us. It may be sickness that comes upon us, or bereavement, or severe loss of some kind. Whatever the trouble may be, a true friend will prove a great comfort to us in the experience.

It is a blessed thing to have one friend that we are sure of, though all others fail us. We can go to him then as David went to Jonathan, telling him all our heart's burden. Young people should seek to have a friend older than themselves, to whom they can fly in trouble or in danger, and in whose faithful love they can find a sure and safe refuge. There is a wonderful strength in the confidence that one has such a friend.

"There is a Friend who sticks closer than a brother." Proverbs 18:24. Christ is the best, strongest, wisest, truest, most helpful friend anyone can have. His friendship is a refuge indeed. We can flee to him in any danger, and find him ready always to comfort, shelter, and bless. However many human friends we may have—we all need Christ.

JUNE

June 1.

Jonathan spoke well of David to Saul his father and said to him, "Let not the king do wrong to his servant David; he has not wronged you, and what he has done has benefited you greatly." 1 Samuel 19:4

One quality of true friendship, is the *loyalty* which speaks out for one's friend in his absence, when derogatory things are said of him. In few ways is human infirmity shown in worse light—than in the too common willingness to hear evil things even of one's friends. We must confess that there is something evil in a great deal of human nature—which delights in learning of faults, mistakes, or lapses in others. At least we must admit that there is a strong tendency in this direction.

But we ought to set the world the example of a friendship free from such malign weakness. We ought to refuse to believe evil of our friend, or even to listen to whispers or insinuations against him. Instead of being *delighted* at hearing injurious things about him, hints of wrong-doing in him, or of flaws in his character, such things should *grieve* us. The *law of Christian love* requires us to defend the character of our friend—as we would our own character. We are our brother's keeper.

June 2.

Jonathan said to David, "Whatever you want me to do—I will do for you." 1 Samuel 20:4

Friendship is *helpful*. We never know what our friends do for us. They are advocates for us, speaking strong, earnest words for us to others. They defend us from false things which others may speak of us. Since I began to write this paragraph, I have had an opportunity to tell the truth about one of my friends to another who had heard certain charges against him, thus removing the false impression concerning my friend—at least from one man's mind. None of us know how much of our success, we owe to the loyal words of our friends.

Friends help us in our personal life. A pure-hearted friend is continually leaving *touches of beauty* on our character. We get from him good thoughts, wholesome influences, fresh inspirations, continual incitements. Longfellow tells us of a song breathed in the air which he found long, long afterward in the heart of a friend. So it is continually with the sweet songs, good words, and holy influences of friendship.

Friends are helpful also in the ministry of kindness which they render as two walk on together. A true friend is unselfish, thoughtful, ready always to render aid in every possible way. Especially should friendship show itself in time of trouble. "A friend is born for adversity."

June 3

The men said, "This is the day the LORD spoke of, when he said to you, 'I will give your enemy into your hands for you to deal with as you wish.'" 1 Samuel 24:4

So far as we know, the Lord had not said this at all. The men put their *own interpretation* on the opportunity, and called it providential. We are all too apt to *interpret providences* in accordance with our own wishes. When we are desiring to be led in a certain manner, and there is one way *we desire* very much to take—we are quite sure to find *providences* that seem to favor our preference.

But *opportunity* does not always indicate *duty*. When the merchant by mistake gives back a dollar too much change, there is an opportunity to make a dollar; but who will say that we ought to accept it? When you find in trouble, one who has done you a wrong, there is an opportunity to have revenge. But does the opportunity justify retaliation? The duty in the former case is honesty, arid in the latter is the showing of love to an enemy.

In reading providences, we must remember that no opportunity to do anything in itself *wrong*—is ever to be regarded as a *divine leading*. It is a sin to take revenge, no matter how much our enemy deserves punishment, or how good a chance we have for punishing him. It is a sin to steal, even though an opportunity makes it very easy to do it. God leads us by his *providence*—but never into sin!

June 4.

David said to Saul, "Why do you listen when men say?" 1 Samuel 24:9

There was someone who in the dark, was stabbing David's name. It is probable that Saul was made to believe that David was his bitter foe, and was plotting all manner of evil against him. There are people in every community who are slanderers. They go to this one and that one, and drop *dark insinuations* about some other person, whose shoe's latchet they are not worthy to unloose. They come to one of two friends, and let fall some hint only that the other is not faithful as a friend, perhaps relating something in a *perverted* way, so as to leave an impression of faithlessness. "A whisper separates chief friends." The ruin wrought by the slanderer in this world, cannot be computed, characters blackened, friendships broken up, jealousies aroused, homes destroyed, hearts broken. *Slanderous words* have measureless power for evil.

June 5.

"The Lord forbid that I should do this thing!" 1 Samuel 24:6

"Would it not be *human* to resent it?" said one who had received an insult. "Yes," was the reply, "but it would be *godlike* to forgive it." David did the godlike thing. He had a chance to *avenge* himself. He had his cruel enemy in his power. One stroke, and Saul would never have troubled him any more. David's life would then have been safe. He would have become king at once. His men were urging it, and he himself was tempted to do it. Yet he overcame the temptation, and allowed Saul to pass out of his hand unharmed. He listened to the voice of God speaking in his own conscience, and restrained the impulse to avenge himself.

The first impulse of a child, when wronged or hurt by another, is to seek revenge. Sometimes older people encourage this evil spirit in children, by telling them to whip the chair or the rocking-horse by which they have chanced to be hurt. In older people, too, the desire for *revenge* is natural, and can be repressed only by the higher law of *love* which Christ teaches. The lesson is, that *the punishment of sin must be left in God's hands*. Our duty is to bear patiently the wrongs and injuries others may inflict upon us, not giving reviling for reviling, to repay unkindness with kindness, to overcome evil with good.

June 6.

"I will not lift my hand against my master, because he is the LORD's anointed." 1 Samuel 24:10

David seemed now to have a short, quick way to the kingdom—but he would not dare to take it. Now the throne was Saul's—he was the Lord's anointed. David would not lift a finger to hurry God's providence, and to become king before God made him king. There often are things that God intends to give us—but which we must *wait* to receive in *his way. Short-cuts in life's paths* are always mistakes in the end. Jacob's mother knew that Jacob was to have the blessing of the firstborn—but if she had waited it would have come to him without being stained, as it was by her own and Jacob's deception.

Young men are ambitious, and their ambition may be right; but too often they are in such feverish haste to reach what they wish—that they take the *shortcut of dishonesty* to get the sooner to the coveted place. It never pays.

David could have been on the throne the next day—but he would have left stains of guilt on the steps as he ascended; it was better far for him to wander on in exile for a time longer, and then reach the throne by a clean path. It is pleasant to see young men get on in life; but we must always ask *how* they have gotten on, to know whether their elevation is really an honor. The only way to true success—is God's way. We must learn to wait for God.

June 7.

"May the LORD judge between you and me. And may the LORD avenge the wrongs you have done to me—but my hand will not touch you." 1 Samuel 24:12

There are apt to be wrong views about *bearing injuries.* People ask, "Is there to be no justice in cases like David's? Must we quietly bear wrong? and must the person who does the wrong never receive any punishment?" Our *sense of right* is sometimes so outraged, that our soul cries out in remonstrance, when we are told that we never should resent nor resist—but *turn the other cheek* when one cheek has been smitten. The Bible teaching is, that it is not our part to punish those who wrong us. Our clumsy hands are not skillful enough to adjust such delicate matters.

We are not required to say that a certain person's treatment of us was right, when it was manifestly wrong—but we are to recognize the truth that the *question of justice is God's matter*, not ours; that our part is to be patient and meek, leaving in God's hands the whole adjustment of right and wrong.

Two Scripture passages help to make this plain: "Do not take revenge, my friends, but leave room for God's wrath, for it is written: 'It is mine to avenge; I will repay,' says the Lord." Romans 12:19. "When reviled, He did not revile in return; when suffering, He did not threaten, but committed Himself to the One who judges justly." 1 Peter 2:23.

June 8.

"Then King David went in and sat before the Lord and prayed." 2 Samuel 7:18

We can get before the Lord anywhere—by shutting our eyes to the world and looking up into our Father's face. Even in a crowd we can be really alone with God.

We can commune with him, too, in his works:

Sweet wayside flowers whisper to us tender thoughts of God.

The sea tells us of his power.

The deep blue sky has its suggestions of God's peace.

The mountains speak of his stability and unchangeableness.

But there are other ways of going in before God.

We open our Bible, and look into its pages with reverent heart and with open ear; and as we read the sacred words, God talks to us.

When we enter into our closet of prayer and shut the door—we are in a very real sense sitting before him. We bow in prayer; and we are lying at Christ's very feet, so close to him that we can reach the hem of his garment, and feel the touch of his hand upon our fevered hearts. How near we get to our Savior in such moments, and how his touch thrills us!

June 9.

"I am the one who has sinned and done wrong! But these people are innocent—what have they done? Let your anger fall against me and my family." 2 Samuel 24:17

It is human and very common to try to *lay the blame on others*—when we have sinned. Compare Saul's conduct when Samuel accused him of disobedience in sparing the king and the best spoil of the Amalekites: he charged the blame on the *people*. How much nobler is David's behavior in this case! The sin had not been his alone—but he sees only his own share in it. He sees the people suffering under a heavy stroke which he feels he ought to be bearing himself, and he cries to God to lift his hand from them—and let it fall upon him.

The lesson is for all of us. We should never try to *shift the blame* of our sins or mistakes upon others—but should take it upon ourselves. If penalties or sufferings come through our mis-doings we should bear them, and not allow them to fall upon innocent people while we escape.

Another thing to notice here is, that David's penitence deepened under the divine judgment. Some people grow rebellious when chastened; but the true way, when we have sinned and when punishment comes, is to creep closer to God, and to get down lower before him. This is the spirit that pleases God and receives blessing from his hand.

June 10.

"The Lord ... who had appeared unto him *twice*." I Kings 11:9

Matthew Henry says: "God keeps account of the *gracious visits* he makes to us, whether we do or not. He knows how often he has appeared to us, and for us, and will remember it against us, if we turn from him." Every such *gracious visit* to us, adds to our responsibility for obedience and holy service.

When Solomon had seen the Lord in vision, he should have been forever a consecrated man. The eyes which had looked upon the Lord, should never have *lusted after earth's pleasures*. The hands which had fashioned a temple for God, should never have built chapels and altars for heathen deities. Solomon's sins were far greater, because of the special favors God had granted to him. *Seeing Christ should set us apart forever for holy living.*

June 11.

"But for the sake of your father, David, I will not do this while you are still alive. I will take the kingdom away from your son." 1 Kings 11:12

In this Word of God, we have a double illustration of *the way our lives cast shadows*. A *godly* man transmits blessings to his children; and *godless* man robs his children of blessings that ought to be theirs. David's godly life kept from Solomon, the visitation of the full consequences of Solomon's sin.

There are many of us who are enjoying blessings, which have come through the faithfulness of our fathers. But there are many who, like Solomon, live so as to rob their children of the honors and privileges which they ought to transmit to them.

Solomon's son did not get the kingdom of all Israel. He received but a fragment of it, and it was his father's fault that the kingdom was divided. The man who by indolence or extravagance wastes the fortune which God has given him, and transmits poverty or beggary to his children, is guilty of a like sin. Still more guilty is he who by wrong or shameful living, brings dishonor upon his own name, and thus bequeaths a *heritage of dishonor* to his descendants. It is not merely our *own* life which is affected by our *conduct*; we are so *tied up in bundles* that others are made or unmade, by our making or unmaking of ourselves. We are under the most sacred obligations to live worthily, so that we hurt not—but bless those coming after us.

June 12.

"I will sing a new song unto you, O God!" Psalm 144:9

Ruskin says, "Many mighty harmonies have been discoursed by instruments that had been dumb or discordant." This is very true, and is most encouraging to those who are conscious of the imperfection of their own lives. One says, "I never can live a truly sweet or beautiful life, for sin has so marred my soul and jangled all its chords." True—but God can take the instrument with the broken keys and the discordant strings—and put it in perfect repair. "He restores my soul;" and under his touch and his breath—it may give out music that will thrill men's hearts, and delight the angels and God himself.

Some of the worst tempered people may be made gentle and loving in speech, act, and disposition, by the transforming power of divine grace. The selfish nature may be tuned into sweetest unselfishness and charity. So with all jangled life-keys. God can put them in tune—if we will but leave them in his skillful hands.
The *possibilities of beautiful living*, in even the most marred and imperfect souls—are almost infinite. None need ever despair, who will accept the divine grace, and profit by the divine teaching and discipline.

June 13.

"The law of the Lord is perfect, restoring the soul." Psalm 19:7

The *works* of God declare his *glory*—but not his *will*. We could never learn—by studying the stars, the flowers, or the rocks—how we ought to live, what is right, and what is wrong. We could never learn what God himself is, what his attributes are, how he feels toward us. We may learn from his works—that he is great, wise, unchanging, good; but we could not learn that he loves us with a tender, personal affection. We could never find a gospel of salvation for lost sinners—in the *works* of God.

How thankful we should be for *his Word*, which tells us all these things! It teaches us how to live. It is a perfect law; not perfect only in that it is without flaw or mistake—but also in that it is complete as a revelation, containing all we need to know to be saved and to reach the full stature of godly men. We may turn to the law of the Lord with every question of duty, and we shall always find the right answer.

June 14.

"The precepts of the Lord are right, rejoicing the heart." Psalm 19:8

Many people think that a godly life—must be a sad and gloomy life. They suppose that Christians have no joy. They have to deny themselves many pleasures. They have to live strictly and soberly. They have to follow the Scriptures. Life must be dreary and joyless to Christians.

So the people talk, who boast of being free from the restraints of the Bible. But, as a matter of fact, the happiest people in this world are those who are keeping God's commandments. Who ever heard of sin "rejoicing the heart"? Disobedience never made anyone happy—but obedience always gives peace.

There are fresh-water springs in the sea, which continually pour out sweet water beneath all the brackish tides. So in the obedient heart, under all self-denials, there is a spring of joy ever flowing. It is the peace of God which nothing can disturb, a holy fountain whose flow nothing can ever check.

June 15.

"Many, O LORD my God, are the wonders you have done."

"I am poor and needy—yet the Lord thinks upon me." Psalm 40:5, 17

Does the great, glorious, eternal God ever think of us—of us sinful, unworthy beings? We admit that he may think of our earth, for that is something large enough to be worthy of divine thought. He may give thought, too, to some distinguished man, who rises above the masses, as Mont Blanc towers above the common hills of earth. But here am I, a little child, living in a lowly street in a great city with its teeming millions; surely he never thinks of me. Of course my mother thinks of me, because she is my mother, and she has only me; but God has millions more children; it cannot be that he ever gives any particular thought to me, one of the least of these.

The Bible says that he does! Think of a parent's thoughts of his child, a father's, a mother's thought. Just so, does God love, watch, think, plan, and care for each one of his children.

Then, his thoughts are both *loving* and *wise*. He says, "I know the thoughts that I think toward you, thoughts of peace and not of evil." There is not a moment when we are not in God's thought. He has plans for each life, taking in its smallest events as well as its greatest. How secure it should make Christians feel at all times—to know that God is thinking of us, caring for us!

June 16.

"Behold, you desire *truth in the inward parts*." Psalm 51:6

No doubt *being* is better than *doing*; that is, if it were possible to separate the two. The worth of a deed, depends largely upon *who* does it. The force of a word, depends upon the character and standing of the speaker. We must *be* good, before we can *do* good.

Yet to *be good* is not a sufficient aim in life; there must also be the *desire to do good*. We are never to live for ourselves alone, even in the seeking of good. We are to desire to be blessed—that we may be a blessing to others. Everything of good we receive from God, should make us able to do more good. It is a new trust from God which we are to hold for him. If our *heart* is right, then our work, little or much— will have a blessing in it for the world.

June 17.

"This is how Aaron is to enter the sanctuary area: with a young bull for a sin offering and a ram for a burnt offering." Leviticus 16:3

The high priest must make an offering for himself—before he could present the sacrifice for the people. The lesson is for all who would intercede with God for sinners, or engage in any way in the Lord's work. They must strive that their own life may be unspotted and their own sins put away—before they go to God for others.

A painter noticed some little blotches on the wall he had painted in delicate tints. Taking a wet cloth he sought to remove the spots; but he only made them worse, for the cloth in his hand was soiled and unclean. So it is when one with *spotted hands* seeks to remove the faults and blemishes of other lives.

A little child reached out his hand to his mother to receive a present she was about to give him; but his hands were soiled, and his mother said she could not give him what she had for him until they were washed clean. We cannot cleanse the lives of others, nor minister in their behalf, nor can we receive gifts and blessings from God for ourselves or others—if our own hands are foul. We must seek forgiveness first for ourselves.

June 18.

"Remember your Creator in the days of your youth, before the days of trouble come." Ecclesiastes 12:1

It is easier to begin a Christian life in youth, than at any other time. It is easy to train the heart's affections around the cross—before they have learned to cling to earth's sordid things. It is easy to teach young fingers to play on the piano or organ—but it is next to impossible to train the stiff fingers of old age to do it. So it is easy for the young to learn to strike the harps of heaven. It is easier to *keep* the heart pure and tender, than to *get back* its purity and tenderness when once they have been lost.

June 19.

"Strengthening the hearts of the disciples by encouraging them to continue in the faith, and by telling them, 'It is necessary to pass through many troubles on our way into the kingdom of God.'" Acts 14:22

The best things of life—come out of *wounding*. Wheat is *crushed*—before it becomes bread. Incense must be cast upon the *fire*—before its odors are set free. The ground must be *broken* with the sharp plough—before it is ready to receive the seed. It is the broken heart, which pleases God. The sweetest joys in life—are the fruits of sorrow. Human nature seems to need suffering, to fit it for being a blessing to the world.

June 20.

"The man who does the will of God lives forever." 1 John 2:17

God's will is always the best; it is always divine love. A stricken wife, standing beside the coffin of her husband, said to a friend: "There lies my husband, my only earthly support, my most faithful human friend, one who has never once failed me; but I must not forget that there lies also the will of God, and that that will is perfect love." By faith she saw good and the blessing, in what appeared to her, to be the wreck of all her happiness. But truly the good and the blessing are in every dark providence which comes into the life of God's child. Our Father never means us harm in anything he does or permits. His word is, "I know the thoughts that I think toward you . . . thoughts of peace."

June 21.

"Everyone should be *quick to listen*, slow to speak and slow to become angry." James 1:19

We miss a great deal—by not being good listeners. The world is full of sweet music, bird songs, the chirping of insects, the sweet murmur of all nature, the breathing of the wind through the trees, the rippling of the waters; and yet some people never hear one melodious sound as they go through the fields and forests. God is ever speaking in our ears, in conscience, in his Word, in the gentle voice of his Spirit; but many of us miss all this wonderful divine speech. We ought to train ourselves to listen, to hear, to be "*quick to listen*." We learn by hearing. Truth comes to us from all sides. There is nothing so lowly, that it may not have some message for us.

Unless we go about ever listening—we may miss many a rich lesson, turning away unaware, many an angel who comes from God with a message for us.

June 22.

"Unto you who believe—He is precious!" 1 Peter 2:7

The close friends of Christ have found no other influence in their life, so strong as his precious friendship, in forming and transforming their lives. Continually before them in all its purity and spotlessness, in all its strength and heroism, in all its gentleness and beauty—that fair life has shone, a pattern in the mount, let down from heaven, brought close to them, and winning them by its loveliness. The vision has hung before them continually, and has lifted them up. No one who has had Christ for a friend, in any true, real, vital sense—has failed to be blessed by him, in the way of growth into nobler, richer life.

Gentle, sympathetic, strong human friendships can do much for us. You can tell me how in your life, in some time of grief, certain friends came to you, and how by their sweet sympathy, their quiet peace, their strong comfort, they helped you through some *valley of trouble*. But tell me, rather, what Christ did for you, in your hours of sorrow. When the shadows hung over your home, when your heart was bowed in grief, when a life dearer to you than your own hung trembling in the balance, when at last death came and your heart was broken—what was Christ to you then? Was he not precious to you in those dark experiences? *We find the best things of Christ's grace and love—only in life's experiences of trial.*

June 23.

"Do you see a man diligent in his work? He will stand in the presence of kings." Proverbs 22:29

Men like to rise in the world; but there are different kinds of elevation. One is that which *money* gives. Then, there is elevation which comes through *social recognition*. But true elevation is of *character* and *worth*. It can be obtained only by being diligent. We are not to wait idly for promotion—but are to be busy at our lowlier duty until the larger is ready for us. Because Moses could not be an emancipator at once, he did not spend his time in idleness—but was faithful as a shepherd; and when God wanted him, he found him at his work. Jesus found Peter, James, and John *fishing*. The way to make sure of being needed for a greater work— is to do well your plainer work. Diligence makes men ready to go up higher. Do well today's work, however lowly; perhaps tomorrow God will have something larger for you.

June 24.

"He summoned the priests and Levites and gave them these instructions: Go at once to all the towns of Judah and collect the required annual offerings, so that we can repair the Temple of your God. Do not delay!" *But the Levites did not act right away.*" 2 Chronicles 24:5

The Levites seem to have been indifferent and negligent. No reason is given for their lack of energy—but we see its consequence. The house of the Lord remained year after year in its condition of decay, a *standing dishonor* to the name of God, and a reproach to those who had been commanded to repair it.

This is quite an old story; but we may take for ourselves a lesson on the *sin of indolence* in doing God's work. Whatever we are bidden to do—we should do at once. *Promptness* is half of obedience. *Procrastination* is a sad sin. It takes out of life much of its power for good. It grows into a fearful habit, if it is encouraged. A boy who is slow and loitering, will always be behind time, and when he becomes a man will accomplish but little. Many men, even good men, fail to do all that they might do with their life—if only they were always prompt. They lose time, not by being idle—but by *loitering*, by failing to work intensely.

June 25.

"Then He said to Moses—Come *up* to the Lord." Exodus 24:1

God is always far *above* us. We can get nearer to him only by rising out of sin and earthliness, into holier, purer life. It was not easy to climb up the steep side of Sinai; it is not easy to rise nearer to God. It costs pain and struggle. We must make stepping-stones of our dead selves—if we would ascend in life and character. We must climb upward *step by step.*

Jacob saw life visioned before him as a ladder. That is the true vision in every case, not a level path, through grassy meadows—but rocky steps up a mountain-side. We sing:

"Nearer, my God! to you, Nearer to Thee!

E'en though it be a cross, That raises me!"

A child lay dying, and said plaintively, "Lift me higher! Lift me higher!" The father took the little one in his arms, and lifted her up high as he could raise her, as she continued to plead, with failing strength, "Lift me higher!" Soon she was gone, lifted out of her earthly father's trembling arms, into the bosom of her heavenly Father. On the child's grave they cut her name and the words: "Lifted higher!" God wants us all to come up to him, to get closer to him, to be lifted higher into life's better things.

June 26.

"As a man thinks in his heart—so is he." Proverbs 23:7

Our thoughts make us. They are *the silent builders* on the 'temple of character' which we are constructing. They give color and form to the whole building. If we *think* purely and truly, we are rearing up a holy fabric. If our thoughts are evil, the fabric that is rising within us is blemished.

The inner and the outer life will always correspond in the end. A bad heart—will work through to the surface. If a man's life is righteous, you know his thoughts are holy. Unholy thoughts will never yield righteousness in conduct.

Thoughts seem mere nothings; flecks of cloud flying through the air; flocks of birds flitting by, and gone. But they are the most real things about our life. All things we do—are thoughts first. Our thoughts fly out like birds, and take their place in the world. Then our heart is still their home-nest, where they will return at last to dwell.

June 27.

"A good man obtains favor from the LORD, but the LORD condemns a crafty man." Proverbs 12:2

It is certainly worth while to have the Lord's favor. If we know that *he* is smiling upon us, we need not much mind what the *world* thinks. Christ's commendation sweetens even the bitterest of unjust blame. It was very comforting for Mary when the disciples were finding fault, to have Jesus say, "She has wrought a good work." This approval healed the hurt the disciples' unfit words had caused.

A good man obtains God's favor. A good man is one who loves God and does his will. The Scripture does not say a *great* man, a *rich* man, a *strong* man, a man of *rank*. If any of these were the qualification required, there would be very many people who never could obtain the divine favor; for not many of us are either great, rich, strong, or noble. The qualification is a "good" man. Goodness is within the reach of all of us. If only we are good, it matters little what our condition in other regards may be.

The other side of this proverb is also instructive: "but the LORD condemns a crafty man." Again, it is not poverty, nor ignorance, nor commonplace condition, which misses the Lord's favor—but a bad heart, one full of deceit, scheming, and evil designs against others. If we would have God's favor—we must keep a sincere and pure heart.

June 28

"The child grew, and one day he went out to his father, who was with the reapers. "My head! My head!" he said to his father. His father told a servant, "Carry him to his mother." After the servant had lifted him up and carried him to his mother, the boy sat on her lap until noon, and then he died." 2 Kings 4:18-20

The child went out with glee from the home door into the harvest-field, where his father and the reapers were busy. The sun was hot, and it was not long until the little one was crying in great pain. The father was too busy to give much thought to his sick child. The mother was the person to do that, and he sent the boy home by a servant. The mother was not too busy to attend to her child—mothers never are. With maternal tenderness she took her stricken boy on her knees, doing all in her power to restore him. But when noon came—he was dead in her arms!

What a change a few hours made in that home! We are never sure when we leave the breakfast table and scatter to our several tasks, that our merry laughter shall not be turned to grief before nightfall. This consciousness should make our home fellowship very affectionate, since any hour we spend together, may be the last. The scene in this old Shunammite home, is one which has been repeated in so many households, that, as we linger on it, it touches all hearts, and makes this ancient mother kin to thousands of other mothers. No matter that she lived twenty-seven hundred years ago. To us she is a mother with her dead child in her arms, and our hearts are touched by her grief down through all these centuries!

June 29.

"O LORD, God of Israel, there is no God like you in heaven above or on earth below—you who keep your covenant of love with your servants who continue wholeheartedly in your way." 1 Kings 8:23

Prayer is not all *request* and *supplication.* We ought not to speak to God merely and only—when we want some favor from his hand. Much of all true prayer is *adoration* and *praise.* A loving child-heart always seeks to express its love and confidence.

"There is no God like you." The heathen have their idols—but our God is not like them. They see not, hear not, love not, care not for those who worship them. Our God loves and keeps covenant. What he promises he performs. His Word never fails, is never broken. What a strong confidence it gives us—to be sure that the God in whom we trust always keeps his Word! Not a promise of his ever has been broken.

There is something else here which we must not overlook. We should never cut Bible sentences in two in the middle, for if we do we shall get only *half truths.* God keeps covenant; but to every covenant there are two sides, and we have something to do to secure what he has promised. He keeps covenant with those who "continue wholeheartedly in your way." That is our part, and it should be our continual care to be faithful to God in all our ways. There is no danger that he will fail us; let us take heed that we do not fail in our part.

June 30.

"Listen as wisdom calls out! Hear as understanding raises her voice! My mouth speaks what is true, for my lips detest wickedness. All the words of my mouth are just; none of them is crooked or perverse." Proverbs 8:1, 7-8

In this world's counsels—there is a great deal of guessing and speculating. Friends advise us, and intend to speak only what is true; yet by reason of the limitation of their knowledge, they may often give wrong counsel. *Bad advice*, though well meant and honestly given, has wrecked many a life. But here is counsel that is always absolutely true. The words that this divine Wisdom speaks to us—are always infallibly right words. Here is a *Guide,* in whose leading we may put implicit confidence. Here is a *Counselor*, whose counsel is always safe, because always right and true.

Those who abandon themselves utterly to the Word of God, follow its counsels and obey its every precept, are sure of blessedness in two worlds. It never has been heard that the Bible took any person on a course which ended in disaster, or in any loss or dishonor. It always leads in right paths; and these right paths are safe throughout, and have their unvarying destination in the highest good and blessedness of those who pass over them.

JULY

July 1.

The LORD says, "I will restore what you lost to the stripping locusts, the cutting locusts, the swarming locusts, and the hopping locusts. It was I who sent this great destroying army against you!" Joel 2:25

It is God who says, "I will restore." Only the *divine hand* can do it. Christ is the restorer, for he has made atonement for us.

Wherever there is a Christian who is hurt by sin or sorrow—the face of the Christ on the cross, beams on it with healing in its beams. "By his stripes—we are healed." By his wounding—our wounds are cured. His visage was marred—that the marring of sin in our faces might be changed to beauty. By his sorrows—our sorrows are comforted.

July 2.

"Then he said, "Take the arrows," and the king took them. Elisha told him, "Strike the ground." He struck it three times and stopped. The man of God was angry with him and said, "You should have struck the ground five or six times; then you would have defeated Aram and completely destroyed it. But now you will defeat it only three times." 2 Kings 13:18-19

Character comes out in little things. It seemed a small matter, there in the prophet's dying chamber, whether the king shot three arrows or six—yet the future successes of his army depended on it. Unconsciously, he was undergoing a critical test. His lack of energy in shooting the arrows, betrayed a fatal weakness of character. And when the test was over the measure of his success in life was unalterably fixed. No doubt he would have given large sums for a repetition of the testing, now that, he knew what depended on it; but it was too late.

Every life is full of just such *testings*. Destinies are forever turning on events too trivial for record. Our characters are ever being put to proof in the smallest things, and the result settles important matters for our future. He who improves his one talent, receives more. He who is faithful in things that are least, is entrusted with greater things. On the other hand, unfaithfulness in the smallest things, is forever keeping men out of greater trusts. The picking up of a pin in a merchant's office, has made a great destiny for a boy. There is not a lad who may not make or unmake his fortune any day, by some unconscious acts.

God also is continually putting us to the test to see how we do this or that little thing; and he determines thereby whether or not he can entrust great things to us.

July 3.

"He has put a new song in my mouth!" Psalm 40:3

The ancient statue of Memnon was fabled to become *musical*, when the sun rose and the beams of morning light fell upon it. Just so, when the light of the gospel falls upon a darkened heart, it begins to sing. No wonder salvation gives joy! Only think of what we are saved from—the horrible pit of sin; and of what we are saved to—childship in God's family. Can we but rejoice, if we realize our full deliverance?

Every Christian should be a singer. If we cannot acquire the vocal art, we should at least sing and make melody in our heart unto the Lord. God wants to put a song into the mouth of every child of his. Our song should be one that nothing can check. Paul sang in prison with his feet fast in the stocks, and his back gashed with stripes. No trouble or pain should have power to hush the song in a Christian's heart.

Then, our *lives themselves* should be songs. We cannot all be poets, to write glad hymns of praise for others to sing; or singers, to thrill hearts by the sweetness of our voice; but we can *live* hymns and songs, and that is just as pleasing to God!

July 4.

"For seven days they celebrated with joy the Feast of Unleavened Bread, because the LORD had filled them with joy." Ezra 6:21-22

The Lord is always doing things to make us joyful, if only we will accept the love he sends us in them, and rejoice. Christian life ought to be one of joy. Christ said he wished his disciples to have his joy in them, and wished their joy to be full. There are a great many reasons why we should be joyous Christians. The greatest is that we are saved from sin and are in God's family. Our privileges, blessings, and hopes—are enough to fill our hearts with gladness.

We ought to show our joy in gratitude. Some people take all God gives them, accept all he does for them, and yet go through life *grumbling* and *complaining* all the time! Every little trial or care counts for more with them, than all the multitude of God's goodnesses. There is never any sunshine in their faces, for they can always find something that is not satisfactory, to make a *cloud* of, and to give them excuse for being unhappy. This is a poor, miserable way to live. These people are neither joyful themselves, nor do they help to make the world brighter. We ought to be ashamed to live so unworthily and unbeautifully. God wants us to be burning and shining lights, and to scatter happiness and good cheer wherever we go. Instead of being *croakers*, he wants us to be *sweet singers*. **It is a sin not to live cheerfully!**

July 5.

"Praise be to the Lord! Not one word has failed, of all the wonderful promises He gave!" 1 Kings 8:56

It is nearly three thousand years since Solomon uttered this testimony; but we can say now, just as confidently as the king did that day, that in all these centuries since not one word of all God's good promise has failed any one of his people. No one has ever trusted a promise of God—and had that word fail of fulfillment.

The most real and sure things in this world—are the words of God. In every one of them, God's own almighty hand is gloved. We *clutch* them—and find ourselves clutched in turn by divinity, out of whose clasp we never can fall, nor be torn away. We *lean* upon these words—and find ourselves encircled and upborne by the everlasting arms. We pillow our head in weariness or sorrow upon God's words of love and comfort—and find ourselves drawn close to our Father's heart, held in his warm bosom, and soothed by his tenderness, which is gentler than a mother's.

So all through life, in every experience, we may trust the promises of God, and commit all our interests to them, and be assured in our heart that not one of them will ever fail us. We may trust them, too, in death, and we shall find everything just as God has said: the divine presence with us in the valley, dying but a going to be at home, absent from the body at home with the Lord, in eternal blessedness. Not one Word of God can fail.

July 6.

"This became a great sin!" 1 Kings 12:30

The king's plan was successful. The people did not go back to the temple at Jerusalem—but bowed down before the calves. The separation was thus made complete. No only so—but the false leading of the king, turned the ten tribes into a path that took them farther and farther away from God.

Twenty times the Scripture records that "Jeroboam made Israel to sin." The name of *Jeroboam* is held up to execration through all the after history—as a man who made others sin!

Sin grows from small beginnings—until it attains giant proportions. The man who starts an error, knows not what moral ruin will come from it. To teach one child falsely, may be to blight thousands of lives. Those who begin new enterprises set in motion streams of influence, good or bad, which may continue to flow forever. Jeroboam gave character to this new kingdom, and all the nineteen kings who followed him walked in his wicked steps.

There is a story of an abbot who coveted a piece of ground. The owner consented to lease it to the abbot for one crop only. The abbot sowed *acorns*, a crop which took three hundred years to ripen. Jeroboam's one sowing of sin, burdened the new kingdom with evil through all its history. Satan begs for *one crop* only, and then sows seeds whose harvest will fill all the life to the end. We do not know what we are doing—when we start a wrong thing.

July 7.

"Whoever drinks the water I give him will never thirst. Indeed, the water I give him will become in him a well of water welling up to eternal life!" John 4:14

If you are a true believer in Christ, your new life will become a spring of water in you. Wherever you go, into the driest desert, into the hottest plain, far away from the means of grace and from spiritual privileges, into the dark paths of sorrow—your life shall not waste nor fail, for its fountain is within you. It is not fed from without, nor is it dependent upon ordinances and 'means of grace' as sources of nourishment along the way. The fountain of your life, your comfort, your joy, your strength—is fed from the mountains of heaven, from the fullness of Christ; hence it can never waste. Thus from this well of water in the heart of the Christian, flows out a perpetual stream of life, with blessing for the world.

If you can be only a little spring, with but water enough to fill a pilgrim's cup, do not be discouraged; be the sweet blessing that you can be, and thank God for the privilege. Yet Jesus says that "*rivers* of living water" shall flow from this well in him who believes—not a mere trickling rill—but large rivers, to bless a whole community. We should not be satisfied with any small measure of usefulness. We should seek to bear much fruit. We should always abound in the work of the Lord. We should seek to be the largest blessing we can be.

July 8.

"The secret of the kingdom of God has been given to you. But to those on the outside everything is said in parables." Mark 4:11

It is astonishing how differently the truth of Christ looks from within and from without. It is like the stained-glass windows in a church. One who stands outside and looks at them sees none of their rich beauty. They seem dull, opaque, and without meaning. But let one stand within the building and look at the rich windows, and all is transformed. The lines and figures appear in all their rich loveliness.

It is the same with the truths of God's Word. They are not attractive to those who are without. People sometimes sneer at the faith of Christians, as they find them leaning upon an unseen God, and clinging to intangible hopes. But when one becomes a Christian, all is changed. Where there was no loveliness, there now appears the loftiest beauty. What was laughed at before, is now seen to be worthy of highest admiration. Only those who have received Christ, can really understand the wonderful things of his love.

July 9.

"The LORD upholds all those who fall—and lifts up all who are bowed down." Psalm 145:14

God never gets tired helping us learn our lessons. No matter how often we fail, he is ready to give us another chance. When we fail to have our lesson learned, he does not give us up, putting us out of his school—but tells us to take the lesson over again and try to get it better. Only think how often we have to try—before we do things as he wants us to do them, how often we fall in trying to walk, before we learn to walk. If our great Teacher were not patient with us—we would never become like Christ; but he never wearies of our slowness. He is pleased with our efforts, however faulty they are, and has for us always an encouraging word.

July 10.

"By this all people will know that you are My disciples: if you have love for one another." John 13:35

There is one unfailing mark of Christian character, wherever it is found: Love is always in it. Whatever else may be or may not be in the new life of the Christian— the scarlet thread of love is always woven into the character. God is love, and the believer in Christ, is in a measure, like God. To be a Christian is to have Christ in the heart; and Christ is love. Not to have love—is not to be a Christian.

The first effect of *faith* in Christ—is the springing up of *love* in the heart of him who believes. This love does not lie hidden—but is revealed in the life. It shows itself in love for *God*; but there is no love for God—which does not also make the heart warm toward *man*. He who loves not his brother, whom he has seen, cannot love God, whom he has not seen.

Christian love is not a mere beautiful sentiment, glowing like a radiant vision in the soul—but fading the moment we meet our brothers in actual life; it is a love that becomes the very mainspring of all action, the burning heart of all ambition. It is a love that makes us *pitiful* toward all human sorrow, *gentle* toward human infirmity, *helpful* toward human need, *patient* under human unkindness and injury, and ready at every call to do and suffer and sacrifice.

July 11.

"We who are strong ought to bear with the failings of the weak—and not to please ourselves. Each of us should please his neighbor for his good, to *build him up.* For even Christ did not please himself." Romans 15:1-3

There are some people who are anointed to be *helpers* of others—to build them up. Those who have questions or perplexities, those who are seeking light or guidance, turn to them instinctively, with confidence, sure of finding what they seek.

There is need for such helpers. There are questions which books or sermons do not answer; it is a friend that is needed, one who can understand and sympathize. No other ministry to which men are ordained in this world, is so sacred as this, which comes into lives in their deepest experiences, at times when, without wise help, they may be wrecked. There is not one of us who may not be such a *helper.*

July 12.

"I tell you the truth, we speak of what we know, and we testify to what we have seen." John 3:11

The things that Christ teaches are certainties. Very much *human science* is only guessing; we cannot be sure of it. Every now and then some new discovery is made, which sweeps away whole volumes of boasted theories. We have to be all the time buying new books—just to keep up with the times; and we are afraid to quote from any but the newest editions, lest there has been some recent discovery which contradicts the older.

But Christ's teachings are certainties. He came down from heaven, where from all eternity he had dwelt, and he knew the things he taught. We may accept his words without the slightest doubt, and may build our soul's hopes upon them. What he said about God, about God's love, about heaven, about the judgment, about the future life, about the way of salvation, is all certainty! As we go on into the future, we shall find everything just as he has described it.

This fact should give us deep and strong confidence—if we are reposing upon Christ's promises for salvation and life. It should drive us speedily to his cross for refuge—if we are still unsheltered, for he has told us of condemnation abiding upon all who do not believe on him. We may not disregard a single word that Christ spoke, for all his words are all true and eternal. Not one of them can ever fail him who leans upon it.

July 13.

"Joshua son of Nun, the servant of the LORD, **died** at the age of a hundred and ten." Judges 2:8

We have no elaborate account of the *closing* scenes of this godly man's life. Many chapters are filled with accounts of his life, his work, his wise words, and his many activities; but all we know about his death is told in this one little phrase. If he had lived in these days—the scenes of his death would have been described with glowing pen. We would have known what his last words were, how he met the end, whether with or without fear; what dying testimony he left to the power of divine grace. But not a word have we, about any of these things. We are told simply, in the briefest possible words, that 'he died'.

The same is true of all Bible saints. We have no death-bed scenes, no descriptions of dying experiences. The meaning of this, is that it matters very little how a man dies; *living* is the important thing. Not many people have raptures in the last hour. Some, whose lives have been very Christly, die without any remarkable manifestation of faith or any joyous experiences. Then sometimes those who have not lived a Christian life at all—seem to have the greatest raptures in their last hours. All this proves that it is living, not dying—which tests one's character. In such a man as Joshua, it mattered not whether he had a triumphant end, or sank away in the shadows of old age, and died without a word of ecstasy. His life was his testimony. He needed no other.

July 14.

"Joshua ... died . . . and the children of Israel did that which was evil . . . and they forsook the Lord." Judges 2:8-12

That is too often the way. So long as the godly parent or the faithful friend lives, it is not hard to do right; but when the human guide is gone—the restraining hand is withdrawn, and the child or friend drifts away from the holy influence. Many a boy begins to drift away from God—at his mother's grave.

There was a man whose besetting sin was strong drink. He said to a friend one day: "When I am with you, I feel strong; if I could always be with you, I would never give way to my terrible passion." Said his friend: "Whenever you feel the temptation getting the mastery over you, come to me and I will help you." So, many a time this poor man might have been seen hurrying toward his friend's office. Once in that helpful presence, he soon grew strong.

But death came to this friend, and among those who wept at his grave—none shed bitterer tears than he who had so often run to him for the sympathy and help that saved him. Soon the temptation came again, and there was no one to whom to go. In his despair he fell into the old sin, and sank down to ruin! If he had known Christ, when his friend died he would still have missed him, and would have found living harder without his help—but he would not have sunk down in utter helplessness. He would then have had the strength of Christ to support him in his temptation.

July 15.

"Jesus gave him no answer." John 19:9

The *silences* of Jesus are as significant as his *words*. He was silent before Pilate. He understood the governor's miserable insincerity. Pilate had had opportunity enough to do the right thing—but he had thrown away his chance. Now Jesus would answer no more of his questions. It was not worth while.

One lesson we get from this *silence of Jesus* is, that if we reject his offers of grace over and over—the time may come, will come, when he will be silent to us. And of all calamities that can possibly ever come to any man, no other could be so great as that Christ should be silent to his prayers, turning his back and answering no more when he calls.

Another lesson from Christ's example is, that there come times in every life when silence is better than speech. Ofttimes to words of reviling or insult, silence is the only true answer. To many of the assaults made by sceptics on our religion, it is better that we remain silent. There is a time to speak boldly in the presence of Christ's enemies; but there also are times when we should keep silence, attempting no answer.

July 16.

"Some of those present were saying indignantly to one another, 'Why this waste of perfume? It could have been sold for more than a year's wages and the money given to the poor!' And they rebuked her harshly." Mark 14:4-5

It is very easy to yield to the temptation to criticize others, and find fault with their way of serving Christ. There are many motives which come in to promote this unchristian habit. We are all prone to be *envious* of others, and hence to form *unjust opinions* of what they do. One of the last graces to ripen in a Christian, is usually that of *rejoicing in another's good work*. It is very hard, too, to learn our Lord's lesson: "Do not judge—or you too will be judged." It seems natural, too, as sad as the confession may be, for us to *disparage* what others do, and to *underestimate* it.

But we should learn the sinfulness of murmuring against others. We see how unlovely, how unChristlike, it was in these first disciples. Is it any less so in us when we allow ourselves to criticize our fellow-Christians, finding fault with the way they show their love for Christ? Even if they do not do their work as we do ours—have we a right to judge them and blame them, and speak unkind things about what they have done? Between them and their Master, rests the matter, and it is not our duty to make *ourselves* judges and condemners of their acts. They are responsible for what they do—not us. There are few lessons more needed than this, for there are few faults more common than that which we see here in these first disciples.

July 17.

"No chastening seems pleasant at the time, but painful. Later on, however, it produces a harvest of righteousness and peace for those who have been trained by it." Hebrews 12:11

We have all known Christian sufferers who have grown into rare, sweet beauty—as they have suffered.

They have lost their earthliness—and have learned heavenliness.

Pride—has given way to humility.

The harsh music—has grown soft and gentle.

The rough marble—has taken the shape of graceful beauty.

There are elements of loveliness in the depths of every life—which pain alone can bring out. God often chastens His children—to bring out more clearly in them, the features of His own lovely image.

Yet afflictions do not always make people better. Not all suffering yields the harvest of righteousness and peace. We have all seen people suffering, who became only more impatient, selfish, and cold. Their trouble hurt them.

As I watch the effects of suffering upon men and women, I find that it is only in the fewest cases—that the life is made more radiant by pain. There are dangerous shoals skirting all the deeps of affliction, and many frail barks are wrecked in the darkness! In no experience of life, do most people need wise friendship, and firm loving guidance—more than in their times of trouble.

July 18

"As the Lord, the God of Israel lives, *before whom I stand.*" 1 Kings 17:1

"You are the God who *sees* me!" Genesis 16:13.

We all stand in the presence of God. His eye is ever upon us. His face ever beams its light upon us. We all believe this, and say it often with our lips; yet many of us do not really get the truth into our heart! If we did—it would make holier people of us. We would not slight our work as now we do so often, if we were truly conscious that God is looking on us as we work!

This consciousness of the presence of God, would also give us hope and courage in darkness or danger; like Hagar, who said, "You are the God who sees me!" Some people think of the omniscience of God—as a reason for fear and terror. But to Hagar, it meant divine love and care. God had not forgotten her, nor forsaken her. She was cast out of her earthly home—but the Lord saw her and took her up.

If we are God's children, the thought of our Father's presence should always bring us comfort, assurance, and a wonderful sense of security. It is a great thing to stand before God, to be conscious of His eye upon us, and to know Him so well as not to be afraid of Him.

July 19.

"You are to drink from the *brook*. I have commanded the *ravens* to provide for you there." 1 Kings 17:4

God is never at a loss for a way of providing for His children. The brooks of water, the birds of the air, the beasts of the field, the winds of heaven, the waves of the sea—all creatures belong to him, and are under His direct control. He has no trouble, therefore, in getting food to His children, wherever they may be.

Perhaps none of us ever had ravens carry our daily bread to us—but God sends it to us in other ways; and it is just as really HE who sends it, whether railroad trains carry it across a continent, or ships bring it half around the globe, or birds convey it to our windows, or it comes through hands of loving friends.

Many of us know too much for our good, these 'modern days'. We are so wise about "laws of nature" that we can account for everything on *scientific grounds*, and have no need for God's assistance anywhere! Consequently we forget, some of us, that God has anything to do with this world. What poor fools we are! What are the *laws of nature*—but God's established and common ways of doing things? If I sow wheat-seeds on a little patch of soil, and in a few months reap a harvest, and then, taking the wheat to the mill, get fine flour and have good bread on my table. Had God nothing to do with sending it to me? Did not he provide it as really, as when he sent the ravens to Elijah day by day, with food for him?

July 20.

"It came to pass after a while, that the brook dried up!" 1 Kings 17:7

That is the way *this world's brooks* always do. For a time they flow full; then they begin to waste away, and at last dry up altogether. This is true of all *earthly* joys. There is a comfort, however, in what comes after the statement made in these words. When the brook dried up, God had another place ready for his servant. "Arise, and go to Zarephath." There he found other help ready.

It must have been a sore test of Elijah's faith—to watch the stream growing less and less every day. "What shall I do when the brook is dry?" he would wonder. But we need not suppose that he ever *worried* about it. He knew that God was providing for him, and would have something else ready when this supply ceased. One morning there was no water running over the stones, and the prophet had to eat a dry breakfast only bread and meat; but still, I think he did not grow anxious. Then after breakfast the Lord came and told him to move.

The lesson is, that we are never to doubt God, no matter how low the supply gets. Though we have come down to the last mouthful of bread—and the last cupful of water, and still see no new provision beyond, we are to take the last morsel with thankfulness, believing that God will have something else ready in time. It will be soon enough if it is ready when we have eaten the last crust!

July 21.

"So she did as Elijah said, and she and Elijah and her son continued to eat from her supply of flour and oil for many days." 1 Kings 17:15

That is, she took the handful of flour she had and the little oil, and made a cake for her hungry guest first, and then for herself and her son. Then she found that there was as much meal and oil left—as she had before.

There are several things to commend in this woman. One is her faith. She believed what was told her, and acted on it. It is when we do God's commandments, that he blesses us. His promises are conditional, depending upon the fulfillment of our part. Had this woman not believed and obeyed, the wonderful two or three years miracle in her house, would not have been wrought. The woman's unselfish generosity must also be commended. She had enough only for a meal for herself and son—but she fed the stranger first. Had she prepared a meal for herself and son, and left the hungry prophet unfed, there would have been no miracle of increase. We must be ready to share our little with others who need, if we would have the blessing on ourselves.

July 22.

"So she did as Elijah said, and she and Elijah and her son continued to eat from her supply of flour and oil for many days." 1 Kings 17:15

Had not the prophet come to the widow's door, she and her household would probably have perished in the famine. Or had the woman refused the prophet's request, saying, "I cannot spare anything for a stranger; charity begins at home, and I must look first after my own," she and her son would have starved before the rain fell. The meal wasted not, because she shared it with another.

The lesson is plain. There is a *withholding* that tends to poverty; there is a *giving* that enriches. The way to make sure of spiritual blessing is—to seek to be a blessing. If your love is growing cold, help someone, and it will become warm again. We cannot afford to shut our doors in the face of those whom God sends to us for sympathy and for the ministries of love. Such serving brings to us blessings which we must not miss.

July 23.

"He himself went a day's journey into the desert. He came to a juniper tree, sat down under it and prayed that he might die. "I have had enough, LORD," he said. "Take my life; I am no better than my ancestors." 1 Kings 19:4

He was sorely *discouraged*. It seemed to him that all he had done, had come to nothing. There are few things we need more to guard against than *discouragement*. When once we come under its influence, it makes us weak, robbing us of our hope and making cowards of us. Many a life is discrowned and drawn down to failure, through discouragement.

It is surely a sad picture: this greatest of the old prophets lying there under the little bush, in the wilderness, longing to die! If he had died then and there, what an *inglorious ending* it would have made of his life! As it was, however, he lived to do further glorious work and to see great results from his contest with idolatry. God was kinder to him, than he knew.

It is wrong to wish ourselves dead. Life is God's gift to us, a sacred trust for which we shall have to give account. While God keeps us living—he has something for us to do. Our prayer should be for grace to do our duty bravely and well unto the end. From Elijah's after-experience, we learn that we would never be cast down by any discouraging experiences. The things we think have failed are often only slowly ripening into rich success. We have only to be faithful to God and to duty, and we may always rejoice. What seems failure—is often best success.

July 24.

"Then he lay down under the tree and fell asleep. All at once an angel touched him and said, "Get up and eat." He looked around, and there by his head was a cake of bread baked over hot coals, and a jar of water. He ate and drank and then lay down again. The angel of the LORD came back a second time and touched him and said, "Get up and eat, for the journey is too much for you." So he got up and ate and drank. *Strengthened by that food, he traveled forty days and forty nights* until he reached Horeb, the mountain of God." 1 Kings 19:5-8

Behold the loving gentleness of God. He followed his discouraged servant in his flight, kept watch over him all the way, and did not cast him off. There is great comfort in this for us all. God is very patient with us in our weaknesses and faults. He does not break bruised reeds.

Then it must be noticed that when God would restore his servant's soul—he began with his body. He gave him *sleep* and then *food*, until his exhausted nature was refreshed. Much spiritual depression is caused by the bodily condition. Ofttimes the best cure for despondency, is sleep and rest, until the body is restored to healthy conditions.

This incident is typical. God is continually preparing a table in the wilderness where he feeds his weary ones. In their sorrows, he provides for them food which the world knows nothing of; they rise up and go on their journey with joy, sustained by the secret strength which divine grace supplies. Many people whose lot in life is hard—go through the days with cheerful, songful spirit, because every morning in the closet, God gives them food which makes them strong.

July 25.

"I have been very zealous for the LORD God Almighty. The Israelites have rejected your covenant, broken down your altars, and put your prophets to death with the sword. **I am the only one left**, and now they are trying to kill me too." 1 Kings 19:10

There is something very pathetic in this verse. Elijah really thought he was alone. He did not know of one other man in all the land, who was loyal to God. This made it all the harder for him.*Companionship* strengthens us. It is comparatively easy in battle for one to march and fight in the ranks, with others all around him; but to move out *alone*, old soldiers say, is a sore test of courage. It is easy to be good, faithful, and loyal in duty, diligent in Christian service—when one has companionship. But it tests one's life to have to stand alone, the only Christian in the family, the workshop, the store, the school. But many have to stand just in this way. They are really the only one who is in their place to stand for God. If they fail, God's work there will suffer greatly.

But we see also the value of a single life. For years Elijah was the only one who confessed the Lord and was faithful to him. Yet though utterly alone, and not knowing of any others who even secretly were true, he yet stood firm, and bravely maintained the honor of Jehovah in the face of a whole nation. As we read the story through to the end—we see the outcome of his faithfulness. He alone wrought a great reformation. We sometimes find ourselves alone—the only one to witness for Christ in the place where we stand. If we simply stand and falter not, we shall by and by see the triumph of that for which we stand.

July 26.

"Yet I reserve seven thousand in Israel—all whose knees have not bowed down to Baal and all whose mouths have not kissed him." 1 Kings 19:18

Things were not so bad as Elijah had thought. He supposed he was the only one left; but there were seven thousand more, scattered here and there through the land, who were still loyal to God. God's cause in this world is never hopeless. He has others, where we think we are the only one.

There is an experience of Luther's which is suggestive: "At one time," he says, "I was sorely vexed and tried by my own sinfulness, by the wickedness of the world, and by the dangers that beset the church. One morning I saw my wife dressed in mourning. Surprised, I asked her who had died. 'Do you not know?' she replied; 'GOD is dead.' 'How can you talk such nonsense?' I said. 'How can God die?' 'Is that really true?' she asked. 'Of course,' I said, not perceiving her aim.' How can you doubt it?' 'Yet,' she said, 'though you do not doubt that—yet you are so helpless and discouraged.' "

July 27.

"The time had come for the Lord to take Elijah up to heaven in a whirlwind." 2 Kings 2:1

When a godly man leaves the world—he does not cease to live. The Lord took Elijah to live in another country, a heavenly one. We are able actually to verify this statement. We have but to turn over to the Gospels to see him again, nearly nine hundred years later, alive, and active still in God's work. "Just then there appeared before them Moses and *Elijah*, talking with Jesus." Matthew 17:3

It is just as true of the Christians who die in our homes—as it was of this old prophet, that the Lord takes them up into heaven, and that they live on in blessedness forever.

One cold autumn day I saw an empty bird's-nest on a tree. It looked desolate and forsaken. But I knew the birds that once were there were living yet, living now in the warm South, beyond the reach of winter's storms, and singing there then sweet songs. There is an *empty love nest* in many a home, in many a heart—but we know that the dear Christian who is gone—is living with God in heaven. There is comfort in this.

There is a suggestion in the way God took Elijah from earth. It was "in a whirlwind." A whirlwind suggests terror. But this wild storm was God's chariot, and it took the prophet up into heaven. Death always seems terrible to nature. Sometimes it comes in form of great terror. But however it may come, it takes God's child home to glory!

July 28.

"As they were walking along and talking together, suddenly a chariot of fire and horses of fire appeared and separated the two of them, and Elijah went up to heaven in a whirlwind!" 2 Kings 2:11

So the most loving friends must sometimes be parted. We walk on together, talking of a thousand things, not dreaming of separation, when suddenly, as we turn some sharp corner in the way, the 'chariot' is waiting, and one is taken and the other left! We ought not to forget the *certainty of separation* in every friendship we form. Some day one of the two will be taken, and the other must be left to weep by a grave and to walk on lonely and sorrowing after that.

Another thought suggested here is, that heaven is not far away. One of the 'chariots' from the King's country came down that day to carry Elijah home. Another came down to the door of your house when your godly father died, or when mother or brother or sister died. We shall not leave this world as Elijah did, missing death; we shall have to pass through the valley of the shadow of death; but we shall have the heavenly chariot to bear away our freed spirit just as truly as he did.

July 29.

"When they had crossed, Elijah said to Elisha, "Tell me, what can I do for you before I am taken from you?"

"Let me inherit a double portion of your spirit," Elisha replied. 2 Kings 2:9

Elisha's choice shows where his heart was. He did not ask for position, for wealth, for ease, for honor—but for more spiritual power. He had watched his master in his great work, his zeal for God, his heroism, his intense earnestness, and he wanted to have a large measure of the same spirit. He wanted most of all to be a better man, a more useful man, more active and mighty in the Lord's work. Here is a good lesson for us. We ought to seek above all other things—the qualities and graces and beauties which make a noble character.

There is something else. Elisha greatly admired his master, Elijah, and his chief desire was to be like him. This is commendable. Christ, our Master, is the one great and perfect example, and all of us should imitate him. Any other model is too low. Yet he gives us in his true followers *pictures* of at least some fragments of his own beauty, and it is right for us to imitate these. Paul said: "Be imitators of me." Every parent should live so that his child, imitating him, shall be ever following Christ and growing more like him. It is right when we see anything beautiful in another—to desire to have the same beauty in ourselves. Whether we will or not, we grow, even unconsciously, like those whom we admire and love.

July 30.

"He picked up the mantle that had fallen from Elijah." 2 Kings 2:13

We are continually seeing useful lives removed from earth. The loss seems irreparable. But *there are no accidents in God's providence*. Everyone's life is a plan of God, and no faithful servant is taken away—until his part in the great plan is finished. There is abundance of work remaining—but it is the work of others, not of him who is gone. His mantle falls at someone's feet— yours, perhaps.

A godly *father* dies, and there is grief in the home. How he will be missed! Yes, but an elder son stands by the coffin, strong and gifted, blessed with the blessing of the father's life and teaching. At his feet the mantle falls from the father's shoulders. He must take it up, and with it lift the burdens and responsibilities of manhood. He must become now his mother's protector, and the shelter and defender of his younger brothers and sisters.

A godly mother dies, and when a gentle mother goes out of a home—the loss indeed seems irreparable. But if there is an elder daughter in the sorrowing group at the grave, at her feet the mantle falls.

So it is in all the breaches which death makes in Christian homes and communities, in every case the mantle falls at someone's feet. God makes provision that his work shall not suffer, unless his servants fail in their duty. We must be ready always to take up what is ours.

July 31.

"But his delight is in the law of the LORD, and on his law he meditates day and night." Psalm 1:2

A perfumer bought a common earthen jar, and filled it with fragrant flowers. Soon every particle of the substance of the jar, was filled with the rich perfume; and long afterward, and even when broken, the fragments retained the fragrance. So it is that a human life becomes filled, saturated, with the Word of God, when one loves it and meditates upon it continually. The thoughts, feelings, affections, dispositions, and the whole character become colored with the spirit of the Word.

Such a filling of the heart and memory with the pure words of God, is the best way to prepare for any future of darkness into which the life may pass. It is like hanging up a hundred lamps while the light of day yet shines, to be ready to pour down their soft beams the moment daylight fades.

AUGUST

August 1.

"The Lord has sent me to *Bethel*."
So they went down to Bethel.
"The Lord has sent me to *Jericho*."
So they went to Jericho.
"The Lord has sent me to the *Jordan*."
So the two of them walked on.
"Elijah went up to *heaven* in a whirlwind!"
2 Kings 2:2, 4, 6, 11

God leads us on step by step, each step a new revelation. He led Elijah on with new calls to new errands, from Gilgal to Bethel, from Bethel to Jericho, from Jericho to Jordan, and then over the river and up among the hills, until at last, as he went on, the chariot came down and lifted him away to heaven! In this same beautiful way, does God lead each one of his children through life. We know not what any day may bring forth. But God knows; and he calls us forward, to this duty and experience today, to others tomorrow, and so on and on, and on and on, until we come to the last step, and that will be into glory!

Elijah's prompt obedience, teaches us our side of the lesson. He went swiftly from task to task. He would finish his work, before the end came. It was to visit the schools of the prophets that he went to Bethel and to Jericho. He wanted to give his last counsels to the young students whom he had been training, and on whom the future religious work among the people would depend.

The nearing of the end of life, should intensify our earnestness. A godly woman was told that she could not live more than six weeks. "Then I must arise, and hasten to finish my work!" Leaving her bed, she went out and hurried from place to place, laboring intensely until the very end came.

August 2.

"Then they took their bones and buried them under a tamarisk tree at Jabesh, and they fasted seven days." 1 Samuel 31:13

It has been said, that everyone lives for a funeral; that the burial one has—tells the story of one's life. One man amasses great wealth, and when his body lies in state, the rich come and look at him and pass on with their tearless eyes. Another devotes his life to doing good. His hands scatter blessings. The needy are cared for, the hungry are fed, the sick are visited, the fallen are lifted up. When he lies in his coffin, the poor come, the widow and the orphan, those whom his hands have relieved and helped, and with grateful hearts and tearful eyes take their farewell.

It is a beautiful sight this rescuing of the body of King Saul from dishonor on the field where he had fallen, and it is especially so when we learn that it was an act of kindness which he had done many years before, which secured for his dead body the gentle thought and care it received that day. Had Saul's life been filled to its close with such deeds of true valor as marked its beginning, he would have had the gratitude of a whole nation when he came to die.

We should try to live—so that we shall be remembered with gratitude. Also, we would never fail to show gratitude to anyone who has conferred a favor upon us. Let us be sure, too, that we live so as to obtain honor from God, when we come to the end of life. If we miss that, earth's honor will be an awful mockery.

August 3.

"When I kept silent, my bones wasted away through my groaning all day long. For day and night your hand was heavy upon me; my strength was sapped as in the heat of summer." Psalm 32:3-4

Sometimes we would better be *silent* to God. When sore trials are upon us we should not say a word in resistance. But there is a silence to God which does not bring blessing. Unconfessed sins, produce bitterness. David's words tell a sad story of the suffering of the days when he kept silent about his guilt.

He could not put away the *memory* of his sin. It stayed in his mind, saddened every joy and embittered every sweet thing in his life. His very body suffered, and his heart cried out continually in anguish.

Unconfessed sins are a burden too great for mortal to bear. We should never keep silence for a moment, about a sin which we have committed. The only godly thing to do—is to confess it instantly, and put it out of our life utterly and forever.

Sin is a *demon from the dark abodes*, and must be expelled—or it will take up its home in the heart and destroy the life. Sin is *poison of eternal death*, and if not cast out—it will spread its death through the soul. The only safety is, by confession and repentance, to thrust out remorselessly every sin that has overcome us!

August 4.

"The Babylonians broke through the wall—and the city fell!" Jeremiah 39:2

When even the smallest breach is made in a wall—it is the beginning of the end! The breach is easily increased, until, where at first only one or two men could enter—now a whole army pours through.

Each of us lives 'within walls'. There is the wall of innocence, which God sets around every human soul. So long as it remains unbroken, we are safe; but when once a breach is made—enemies pour in! It is then easy to break down the whole wall, leaving the life exposed to every temptation. Then, every wild beast enters the garden at will.

Conscience is another of the walls which God builds around each soul. So long as it is kept inviolable, it is an impregnable protection. But this, too, may be broken; and when one small breach has been made in it—it is easy to make it larger breach. It is not as hard to violate conscience the second time, as it was the first time. It is easier still the third and the fourth time. By and by the whole wall is broken down! When this time comes—the citadel of the heart is utterly in the enemy's hands! Everything beautiful is destroyed. The temple is in ruins, the altar is torn away, the fires are out—and there is only darkness in the place once sacred and bright with God's presence. It is well that we look after 'the walls of our life'!

August 5.

"After leaving them, He went up on a mountainside by himself to pray.

He saw that they were in serious trouble, rowing hard and struggling against the wind and waves. About three o'clock in the morning He came to them, walking on the water." Mark 6:46, 48

He did not come immediately; indeed, it was almost morning when He came, and the disciples had been struggling all night in the storm. Yet He had not been indifferent to them meanwhile. From the mountainside where He was praying—He kept his eye upon them. "He saw that they were in serious trouble." All that dark night, He kept a watch upon that little boat that bore His disciples in the midst of the waves.

There is something very suggestive in the picture. This 'boat in the storm', is a picture of 'Christ's friends in this world, in the storms of life'. Sometimes we think we are forgotten—but from His place in glory, Christ's eye is always on us! He sees us struggling, battling with the waves, beaten, and distressed. He has full sympathy with us in all our struggles. It ought to be a great strength and comfort to us in trial, to know this. Jesus intercedes for us in our distresses!

It may not be best always to deliver us immediately—but His prayer continually ascends, that our faith may not fail in the struggle. This also should encourage us.

Then, He always comes in time. He may delay long—but it is never too long. If we call upon Him in trouble—we may be sure that He hears and sees us, and knows just how hard it is for us to endure; that He prays for us that we may not fail, and that He will come at the right time for our deliverance!

August 6.

"Jesus did not answer a word." Matthew 15:23

Jesus is not so tender-hearted, that he cannot tolerate to see us suffer—when suffering is the best experience for us. He does not immediately lift burdens from our shoulders when it is needful for our growth that we bear the burdens longer. There is a mushy sentimentality in many people's ideas about Christ—as if he were too gentle to endure the sight of suffering. It is possible to be too tender toward pain. It is possible for parents to be too emotionally kind to their children. Uncontrolled pity is great weakness, and it is ofttimes very injurious.

Christ's tenderness is never too tender to be wise—as well as tender. He never makes the mistake of yielding to anyone's entreaties, when denial would be better than acquiescence. He never lets us have what we want—because he cannot bear to say "no" to our tearful cries. He is not so tenderhearted as to allow his own disciples to go unchastened, when only by chastisement can he promote their spiritual growth.

But one thing we must not forget, it is love which prompts his severity. He was silent here, that, in the end, he might give the full, rich blessing he wanted to give this woman—but which she could not receive at the first. He denies us, and is silent to us when we cry—that he may draw out our faith, and give us his best blessings by and by.

August 7

"Servants, obey in all things your masters according to the flesh; not with eye-service, as men-pleasers; but in singleness of heart, fearing God." Colossians 3:22

Paul speaks of "eye-service" as a kind of service that is not the truest. There always are those who work well when they are under the eye of a master—but who fall off in diligence and faithfulness when the watching eye is absent. This is very imperfect serving. The person who takes advantage of an employer and does his work slowly, or loiters at his tasks, or shortens the time he is expected to be at his post, or in any way is less faithful or less diligent and careful than if his employer were beside him—is yielding to a temptation which will hurt his own life immeasurably. The wrong he does to another by skimping his work, is sin enough; but the injury done to himself is far more serious. The former is only in *money*; the latter is in *character*. The man who does a dishonest thing, or is in any way unfaithful in duty, has lowered the tone of his own life, and blighted irreparably some portion of the possibilities of his being.

August 8.

"After Hezekiah received the letter and read it, he went up to the Temple and spread it out before the Lord." Isaiah 37:14

That was Hezekiah's way of laying his troubles in the Lord's hands. He could not do anything, and so he gave the matter to God. We all have our cares. Sometimes it is a business perplexity, sometimes it is a temptation; or it may be a combination of circumstances that seems about to crush us.

What is our duty? what is our privilege? We may take the matter directly to God! We may cast the burden upon him. That is what Paul tells us to do with all our anxieties; and he says the peace of God shall then guard our heart and thoughts in Christ Jesus.

Peace, perfect peace, in this dark world of sin?
The blood of Jesus whispers peace within.
Peace, perfect peace, by thronging duties pressed?
To do the will of Jesus, this is rest.

Peace, perfect peace, with sorrows surging 'round?
On Jesus' bosom, naught but calm is found.
Peace, perfect peace, with loved ones far away?
In Jesus' keeping, we are safe and they.

Peace, perfect peace, death shadowing us and ours?
Jesus has vanquished death and all its powers.
It is enough; earth's struggles soon shall cease,
And Jesus calls us to heaven's perfect peace.
Edward Bickersteth

August 9.

"In those days king Hezekiah became ill and was at the point of death." 2 Kings 20:1

Palace walls cannot shut out sickness. Kings and queens, as well as peasants, must yield to the touch of disease and pain. People who live in a plain, humble way—very often feel that somehow this world's troubles have easier access to them than to the rich, who live in a grand way. Sometimes they envy those who dwell in the great houses, and imagine that palace walls exclude most of the ills of life.

But they make a mistake; no splendid doors can shut out trouble. The healthiest people in the world—are working people, who earn their bread by honest toil—the healthiest and the happiest too. Wealth and high station bring more *cares* than they shut out! The *tall peaks* are more conspicuous than the little hills—but they are swept by more storms. Contentment, with plainness and God's blessing, is the lesson. "If we have food and clothing, we will be content with these. But those who want to be rich fall into temptation, a trap, and many foolish and harmful desires, which plunge people into ruin and destruction!" 1 Timothy 6:8-9

One stormy night during the American civil war someone in conversation with Mr. Lincoln was pitying the soldiers in the field. The President replied, that there was not one of them with whom he would not gladly exchange places that night. Responsibility brings burdens.

August 10.

"Turn my eyes from looking at what is worthless." Psalm 119:37

We must be always *turning*—if we would keep our life true and according to God's commandments. There are some flowers which always turn toward the sun. There was a little potted rose-bush in a sick-room which I visited. It sat by the window. One day I noticed that the one rose on the bush was looking toward the light. I referred to it; and the sick woman said that her daughter had turned the rose around several times toward the darkness of the room—but that each time the little flower had twisted itself back, until again its face was toward the light. It would not look into the darkness.

The rose taught me a lesson—never to allow myself to look toward any evil—but instantly to turn from it. Not a moment should we permit our eyes to be inclined toward anything sinful. To yield to one moment's sinful act—is to defile the soul. One of the main messages of the Bible is, "Turn from the wrong, the base, the crude, the unworthy—to the right, the pure, the noble, the godlike." We should not allow even an unholy thought to stay a moment in our mind—but should turn from its very first suggestion, with face fully toward Christ, the Holy One.

"I will set before my eyes no vile thing!" Psalm 101:3

"Finally, brothers, whatever is true, whatever is noble, whatever is right, whatever is pure, whatever is lovely, whatever is admirable—if anything is excellent or praiseworthy—think about such things!" Philippians 4:8

But we should train ourselves to turn also from all discouragements. There is always a bright side, and we should find it. Discouragement is full of danger. It weakens and hurts the life.

August 11.

"Choose my instruction instead of silver, knowledge rather than choice gold; for wisdom is more precious than rubies, and nothing you desire can compare with her." Proverbs 8:10-11

It is hard to convince people in these days, that anything is or can be better than silver or gold or rubies. The best way, however, to look at this subject—is to think of some of the greater and deeper needs of life, and ask what these earthly gems can do to meet them.

One writer represents a party of emigrants wrecked on a desert island, far from the tracks of men. They have food to last for a time. The soil is rich and the climate fine. Soon, however, they find gold, and instantly they all begin to search for the precious metal. They gather much, and are rich; but they have not sown a grain of seed, and no harvest is coming, for the season for sowing was now past. Famine is upon them, and their gold will not feed their hunger.

This illustrates the value of godly wisdom. In the great needs of life, riches and jewels amount to nothing; only the grace of God will do then. In the time of great sorrow, no one turns to gold or diamonds for comfort. In the sore struggles of life, in its temptations, trials and perplexities, these symbols of earthly wealth will not meet the needs of the soul. When death comes, these things are utterly worthless, are indeed bitter mockeries! We need a help greater than earth's glittering baubles, in these solemn experiences!

"But if we have food and clothing, we will be content with that. People who want to get rich fall into temptation and a trap and into many foolish and harmful desires that plunge men into ruin and destruction. For the love of money is a root of all kinds of evil. Some people, eager for money, have wandered from the faith and pierced themselves with many griefs!" 1 Timothy 6:8-10

August 12.

"All your robes are fragrant with myrrh and aloes and cassia." Psalm 45:8

We cannot guard too carefully, the *influences* which we allow to play upon our life, for all of them leave their hue and impress upon us, either for beauty or for marring. A great artist refused to look upon the works of inferior artists, saying that they would affect his style. We should seek continual fellowship with the good, the pure, the holy; for in close, sympathetic mingling with them, we unconsciously receive into our own spirit something of their sweetness, their beauty, and the aroma of heavenliness that surrounds them. We absorb something of whatever we see or touch.

August 13.

"Teach me to do your will, for you are my God. May your gracious Spirit lead me forward on a firm footing." Psalm 143:10

There are so many possibilities in life, in attainment and achievement, and so many opportunities of doing good, that it is a glorious thing to live. Surely, then, we ought to make the most of our life, not failing to become what Christ would have us to be, or to do the sweet things he would have us do—as we pass along the way.

Yet life's lessons must always be learned slowly. Paul was well on in life when he said, "I have *learned*, in whatever state I am, therein to be content." The words suggest that the lesson was not easily learned; that it required time and struggle. It is only fair to infer that Paul could not have written thus in his earliest epistles. These is comfort in this for us common mortals, who in younger or middle life grow discouraged because we have not Paul's contentment. If only we are really *learning* the lesson, there is hope that some day we shall be able to say we *have*learned it.

August 14.

"Each one helps the other, and says to another, *Take courage!*". Isaiah 41:6

It was Charles Kingsley who said, "We become like God—only as we become of use." The saying is truer than at first we may think. Every glimpse we have of heaven's life—is a glimpse of usefulness, helpfulness. In olden days, angels sometimes came down to earth, and they always came on some *errand of service* to men. Then, we are told in our New Testament, that the mission of the angels to earth is "to minister to those who shall be the heirs of salvation." Thus these *pure creatures of heaven* live only to serve. God himself is revealed on every Scripture page, and always in the same character of helpfulness. Christ came as God incarnate; and his whole life is summed up in the words, "He went about doing good." Thus the divine life finds its expression in serving, doing good. "God is love;" and love cannot but minister and bless, even to the point of utter self-sacrifice.

August 15.

"I waited patiently for the LORD; he turned to me and heard my cry." Psalm 40:1

Has God taught you some great truth, or revealed to you, in deep personal experience, some new, sweet thought of his love? What is the next thing? Is it not that you shall whisper the blessed secret to some other soul? After Peter's strange vision, he sat pondering what it could mean; and while he thought on the vision, the Spirit said unto him, "Behold, three men seek you." The picture is very suggestive. When we have gotten anything from God—there is always someone waiting to get from us what God has just given to us. Heavenly visions are not shown to us, only to be absorbed in our own soul—but to be translated into some form that will bless the world. That is what the artist does with his visions. That is what we should do with ours.

August 16.

"We know that when He appears, we will be like Him, because we will see Him as He is!" 1 John 3:2

Thoburn tells a beautiful story about *a picture of his dead child*. It seemed a very imperfect photograph, so blurred that scarcely a trace of the beloved features could be seen in it. But one day he took the picture to a photographer, and asked him if he could do anything to improve it. In three weeks he returned; and as he saw the picture in its frame on the wall, he was startled. It seemed as if his child were living again before him. The image had been in the old picture—but was concealed beneath the blurs and mists that were there also. The photographer, however, had brought it out in strong, living beauty, until it was life-like in its tender charm.

In every true disciple of Christ, there is the image of the Master, It may be very dim. Its features are overlaid by blurs and blemishes, and are almost unrecognizable by human eyes. It is the work of Christ in our lives to bring out this likeness, more and more clearly, until at last it shines in undimmed beauty. This is what Christ is doing in many of his ways with us.

August 17.

"While he was in Bethany, reclining at the table in the home of a man known as Simon the Leper, a woman came with an alabaster jar of very expensive perfume, made of pure nard. She broke the jar and poured the perfume on his head. Some of those present were saying indignantly to one another, "Why this waste of perfume? It could have been sold for more than a year's wages and the money given to the poor." And they rebuked her harshly.

"Leave her alone," said Jesus. "Why are you bothering her? She has done a beautiful thing to Me!" Mark 14:3-6

Usefulness is not the only test. Acts may be beautiful in Christ's sight, even though they do not seem to be immediately helpful to others. Mary's deed fed no poor, relieved no sick, clothed no shivering child—and yet Jesus commended it. He is pleased when offerings are made from love to Him, even though the things offered may not be necessary to His work.

We may not measure all our services to Christ, by the standard of direct helpfulness to others. Mary's ointment, spilled over Christ's head and feet, was not a really useful ministry, and yet it was good and beautiful in Christ's sight. What shall we say of the loveliness which God lavishes everywhere in nature? Does the beauty of the flowers, of the skies—feed the hunger of the poor? Evidently it was Mary's love for Christ which pleased him, and made her deed beautiful. She had indeed wrought a good work on Him, one that blessed Him; for in the great sorrow of His heart as He drew near His cross, nothing could so strengthen Him, as love! It made Him stronger for the journey to His cross! Likewise, nothing else that we can give another, will be such a blessing, as love.

August 18.

"About that time the disciples came to Jesus and asked, 'Which of us is greatest in the Kingdom of Heaven?' Jesus called a small child over to Him and put the child among them." Matthew 18:1-2

When the disciples wanted to know who was greatest, Jesus called a little child, and took him on his knee. The disciples were clustered around him, and saw what he did. A little child in the midst, is used ofttimes to teach great lessons to older people. When a new baby comes into a home, God sets it in the midst of a family as a teacher. Parents suppose they are training their children—but the children are also teaching and training them.

I learned more of the meaning of the fatherhood of God, and pf the way he feels toward his children, in one week after the first baby came into my home, than I had learned from teachers and books, even from the Bible, in all the preceding years of my life. Every child's life is a *book*—a new page of which is turned over each day.

Children are not angels, and yet they bring from heaven to earth many fragments of loveliness. Their influence in a home is a blessing. They soften hearts; they change the whole thought of life in their parents. It is no more *SELF*; they begin to live for their children. The children open *love's chambers*. They train their parents in patience, gentleness, thoughtfulness. While a young child is in a home—a school of heaven is set up there. Sad is it for those within, if they miss the chance of learning such blessed lessons.

August 19.

"We also rejoice in our sufferings, because we know
that *suffering* produces *patience*." Romans 5:3

Patience is a great lesson to learn. Any school in which we can learn it, is a good school, and the lesson can scarcely be too costly. Few things mean more in life, than patience. Many people wreck the best hopes of their life, for lack of patience. To be impatient in certain conditions, is to lose all; and to be patient, to be able to keep quiet and still in the presence of things that try us, is to gain all. Thus patience becomes the very key to success in living. It is surely worth while to learn the lesson!

Patience is ofttimes learned in the *school of suffering*. We are there trained to *endure*; not to cry out in the hour of anguish—but to sing instead. Richter tells of the little bird that is shut away in the darkness, to learn new strains, which afterward it sings in the light. Many Christians are taken into the darkness, and kept there for a time, while they are taught the songs of patience. We look at patient people with admiration, not knowing what it has cost them to get this pearl of the graces.

August 20.

"The Lord gave—and the Lord has taken away; blessed be the name of the Lord."
Job 1:21

God's love is the same in the brightness—and when the brightness fades into gloom. It is the same in joy—and when the joy turns to grief. It is the same when blessings are given—and when the blessings are recalled.

It does not seem so to us; we easily believe that while God showers favors upon us—he loves us; but when he gives suffering and sorrow, we almost feel that he does not love us as before. Yet it may be, that there are even richer blessings in the things which make us grieve—than in those which give us gladness. We know at least that the same love sends both. That should be comfort for us. It is always love that comes from God—in whatever form or guise it comes. We need never doubt that this is true, "For the Lord disciplines the one He loves, and punishes every son whom He receives." Hebrews 12:6

August 21.

"The Word of the Lord came unto Jonah the *second time*." Jonah 3:1

Jonah had failed the first time—but God gave him a *second chance*. This shows the divine patience. Strict justice would have left Jonah at the bottom of the sea, or in the jaws of the great fish; but God was merciful to him. He had now gone through a discipline which left him ready to obey.

That is the way God often deals with people. When they rebel or disobey him—he does not cast them off—but puts them under some discipline, sometimes sore and painful, to teach them obedience, and then tries them again. Many of us have to be *whipped* to duty; but what a blessed thing it is that God is so patient with us! Most of us owe all we are, to God's disciplines. "For the Lord disciplines the one He loves, and punishes every son whom He receives." Hebrews 12:6. Thus even our *sins* may become *blessings* to us.

We should be very thankful to God for these *second chances* that God gives us, when we have failed to improve the first chance. Very few people make of their life, what God first wanted them to make. Then he sets them another lesson, that they may try again. Perhaps the second is not so beautiful nor so noble as the first; still it is good, and if they are faithful and diligent, they can make something worthy even yet of their life. Most of us have to be sent more than once, on our errands for God. Happy are we if we obey even at the second bidding, although it is far better that we go at first.

August 22.

"So Jonah got up and went to Nineveh, according to the Lord's command." Jonah 3:3

Jonah had learned his lesson well. We are not told where he was after his deliverance—but no doubt he had a quiet time for thought. He thought over the story of his wilfulness and disobedience, no doubt, and was ashamed of his conduct. Thus he learned humility, and was ready now to do as God might command him. Indeed, he became eager for another opportunity to do the work which at first he had refused to do.

There is a story of a regiment of soldiers which in some war had been dishonored on a certain battle-field. In the next war the same regiment was again in the service, and at the first opportunity they displayed most heroic courage, thus "burning out the shame" of the former field. So Jonah in his penitence, would long for another chance to go for God to Nineveh, that he might wipe out the dishonor of his former disobedience.

So we see prompt obedience this time, no quibbling, no running away. We ought to get the lesson. When we have failed in any task that God has set for us, or broken any command that he has given to us, not only should our repentance lead us to sorrow and confession—but we should eagerly prepare ourselves for burning out the shame of our past sin and dishonor—by a service and an obedience worthy of sincere love for Christ. Thus alone do we make our repentance worthy.

August 23.

"Now Elisha was suffering from the illness from which he died." 2 Kings 13:14

A death-bed is a good place from which to look at one's past life. In the strange, dim light that pours in from eternity, things do not appear as they did in the common sunlight. Many things that gave pleasure as life went on—now give pain and shame in the retrospect, and appear calamitous. This is true of all sins and follies, of all gains and pleasures that did not have God's blessing, of all things done for SELF and not for Christ, of all quarrels and strifes.

Many things also that seemed hard when they came, and that cost pain and self-denial, in the light of the death-chamber, now appear radiant and beautiful. Thus the dying hour—is the place to test life. If we would always ask, before doing any doubtful thing, "How will this look—when I am dying?" it would save us from many a mistake and sin!

"Now all has been heard; here is the conclusion of the matter: Fear God and keep his commandments, for this is the whole duty of man. For God will bring every deed into judgment, including every hidden thing, whether it is good or evil." Ecclesiastes 12:13-14

But the death-bed is also a good place for other people to study a man's life. When a man is engaged in the affairs of the world, he suffers more or less from the envy of others. The more active and influential he is, the more are men about him envious of him. But when a man lies dying, all this unjust feeling vanishes. All men feel kindly toward him. Whatever has been faulty in him is forgotten in the glow of tenderness that his dying enkindles; and whatever has been beautiful in him shines out in still fairer beauty.

August 24.

"Once while some Israelites were burying a man, suddenly they saw a band of raiders; so they threw the man's body into Elisha's tomb. *When the body touched Elisha's bones, the man came to life and stood up on his feet!*" 2 Kings 13:21

The bones of Elisha had no more power in themselves to give life—than any other dead man's bones. Yet we may get here the lesson of *posthumous influence*. No man ever wholly dies. We have nothing to do with superstitious nonsense about relics, saints' bones, and bits of holy men's clothing or of their coffins; but it is true that a really godly man has influence after he dies. He leaves behind him something which cannot die. His name has power. If he writes good books, these live after him, and give life to the souls that their words touch. We ought ever to seek to live—so as not only to be missed and mourned when we die—but to live on after death in our works, our name, our influence.

August 25.

"Mordecai gave **Hathach** a copy of the decree issued in Susa that called for the death of all Jews, and he asked Hathach to show it to Esther. He also asked Hathach to explain it to her and to urge her to go to the king to beg for mercy and plead for her people. So Hathach returned to Esther with Mordecai's message.

Then Esther told Hathach to go back and relay this message to Mordecai . . ." Esther 4:8-10

We are apt to overlook the minor actors in Scripture stories—in our absorbed interest in the prominent ones. Yet ofttimes these lesser people are just as important in their own place, and their service is just as essential to the final success of the whole—as the greater ones.

The little girl in the story of Naaman the leper, is scarcely seen in the splendors of the Syrian court; but without her part, we would never have had the story at all.

The young lad with the basket, is hardly thought of when we read the account of the miracle; but they were his loaves with which the Master fed all those hungry thousands that day on the green grass.

The smallest links in a chain—are ofttimes quite as important as the greatest links.

Hathach was one of these obscure characters. But his part was by no means unimportant. Without his being a trustworthy messenger, Mordecai's communication with Esther would have been impossible.

If we cannot do brave things like Esther, nor give wise counsels like Mordecai, we may at least be useful, as Hathach was, in faithful service. And perhaps our lowly part may some day prove to have been as essential—as the great deeds which all men praise. We may at least help some others in doing the great things that they are set to do in this world.

August 26.

"If you keep quiet at a time like this . . . you and your relatives will die. What's more, who can say but that you have been elevated to the palace for just such a time as this?" Esther 4:14

The only safe way in life's thronging field—is straight on in the path of duty. He who falters and hesitates even for one instant, is trodden down by the marching hosts behind him. No danger of the battle is so great—as that of *halting* and trying to turn backward.

The same is true in all the paths of life. No duty, however hard and perilous, should be feared one-half so much as *failure in the duty*. People sometimes shrink from responsibility, saying they dare not accept it because it is so great. But in shrinking from duty—they are really encountering a far more serious condition than that which they evade. It is a great deal easier to do that which God gives us to do, no matter how hard it is—than to face the responsibility of not doing it. We have abundant assurance that we shall receive all the *strength* we need to perform any duty God allots to us; but if we fall out of the line of obedience, and refuse to do anything which we ought to do, we find ourselves at once out of harmony with God's law and God's providence, and cannot escape the consequences of our failure.

So it is always in the end easier and infinitely safer to do our duty, whatever it may involve of cost or peril, than not to do it. To drop out of the ranks in life's crowded pathway—is to lose all. To neglect opportunities, is to throw away honors and crowns.

August 27.

"If you *keep quiet* at a time like this . . . you and your relatives will die! What's more, who can say but that you have been elevated to the palace for just such a time as this?" Esther 4:14

Often we sin by *speaking*, and do incalculable harm with our words. But there are times when it is a sin *not* to speak—when to be *silent* is to fail in duty. We are not to speak out the *wrong* thoughts that may be in our heart—but the *good* thoughts and feelings which burn within us it is usually our duty to utter. We should never hesitate to speak out boldly in confession of Christ, when his honor is assailed by his enemies. To walk with an impenitent friend day after day and year after year, in close association with him, and never to speak a word to him about his spiritual life—is to commit a grievous sin against him.

We have many cautions about watching our speech, and withholding words that are not good; but we need to beware also lest we fail to speak the *words we ought to speak*. Especially should we beware of silence about spiritual and eternal things.

God gives to each of us a message—a gospel message to others—and we dare not fail to deliver it. We scarcely ever lack words when the themes are trivial; but amid the trivial talk, let us not fail to speak some word which shall not be forgotten.

August 27.

"Perhaps you have come to royal position—for such a time as this!" Esther 4:14

One reason Esther was in the palace at this time as queen, was for this very mission—to save her people by interceding for them. She was not there by accident. We know the singular providences by which she came to her circumstances.

We live under the same providence, and nothing is 'accidental' in any of the circumstances of our lives. If we are true to God, doing His will day by day, we are always in the place where He wants us to be; and wherever we are—He has something for us to do there. Each day God sets our work for us. When we find ourselves in the presence of any human need or sorrow, we should say, "Perhaps God sent me here just now—to bring relief or to give help or comfort." Sometimes we wonder at the strange ways of God's providence, by which we are carried into this place or that circumstance; is there not a 'key' to this mystery?

It certainly was a strange providence that led Esther—the lowly, simple-hearted Jewish maiden, into the palace of the great Xerxes to be his queen; but there was a divine purpose in it. She was sent there—because she would be needed there by and by.

Likewise, when God, by some strange providence, brings us into peculiar circumstances or associations, it is because at some time there will be need for us there. We must be careful that we do always the thing, we find there to do.

August 29.

"When I heard these things, I sat down and wept. For some days I mourned and fasted and prayed before the God of heaven!" Nehemiah 1:4

Tears were not all. Nehemiah also carried the burden to God in prayer. He did this before he took any step himself for the relief of the suffering, and the advancement of his work. Compassion is Christlike; but tears alone are not enough. This is a lesson we should not forget in our compassion for others: God cares more for them than we do, and his compassion is deeper than ours; we may, therefore, be sure of interest upon His part—when we speak the names of our friends in His ear. Besides, He knows best how to help. We should take the burden to Him first—and then be ready to do whatever He may tell us to do.

The best way for us to help others—usually is to PRAY for them. Of course praying is not all we should do; Nehemiah did not stop with tears and prayers. He gave himself to the work in behalf of his people. He left his luxurious palace, and journeyed away to Jerusalem, and took earnest hold with both hands, giving all his energy and influence to the cause.

Likewise, more than tears and prayers are needed; there is something for us to DO. Many people can weep over distress, and then pray fervently for the relief that is needed—but never DO anything themselves! Nehemiah's way is better: sympathy, prayer, work. This makes a threefold cord which cannot be broken!

August 30.

"But we prayed to our God—and posted a guard day and night to meet this threat!" Nehemiah 4:9

We are in danger of making prayer a substitute for duty; or of trying to roll over on God, the burden of caring for us and doing things for us—while we sit still and do nothing! When we pray to be delivered from temptation—we must keep out of the way of temptation, unless duty clearly calls us there. We must also guard against temptation, resist the Devil, and stand firm in obedience and faith. When we ask God for our daily bread, pleading the promise that we shall not lack—we must also labor to earn God's bread, and thus make it ours honestly.

A lazy man came once and asked for money, saying that he could not find bread for his family. "Neither can I!" replied the industrious mechanic to whom he had applied. "I am obliged to work for it!"

While we pray for health—we must use the means to obtain it.

While we ask for wisdom—we must use our brains and think, searching for wisdom as for hidden treasure.

While we ask God to help us break off a bad habit—we must also strive to overcome the habit.

Prayer is not merely a device for saving people from toil, struggle and responsibility. When there is no human power adequate to the need—we may ask God to work without us, and in some way He will help us. But ordinarily WE must do our part, asking God to work in and through us, and to bless us through faithful obedience.

"I labor, struggling with all His energy, which so powerfully works in me!" Colossians 1:29

August 31.

"Meanwhile, the people in Judah said, "The strength of the laborers is giving out, and there is so much rubble that we cannot rebuild the wall!" Nehemiah 4:10

There are always croakers and discouragers! They find fault with their part of the work, and object to the methods of those in charge.

We remember how it was with the spies sent to look over the promised land. It was a good country, they said, rich and fertile—but, oh, the giants that were there! So these ten frightened men discouraged a whole nation!

People are forever making it harder for others to live righteously—by going about with their murmurings and groanings!

These people of Judah in Nehemiah's time, seem to have been only half-hearted. They were not willing to make sacrifices to get the city rebuilt.

Nothing good is ever accomplished without cost! Gold is not picked up in the streets! Half-heartedness is not merely weakness; it is sin! All through the ages, men who have been blessings to the world, have been willing to bear burdens that were too heavy for them. Easy living never accomplished much for God or the world!

SEPTEMBER

September 1.

"I stood up and said to the nobles, the officials and the rest of the people, "Do not be afraid of them. Remember the Lord, who is great and awesome, and fight for your brothers, your sons and your daughters, your wives and your homes!" Nehemiah 4:14

Everyone with a spark of manhood in him—will fight to the death, for his family. We are all so tied up together, that this motive is really present in all our defending of 'justice'. We must seek the safety of the town in which we live because our family is in it, and peril to the town—is peril to us. We must seek wholesome water supply, good drainage, and clean streets for the town, because our children and friends live there.

Likewise with the *moral* and *religious* influences of the community; the welfare of our sons and daughters, our brothers and sisters, is involved. A man may have no interest in the fight against the saloon; but if the evil is let alone—by and by his own boys may be destroyed by it!

A distinguished man was speaking at the opening of a reformatory for boys, and remarked that if only one boy were saved from ruin—it would pay for all the cost. After the exercises were over, a gentleman asked him if he had not put it too strongly when he said that all the cost of founding such an institution would be repaid—if only one boy should be saved. "If it were MY boy!" was the answer. It is only when we learn to look at all such movements as if we were working for our own—that we do bur best work.

September 2.

"The laborers who carried the loads worked with one hand—and held a weapon with the other hand. Each of the builders had his sword strapped around his waist—while he was working!" Nehemiah 4:17-18

We should all work on the wall of God's temple, everyone building near his own door. We should never slacken in our diligence; there is some duty for each moment. But we work amid enemies! On every side are those who oppose us, and are ready to assault us and to stop us in our service. The Christian young man in the store or shop, in the school or college, is constantly exposed to temptation. His companions are not all godly. Some of them will seek to draw him away from Christ. In his own heart, too, there are enemies which resist the good that is striving within him—and seek his destruction! So while he works—he must also be ready any instant to fight.

Every Christian should have his sword girded continually by his side. The Christian's sword is "the Word of God." The best preparation, therefore, for meeting the world's enmity—is to become filled with the Holy Scriptures. There come many occasions through life when a verse quoted will be a sword drawn to smite an enemy. Thus it was that Jesus vanquished the tempter, at each temptation drawing out a Word of God, and with it smiting the adversary!

So we all may learn to fight, building ever on the wall of character, and ever thrusting back the enemy that assails us!

September 3.

"And Nehemiah continued, "Go and celebrate with a feast of choice foods and sweet drinks, and share gifts of food with people who have nothing prepared. This is a sacred day before our Lord. Do not be dejected and sad, for the joy of the Lord is your strength!" Nehemiah 8:10

God loves to have us enjoy ourselves. He does not want us to be long-faced!

JOY is the ideal Christian life!

Of course we are to be sorry when we sin; but when we have confessed the sin, truly repented of it, and found mercy—we are to dry our tears—and rejoice! Why should we not be happy when God has forgiven us, made us His children, and assured us of everlasting glory?

But our joy must not be selfish. When we are prosperous—we should not forget those who are poor. When we are happy in our homes of love, with unbroken circles—we should not forget the families that are in sorrow. The good things God gives us—are not meant for ourselves alone. They are given us to be passed on. "It is more blessed to give—than to receive."

People who keep all to themselves, and consume the choice foods and sweet drinks in their own houses, at their own well-covered tables, never thinking of the hungry ones outside—are not the kind of children God wants them to be.

The very essence of Christian life—is unselfishness!

September 4.

"Do not be dejected and sad—for the joy of the Lord is your strength!" Nehemiah 8:10

If we would be strong for service, and would do our best always—we must cultivate a joyful spirit. No duty is urged in the Bible more earnestly, than the duty of Christian joy. Of course we must make sure that it is the 'joy of the Lord' which we have. We must draw the water of our gladness—out of the wells of salvation, and not out of the muddy pools of earth! The 'joy of the Lord' comes from the heart of Christ. When we have this joy—we are strong; for joy inspires us, fills us with hope and courage. When we can sing at our toil, or in our sorrow—we have the Lord's strength—and are in no danger of being overcome.

September 5.

"This is what Cyrus king of Persia says: The Lord, the God of heaven, has given me all the kingdoms of the earth—and He has appointed me to build a temple for Him at Jerusalem!" Ezra 1:2

It comforts us to know that nothing is going wrong in this world, though at times, all seems to be in confusion. It ought to comfort us to know that there is One, greater than men, who rules over all things!

A little boy sat in front of his father in a carriage, and held the reins. But his father held them too, although the boy did not know it. Presently the boy felt one of the reins drawn through his little hands. He understood it then, and said, "Father, I thought I was driving; but I am not, am I?"

Just so, we think that WE are doing great things—but there is One behind us, whose hand really holds *the reins!*

"In him we were also chosen, having been predestined according to the plan of him who works out everything in conformity with the purpose of his will." Ephesians 1:11

"The lot is cast into the lap, but its every decision is from the Lord." Proverbs 16:33

"A king's heart is a water channel in the Lord's hand: He directs it wherever He chooses." Proverbs 21:1

September 6.

"Whoever is among His people, may his God be with him, and may he go to Jerusalem in Judah and build the house of the Lord, the God of Israel, the God who is in Jerusalem." Ezra 1:3

There is another temple to build for the Lord, and builders are needed. The proclamation comes now, not from a heathen king—but from Christ himself. Everyone is invited to take part in this great work. The temple at Jerusalem, on which these builders wrought, has long since perished, and every trace of their work has been destroyed. But the temple for which Christ seeks builders, shall stand forever, and everything anyone may do on it shall be eternal.

How can we build on the heavenly temple? By doing all we can in this world for Christ. *Our own lives are parts of the temple.* We may seek to have our *characters* made beautiful and holy. Then we can strive to bring others to Christ, to make other lives better, to help build up in them a likeness to the Lord Jesus. The smallest things we can do for Christ, will be like the stones laid on the walls of God's great house, which is rising within the veil; or like ornaments, little touches of beauty, on some part of the glorious building. We cannot see now that our work is of any value—but some day we shall see that nothing which we have done with pure motive for our Lord, has been done in vain! No touch laid on another life in love, shall ever fade out!

September 7.

"Then the Israelites, including the priests, the Levites, and the rest of the exiles, celebrated the dedication of this house of God with joy!" Ezra 6:16

It was a glad occasion when that building stood there completed on the sacred mount. It had risen out of ruins. It had cost great sacrifice and toil. It had been built up amid many discouragements and hindrances. Tears had fallen on many a stone, as it was lifted to its place.

Things we do through cost, self-denial, hardship, and hindrance are far dearer to us, and more sacred—than things we do with ease, without feeling the burden or the cost. Churches built by poor, struggling congregations, whose people have to sacrifice and deny themselves to gather the money, yield far more joy to their builders when finished—than beautiful and costly churches reared by the rich. They are built out of people's hearts, and shine in heaven's sight—in love's splendor.

Our joy in doing God's work, and in making gifts to God, is measured by the real cost of the things we do and give. The more heart's blood there is in them—the more precious will they be to us and also to God. The richest treasures of our lives—are those which have cost us the most.

September 8.

"On the twenty-first day of the seventh month, the Word of the Lord came through Haggai the prophet" Haggai 2:1

The Lord always seeks to be an *encourager*. These returned captives were very much discouraged. They had begun with great enthusiasm to build the temple—but difficulties had risen. Then the Lord sent his servant to hearten the governor and the people, to cheer them, that they might go on through all the obstacles which faced them. That is the way the Lord is always doing with his children. He does not want us ever to yield to discouragement. Of course, life is hard at many a point. There are ofttimes difficult tasks to perform, and sore struggles to endure. Things often seem to fail in our hands. Our *plans* miscarry, our *hopes* disappoint us. We meet opposition and enmity, and it seems to us we can never get through with the things we are set to do!

But when we open the Bible, we find encouragement on every page. We are there taught never to yield to despair. There can be no failure in duty—if only we are faithful. We never can be defeated in temptation, if only we stand true to Christ. We never can sink under our burden, if only we cast it upon Christ. The things that seem to be failures, become successes, when God's hand is in them. So God ever comes to encourage us in our difficulties. "Fear not; I am with you!" is the *formula of divine cheer* in every hour of trial. Therefore we should never lose heart.

September 9.

*"I waited patiently for the Lord—*and He turned to me and heard my cry for help." Psalm 40:1

There come times in everyone's life, when no exertion of his own can do anything, and when no human power can help. Then he should commit all to God, and wait for him. And it is no *ignorant confidence* that we may have at such times; for our Father rules this world, and has a plan for each life. We can safely trust him to bring aid, deliverance, or light at the right time.

There are occasions when a *patient waiting* is our highest duty. When we are working for souls—we must present the truth, and then commit the result to God. Time is necessary for some spiritual processes, and the result cannot come immediately. In prayer we sometimes have to wait for the answer, even to wait long—but we should never be impatient.

September 10.

"What do you see now?" he asked. I answered, "I see a solid gold lampstand with a bowl of oil on top of it. Around the bowl are seven lamps, each one having seven spouts with wicks." Zechariah 4:2

A *lampstand* suggests light. Every Christian should be a light-bearer. God wants us to shine. The world is dark, and we are to pour light into its darkness. Our character must shine. That means, to put it very simply, that we must be holy.

To be holy, is to be first pure in heart. A little child said she liked best of all the beatitudes, the one about a pure heart, because if she had that blessing she would have all the others too. A pure, holy, loving heart—will make a life shine. "God is love," and we are like God just so far as we are loving. That means love to God first, and then love to all men. We are therefore to be obedient, trustful, and reverent toward God—and gentle, unselfish, patient, thoughtful, kindly and helpful toward men.

We will find that it is not always easy, to shine with love's light. The *candle* wastes, burns itself up, in shining. So does life. It *costs* to be unselfish, patient, thoughtful, and useful. We have to be forgiving, to bear injuries sweetly, to deny ourselves and make personal sacrifices, continually, in order to be gentle, patient, and kind when others are crude to us. It *costs* to shine; nevertheless we are to shine. Christ gave his blessed life—to be consumed on the candlestick of divine love, to light the world.

September 11.

"Be strong, all you people of the land, and work; for I am with you,' declares the Lord Almighty." Haggai 2:4

There are many times in most people's lives, when this fragment of a lesson ought to be inspiring and helpful. Men are called to do some *work* for God, and their resources of strength appear to be altogether inadequate. They look at the small beginning or the unpromising condition, and say they never can do the work, nor achieve the result expected. Nearly all beginnings of good things, are small. The Christian church began with two followers. Missionary efforts have all had a most unpromising start.

In our individual lives the same thing is true. It does not seem to us that we can ever accomplish anything worthy, with our feeble strength. But the Word of God rings out: "Be strong, and work; for I am with you." God never gives us a duty, but that he means to help us with his *presence* and *strength,* so that we need not fail in it. If we lose heart, and, let our hands hang down in idleness, nothing will come of the little beginning, and God's purpose will fail in our hands through our own lack of earnestness. But if we do our whole duty, the end will be blessing and success.

September 12.

"The LORD said to Satan, "The LORD rebuke you, Satan! The LORD, who has chosen Jerusalem, rebuke you!" Zechariah 3:2

The Lord is the friend of his people, and will not stand by inactive when Satan is plotting against any of them. He is the defender, especially of the defenseless. This characteristic of the divine love, is revealed in all parts of the Scriptures. God is the God of the weak. In the Mosaic laws, definite provision was made for the *widow* and the *orphan*. Something was to be left for them when the harvests were gathered. The poor were put under special protection, to shield them from the oppression of the rich and the strong. God's thought for the poor appeared amid even the detailed laws given for common life.

Every child of God is an object of peculiar divine care. The weakest of his children is safe in his keeping, even amid the greatest dangers. No harm can come to any of them, while nestling in his bosom. We may safely leave our defending in the Lord's hands, when Satan assails us, and when anyone would do us harm.

"For I am persuaded, that neither death, nor life, nor angels, nor principalities, nor powers, nor things present, nor things to come, Nor height, nor depth, nor any other creature, shall be able to separate us from the love of God, which is in Christ Jesus our Lord!" Romans 8:38-39

"I give them eternal life, and they will never perish—ever! No one will snatch them out of My hand!" John 10:28

September 13.

"The child sat on her lap until noon and then died."
"Did I ask you for a son, my lord?" she said.
  2 Kings 4:20, 28

The woman's thought seems to have been, "It would have been better had I remained as I was, with no voice of love in my home, my heart unfilled with affection, than that I should know and experience the gladness of motherhood for this brief time, and then be robbed of the joy." No doubt similar thoughts ofttimes come to those who are bereft of friends. In their deep grief, it seems to them that it would have been better if they had never had their friends at all—than to have had them a little while, to have learned to love them so, and to find such blessing in them—and then to lose them!

But Tennyson's word is far more true:
'Tis better to have loved and lost,
Than never to have loved at all.

Loving itself blesses us. It opens our heart and enriches our life. It teaches us the true meaning of life; for to live truly—is to love.

The taking away of our dear one—does not rob us of the blessings which loving has wrought in us. These we keep forever, though the friend is with us no more. Even if this child had not been restored to the mother in this world, she would still have kept forever the impressions and the influences which the child in its brief, beautiful years had left upon her life.

September 14.

"That they may be ever seeing—but never perceiving,
and ever hearing—but never understanding" Mark 4:12

It is a mistake not to use one's eyes to see things that are to be seen. The result is that in the end—one has *no eyes* with which to see. Refusing to listen to the words of God that are spoken in gentleness and love, results in the loss of the power to hear, so that in all God's universe of love, one shall hear no sweet sound; so that the very *voices of tender mercy* shall become*screams of terror*. Refusing to understand the things of God—leads to the dulling and deadening of the soul, so that at last one cannot understand—even if he would.

We should learn to keep all the gates of our soul open toward heaven. We should train ourselves to see whatever God would show us. Thus shall our eyes become able to see more and more beauty in God and in all his works. We should keep our ears intent to hear every Word that God speaks to us. We should strive to understand what God teaches us; for to those who seek, all hidden mysteries at length become clear.

September 15.

"Who touched Me? Jesus asked." Luke 8:45

The people were crowding against Jesus, and many people touched him; but there was *one touch* different from the others. There was a heart's cry in it, a pleading, a piteous supplication. It was a touch of faith, inspired by a deep sense of need. It was not an accidental touch, a mere touch of nearness; it was intentional.

This incident illustrates what is going on all the while, about Christ. We cannot move without pressing up against him. Sometimes in our heedlessness we jostle him rudely. But when among all earth's millions, one person intentionally reaches out a hand to feel after Christ, to touch him with a purpose, to seek for some blessing, to crave some help—Jesus instantly knows the pressure of that touch, and turns to answer it. He knows when any heart wants him, no matter how obscure the person, how poor, how hidden away in the crowd. Blessing came that day to none in that crowd, so far as we know—except to this poor, sick woman, who touched Christ's clothes. It came to her, because she had a burden on her heart—and sought Christ's help.

So in every company, there are some who are close, and yet receive no blessing, because there is no faith in their touching. Then there are those who are no nearer— but who reach out their hands in faith, and touch Christ's clothes, and go away helped, comforted.

September 16.

"Blessed are you who are poor, because the kingdom of God is yours!" Luke 6:20

The *blessed* ones of the Bible, are not those whom this world considers *happy*. Indeed, in the opinion of worldlings, those whom Christ calls blessed, have a dreary life. He says the meek are blessed, the poor in spirit, the pure in heart, the peacemakers, those who mourn, and those who are persecuted for righteousness' sake. It would be hard to convince the man of this world—that these are the really *blessed* ones. But that is the way it appears to the eyes that look down from heaven—and that is the standard of life by which we must be measured in the divine judgment.

It is assuring to hear Jesus himself speak beatitudes for men. He knew who really are *the blessed*. He knew the difference between the earthly ideals of happiness, and the heavenly ideals. We may safely trust his estimates, and know that they are right. We know, too, that he came into this world to make blessedness possible for men who were lost in sin. On the cross he died to make men happy. It is pleasant to remember, too, that the last glimpse this world had of Jesus—he was in the attitude of blessing men. He had his hands stretched out over his disciples when he began to ascend. Ever since that moment, blessings have been raining down from those pierced hands upon a sorrowing earth. Those who do not receive blessings shut their hearts against them.

September 17.

"When the Lord saw her, His heart went out to her and He said, *Don't cry!*" Luke 7:13

A *sorrow* in a home sends out a wave of tender feeling which impresses a wide community. While the death-crape hangs on a door, almost everyone of the great throng of passers-by is made at least for the moment, a little more thoughtful. Even strangers going by feel the influence, and their hearts are warmed by it. Whatever thus touches men with a gentler mood, though but transiently, becomes a blessing in the world. There is a humanizing influence in *sympathy*. It makes men more tolerant of each other, more patient with each other's faults, more loving and thoughtful. That which is changing the world these days from cruelty and savageness, into lovingness and brotherliness, is a sorrow—the sorrow of Calvary.

September 18.

"Then a voice from the *cloud* said, "This is my Son, my Chosen One. Listen to him." Luke 9:35

Many of the sweetest revealings of comfort, are spoken to God's children out of the *clouds of sorrow*. Many a Christian learns more about God in a brief season of trouble, than he has learned before in years of earthly prosperity. We would never see the *stars*—if the *sun* did not go down. We would never see the promises that gem the Bible pages, like stars in the sky—were there no darkening of the sky of human prosperity and joy. Out of our clouds, too, comes the Father's voice, saying, "This is my Son." It is Christ who comes even in the *shadow*, who for a time hides and darkens his face. HE is in the center of every cloud.

There is significance also, in the message from the cloud, "Listen to him!" We must learn to listen to Christ—and to him only. There are mysteries about Christianity, things hard to be understood—but we may safely wait for the solution of these, meanwhile doing sweetly and quietly the things that Christ bids us do. *Hereafter,* we shall know.

Rain comes out of clouds, and if there is no rain—all nature suffers. So out of sorrow's clouds—the rain falls, and our lives are enriched thereby.

September 19.

"Then He said to them all, *If anyone wants to come with Me, he must deny himself, take up his cross daily, and follow Me.*" Luke 9:23

The more important the *position* we occupy is, and the *greater* its responsibilities are—the more *cares* will it bring. The quiet calm is found in the low valley, not on the mountain-top. As we rise in life—our burdens increase. We need to learn how to carry our load cheerfully when it gets heavy. We cannot reach the higher places, and miss the *steep climbing* that leads to them. If we would gain the heights—we must consent to climb up the steep and rugged mountain. It was not a mere dream, which envisioned life to the patriarch as a *ladder*.

September 20.

"If you love Me—you will keep My commandments." John 14:15

Love is more than a mere sentiment; it is also a life. The proof of it must be in acts. Thus in one of his epistles this *disciple of love* writes: "This is how we know what love is: Jesus Christ laid down his life for us. And we ought to lay down our lives for our brothers. If anyone has material possessions and sees his brother in need but has no pity on him—how can the love of God be in him? Dear children, let us not love with words or tongue but with actions and in truth." 1 John 3:16-18

This same principle applies to our profession of love for Christ. It is not enough that we sing it in our *hymns*, say it in our *prayers*, or utter it in our *creed*; we must *show* it in our life! A fruit-tree proves its usefulness by bearing fruit in the season. The rose-bush puts forth beautiful roses. And when we claim to be Christ's friends—we must show it by doing what he bids us to do.

September 21.

"Yes, Lord—but even the dogs eat the crumbs that fall from their masters' table!" Matthew 15:27

When Jesus spoke to the poor Gentile woman in the language of the time, as if she were but a 'dog'—she was not offended. She was willing to be as *a dog under the Master's table*. She was ready to grant to the *Jews*—the *children's* place. The position Jesus had assigned to her satisfied her. For the dogs under the table did not starve. The children were first served, and then the pieces of food which they let fall, belonged to the dogs. Even the crumbs from that table were enough for her. Thus her *humility* and also her *faith* were shown.

We should come to Christ with a deep sense of our unworthiness, ready to take the lowest place; and we should realize that even the *crumbs of his grace and love* are better than all the feasts of this world.

September 22.

"Follow my example—as I follow the example of Christ." 1 Corinthians 11:1

"Be imitators of me—as I also am of Christ." 1 Corinthians 11:1

One way in which God reveals himself to us, is through the lives of the godly and the saintly. Next to living in direct communion with him—is living with others who thus live with him. Converse with those who lie in Christ's bosom and who know the secret of the Lord, cannot but greatly enrich our own knowledge of divine things. Yet in these busy days we are quite in danger of losing almost altogether out of our lives, this rich means of grace. One has said: "Do not think it wasted time—to submit yourself to any influence which may bring upon you any noble feeling."

September 23.

"Do not be deceived: God is not mocked. For whatever a man sows—he will also reap" Galatians 6:7

People have loose notions about sin. They think they can go on through life in disobedience of God's commands, and defiance of all moral laws—and then, by a single act of penitence, in a moment, have all the *consequences* of their sinning wiped out, all the effects in their own nature of lifelong evil habits reversed, and their character changed into saintly beauty and fitness for the kingdom of heaven.

But the Bible does not teach this. Those who choose sin for their way in life—must eat sin's fruit. The fruit of trees drops off—but *sin's fruits* stay in the life and become part of it. One may sow common seeds, and *others* gather and eat the harvest; but the *sinner* must gather and eat the fruit of his *own* sowing.

We are not through with our life—as we live it. Every act, every word, every thought, every choice, is a *seed* which we drop. We go on carelessly, never dreaming that we shall ever again see our deeds. Then some day, we come upon an ugly plant growing somewhere, and we ask, "What is this?" Comes the answer, "I am one of your plants. You dropped the seed which grew into me." Our lives are the little garden plots, in which it is our privilege to drop seeds. We shall have to eat the fruits of the seeds of which we are planting these days.

September 24.

"Every good and perfect gift is from above, coming down from the Father of the heavenly lights." James 1:17

There are many good things that come to us through our friends. The father toils and saves, and leaves an inheritance for his children. Many rich blessings come to us through human affections. Hands are ever being reached out to us, hands of love and kindliness, offering us good things. We owe far more than we ever can estimate, to those who love us. The *kindly ministry of friends*, brings countless benefits to our lives.

But everyone of these is a blessing sent to us from God. The *human* hands which bring them—are but the hands of messengers. This is only one of God's ways of sending his good things to us.

James tells us also, that *all* that God gives us is good, and that every blessing of his is perfect. Sometimes we think that what we receive from God, cannot be good. We think he must have changed toward us. It is a loss or a disappointment, and it seems unkind. But in whatever form it comes, there is a blessing—some good is wrapped up in everything God sends to any of his children.

September 25.

"But you have now rejected your God, who saves you out of all your calamities and distresses." 1 Samuel 10:19

We are very quick to see ingratitude in those whom we have befriended, who forget our kindness and treat us unkindly. We like to quote in such connection, the fable of the serpent, frozen by the wayside, which the benevolent passer-by took up and put in his bosom to warm—but which returned his kindness, by striking its deadly fangs into his flesh!

Let us be honest toward God. Let us judge ourselves in relation to his mercies and favors to us, by the same rule which we so inexorably apply to our fellow-men. What has God done for *us?* What mercies and favors have we received from him? From what adversities and tribulations has he delivered us? Are we saved? Are we on the way now to heaven and glory? Who forgave us our sins? Who rescued us out of the hands of Satan? Who keeps us day by day?

There is only one answer. How, then, are we treating this Deliverer, Savior, and Friend? Do we recognize him as our King and Lord? Or are we rejecting him and demanding another? It is well that we sit down quietly, while this matter is before us, and see whether we are free from the sharp blame which the prophet here lays upon these ancient people. May it not be that we, too, are neglecting the God who has saved us?

September 26.

"The LORD is the stronghold of my life—of whom shall I be afraid?" Psalm 27:1

The thought is, that God is a fortress like stone walls around His people. The same thought is found elsewhere. "The eternal God is your refuge." "God is our refuge." "Just as the mountains surround and protect Jerusalem, so the Lord surrounds and protects His people, both now and forever." It is not said that the Lord builds a refuge around His people—but that He Himself is the refuge! He puts Himself between them and peril.

The stork and other birds, when there is danger, cover their young with their own bodies, receiving the assault themselves and shielding their brood. So Christ said that He would gather His people as a hen gathers her chickens under her wings. Thus on Calvary, He received on Himself the terrible storm of wrath—that His people, coming under the shadow of His cross, might be sheltered.

So around every individual believer's life—God is a fortress, in which, in every danger, he may hide and be safe. If this is true, of whom indeed shall we be afraid? The only thing is, to make sure that we can say for ourselves the words, "The LORD is the stronghold of my life." It makes a very great difference on which side of a fortress one is on—when the battle is raging. Outside its strong walls one finds no protection, while its missiles fall everywhere, dealing death. It is only inside— that its shelter is enjoyed. Thus, we must be in Christ by a simple faith.

"The LORD is my rock, my fortress, and my savior; my God is my rock, in whom I find protection. He is my shield, the strength of my salvation, and my stronghold!" Psalm 18:2

"He is my loving God and my fortress, my tower of safety, my deliverer. He stands before me as a shield, and I take refuge in Him!" Psalm 144:2

September 27.

"So all the elders of Israel gathered together and came to Samuel at Ramah. They said to him, "You are old . . ." 1 Samuel 8:4-5

They meant that his *old age* made him inefficient as a ruler. It was a suggestion to him that he would better resign and let them choose some other ruler. They seem to have forgotten that *he had grown old in their service*; that they owed to him whatever of grandeur or real glory there was in their land. They forgot, also, that his years had brought him more wisdom, and had fitted him all the better to rule them, and that he could do more for them now—than ever he had done. Their conduct toward him was most ungrateful.

This fault is too common in our own days. *We are lacking in reverence for the aged.* We are too ready to ask them to step aside when they have grown gray in serving us, to make room for younger people to take up the work they have been doing so long and so faithfully.

We ought to venerate old age, especially when it has ripened in ways of righteousness and in service of self-denial for the good of others. Those who have given all their life to God's service, ought to receive honor and affection from younger Christians. Often they are lonely; we know not what sorrows they have endured, what sad memories fill their hearts, how they crave sympathy and love. No sight is more beautiful, than that of a young person showing respect and homage to one who is old.

September 28.

"I stand here, an old, gray-haired man. I have served as your leader since I was a boy." 1 Samuel 12:2

Old age is the test of life. It is the harvest of all the life's sowing. In its evening shadows, the deeds of all the past years appear at their real value. All life's memories gather about the old man's last days, and make either sweetness or bitterness for him. It is a great thing to be able to stand up in old age, and face all one's past without a blush, and challenge everyone to witness if anything wrong is known.

Nothing but well-lived years all along life's way, can yield such a happy consciousness in old age. We must begin in early youth—to grow old; that is, to grow into the beauty and sweetness which we all want to have in our character, when we become old. If we would be able to face our own past without blushing, when we reach seventy years—we must not do anything during the seventy years that we shall be ashamed to face. If we would be able to challenge the scrutiny of the world, turning the light on every chapter of our life, every page and line—we must be careful that we leave nothing behind us as we go on, which anyone can bring up against us. It was because that from a child, Samuel had served God, and had been exemplary in his conduct—honest, faithful, and upright in all his dealings—that he could now so confidently appeal to his record.

September 29.

"Now tell me as I stand before the Lord and before his anointed one—whose ox or donkey have I stolen? Have I ever cheated any of you? Have I ever oppressed you? Have I ever taken a bribe? Tell me and I will make right whatever I have done wrong." "No," they replied, "you have never cheated or oppressed us in any way, and you have never taken even a single bribe." 1 Samuel 12:3-4

It is a noble testimony to the purity and nobleness of a man's life, that in his old age, not a voice can utter a word of complaint against him. Especially is it so, when a man has lived all his days in public, in the eyes of his neighbors, charged with sacred trusts. The life of Jesus was thus unblamable. Even his enemies, searching with all the keenness of their wicked malice, could find not the slightest thing with which to accuse him.

The aim of everyone of us, should be to so live, that when we come to the close of our days—no one can lay any wrong or injury to our charge. It is a sweet joy in our last hours to have others say to us with unanimous voice, "You have never done anything to harm us. You have never treated us unkindly. You never robbed us of anything. You have been only and always kind to us. You have comforted our sorrows. You have encouraged us in our toils, tasks, and trials. You have helped us in all ways, generously, unselfishly, thoughtfully. You have done us nothing but good." To have such a testimony at the last, one must begin early to live an upright, helpful life, and must never allow his hand to slacken until it is folded on his bosom in its final rest.

September 30.

"As for me, far be it from me that I should sin against the LORD—by failing to pray for you. And I will teach you the way that is good and right." 1 Samuel 12:23

We sin against our friend—when we do not pray for him. Of all the ways of doing good and showing kindness to others—prayer is the best. Sometimes we catch ourselves saying to one who is in sore trouble: "I am sorry I cannot do anything to help you; I can only pray for you." But if we really pray for him, we do the very best that we could possibly do! God knows better how to help him, than we do. Ofttimes the help we would give would only harm him. We would lift away burdens, which it would be best if he would carry longer. We would make easy the path, which would better be left rough. We are always in danger of hindering God's work in a man's life—when we come in with our help. The best we can do—is to pray for him.

OCTOBER

October 1.

"My soul thirsts for God, the living God. When can I come and appear before God?" Psalm 42:2

One may have everything else—riches, honor, human friends, social rank, health, home joys—but if he has not God, all these things fail to make him truly and deeply happy. On the other hand, if we have God we are blessed, though we have nothing else.

A gentleman came home from business heavyhearted. Disaster had overtaken him. Throwing himself into a chair, he said, "Everything is gone. We are beggared. There is nothing left." His little child, seeing his distress and hearing his words, climbed up on his knee, and said, "Why, papa, you have mamma and me left." Yes; while such human love remained, was he not still rich? Still more, if everything else is taken, and God and his love remain, are we not rich?

October 2.

"Unless a grain of wheat falls into the ground and dies, it remains by itself. But if it dies, it produces a large crop." John 12:24

Jesus was a very wise teacher. He did not use fine illustrations which the common people would not understand—but took those whose meaning would be plain to them. He pointed to the lilies, to the birds, to leaves, to vines, to the hen and her chicks, and other familiar things.

The illustration here from nature is very simple. The farmer who would keep his wheat in the dry, safe granary, because if it were sown in the field—it would rot and die, would make a very foolish mistake. The only proper thing to do with the grain which the farmer wishes to preserve and take care of in the best way, is to sow it in the ground. True, that seems to be wasting it, losing it, throwing it away. But it is thus it is made to increase. It has to die—to live. This is the law of life.

Our Lord meant here that the only way for him to be glorified—was by giving his life. He could have saved himself from his cross; his sacrifice was voluntary. But suppose he had saved himself—what would have been the result? He would have missed the suffering; but souls would not have been saved, no church would now be praising his name. But in dying, he made blessing for the world. From the one precious seed let fall into the ground on Calvary, has sprung a glorious harvest, whose full fruitage will not be known until all the redeemed are gathered home!

October 3.

"The words I have spoken to you are spirit and they are life." John 6:63

God's own life is in the words of Scripture. Put a handful of flower-seeds in your window-box, under the sunshine, and they will soon become lovely flowers. Put the truths of the gospel into a human heart, and soon the life will begin to grow into the beauty of Christ. Its effects will be seen in the disposition, in the character, in the conduct, in all the daily acts.

At an auction, a crude jar of common earthenware was bought by a seller of perfumes for a penny. But he filled it with *attar of roses*, and soon every particle of the substance of the jar had partaken of the sweetness. The fragrance within it had permeated it. Long, long afterward, when emptied and broken, every smallest fragment was still sweet with the precious perfume.

So it is, when even the most common life is filled with the Word of Christ. It flows out, as it were, in the character, in the feelings and affections, in the thoughts and desires, in the tempers and dispositions, until the whole being is permeated, filled with the spirit of Christ. For where the Word of Christ dwells—the Holy Spirit dwells; and where the Holy Spirit dwells—is the kingdom of heaven, heaven begun in a human life. We see the effects of this indwelling—in the gentleness, the sweetness, the purity of heart, the truth, the patience, the love, which the Word of Christ always produces.

October 4.

"I came that they may have life—and may have it abundantly!" John 10:10

To have abundant life, we must use the life we have. If the child would have his puny arm grow into strength—he must exercise it. The smith wields his hammer—and his muscles become like bands of iron. If you would have your brain develop into mental strength—you must use it. It is so of every faculty and function of the life. If you would have your power of sympathy grow, until you are able to be a true helper and comforter of others—you must find expression for your sympathy. If you would become a true helper—begin in little ways. Every outgoing of love in true service—makes our love itself more abundant.

Begin with the little life you have, accept every opportunity to use it—and by and by you will reach a capacity for helpfulness and service which will amaze you. But sit down and do nothing, put forth no effort, and your little life will dry up and shrivel to a crisp. "If the stars did not move," said Horace Bushnell, "they might rot in the sky!" The curse on thousands of Christian lives, is inactivity. Do not use your hand, and it will wither to death. The same is true of all physical, mental, and moral powers; unused they will die. If you would have abundant life, use every particle of the life you have, and it will develop until it reaches fullness of power.

October 5.

"Then a Samaritan came along, and when he saw the man, he felt deep pity." Luke 10:33

"O Lord, advertise your love through us!" was the prayer of an earnest Christian. A young Christian, when asked if she loved Jesus, was moved to tears, saying in her heart, "What a dim light mine must be, if others are not sure that I love Jesus!" A Christian writer has recently said, that the deadliest heresy is to be unloving.

God advertised his love through the *good Samaritan*. Others needed not to ask him if he loved God. He was not guilty of *the deadly heresy of being unloving*. He had true compassion. He was not content merely to say a few pitying words. His sympathy took the practical form of *doing* something. He bound up the man's wounds—that was help of the best kind. He stopped the bleeding away of the sufferer's life. He rested not until he had him safe in a warm shelter.

He did not even content himself with getting the man into an inn, then throwing off further responsibility. He might have said, "I have done my share; let some other one look after him now." But he was in no hurry to get the case off his hands. He took care of the man for a time, and then provided for the continuation of the care as long as it would be needed. The good Samaritan is Christ's own picture of what Christian love should be in everyone of his disciples.

October 6.

"Jesus wept." John 11:35

This is the *shortest verse* in all the Bible—but it is rich in meaning. It is a great window in Christ's bosom, showing us his very heart. It tells us that our Savior, though so glorious, is touched by our griefs. He is the same now in heaven, that he was that day when Mary lay at his feet and he wept with her. He is with us in all our sorrows, and sympathizes with us. This alone is a wonderful comfort to those who are in trouble.

A little child visited a neighbor who had lost her baby, and came home and told her mother that she had been comforting the sorrowing woman. Her mother asked her how she had done it, and she said, "I cried with her." It does us good when we are in trouble, to know that some other one sympathizes with us. It brings us a sense of companionship in our loneliness. It puts another shoulder under our load. But when it is Jesus who cares and is touched, weeps with us, comes up beside us in gentle companionship, it is wondrous comfort indeed.

October 7.

"Taking him by the right hand, *he helped him up*, and instantly the man's feet and ankles became strong." Acts 3:7

A lady was asked for her ideal of happiness, and gave this answer: "My ideal of happiness, is the helping of somebody up." This has the ring of that word of the Master's, in which he said he came, "not to be ministered unto—but to minister." At first thought, most people would look for their ideal of happiness in some possible good or favor to be received by themselves. But this lady was right. There is more real happiness in helping somebody up—than in the receiving of the largest benefits for ourselves. This glimpse of ideal happiness shows how near the desired blessing lies all the while, to everyone of us. There is not a day nor an hour, when we cannot be *helping somebody up.*

October 8.

"Rejoice with those who rejoice; weep with those who weep. Romans 12:15

Strange as it may seem, it is easier to weep with those who weep; than it is to rejoice with those who rejoice. There is something in sorrow that makes its resistless appeal to every heart, touching it with tenderness, and calling out sympathetic expressions. Suffering in another, disarms all unkindly feeling, and bids a truce, for the time at least, to all bitterness, jealousy, and resentment. We weep even with our enemy, whom we find in pain or sorrow. No one is ever envious of another's grief.

But when we see others rejoicing, it is not so according to nature to rejoice with them. The mood of gladness is not so sure to find *sympathetic chords* in the hearts of others. There are those who are envious of the happiness of others—and are made even more miserable by their joy! This surely is a most undivine spirit, and yet none can deny its existence in many hearts.

Gladness in others makes no such appeal to a heart, as *sorrow* does. It does not need help. Yet we should mark well the lesson that it is as much our duty to rejoice with those who rejoice—as it is to weep with those who weep. It is a close test of character, this being able to be glad because our friend is prosperous, even though at the time we do not have prosperity ourselves. It shows a wholesome spiritual condition.

October 9.

"Affliction produces endurance, endurance produces proven character." Romans 5:3-4

At first we would say that a home into which no sorrow had ever come, is the happiest home. It has had only prosperity. It is a Christian home, too, and has all the blessings of true religion. It is a home of love, ideal in its fellowship. But it has never known a sorrow. The circle is unbroken. No tears have been shed in it. We would say that this is the happiest home we know.

But it takes *sorrow* to perfect 'love's happiness'. There is little doubt that the sweetest home, is one in which there has been grief. We do not find the richest things in the Bible, until we pass into *shadows*. We do not see the stars, until night comes. There is no rainbow, except when there are *clouds*. We do not find out the richest love, even of our human friends, while we are strong and well and prosperous; it is only when we are in some grief or trouble, that we discover how much they love us. And we do not get the best of God's grace—until we are in sorrow.

Besides, grief softens our hearts, makes us capable of deeper affection and sympathy, and draws us nearer to each other. After a household has stood together around the coffin of one of its own—it is a new tenderness that unites the members. Suffering together, brings a new closeness in loving. Thus, even sorrow may be put among the elements of home happiness.

October 10.

"I have had God's help to this very day!" Acts 26:22

It had been through nearly twenty-five years of hard, toilsome life, that the heroic old apostle had stood, never giving up, never faltering in his confession. But he takes no praise to himself. The help came from God.

Many young people are afraid to set out on a Christian life, fearing they will not be able to be true to the end. Here is the word for all such; they will obtain help from God—for every duty, for every struggle, for every sorrow, which they must endure. They need only to be faithful day by day, doing the day's duty, and trusting God for grace. The help will come silently, just as it is needed, always sufficient grace—so that they will ever be able to stand.

God never puts a burden upon us—without giving us the strength to carry it. The way to obtain help from him, is to go promptly forward in the way of duty, asking for the help, and sure of getting it. It will not come if we wait to get it before we set out to obey. It will come only as we do God's will moment by moment.

"But He said to me, My grace is sufficient for you!" 2 Corinthians 12:9

October 11.

"That you may be *sincere* and blameless until the day of Christ" Philippians 1:10

Sincere means 'without wax'. Many people in Rome's palmy days, lived in fine marble palaces. Sometimes a dishonest workman, when there was a piece chipped off a stone, would fill in the chink with a kind of cement called wax, an imitation of marble. For a time the deception would not be discovered—but after a while the wax would become discolored, thus revealing the defect. It became necessary to put in contracts, a clause stating that the work should be '*sine cera'*, without wax. This is the origin of the word sincere. It means that the life thus described, is true through and through. It makes no pretensions. It has nothing to hide.

Insincerity in any form mars the beauty of life. Unreal professions of friendship are to be guarded against. So are over-statements of religious experience. We remember in what scathing words our Lord denounced *hypocrisy*. This was the only sin of which he did not speak with pity and compassion. So in many parts of the Scripture we are cautioned against *insincerity*. We are to have sincere *faith*. We are to have sincere *love* of the brethren. We are to love without hypocrisy. Few things do more harm to the cause of Christ, than insincerity in those who profess to be his friends. Sincerity gives influence and power to life.

October 12.

"Bless the Lord, O my soul; and all that is within me, bless his holy name!" Psalm 103:1

Every part of our being should join in praising God. The song of praise we sing, should not be a solo, or a duet—but a full chorus the feelings, affections, mental powers, tastes, desires—all mingling in praise.

There are some who praise with their *voice*—but not with their *heart*. Others give *intellectual* worship, while their *affections* are not engaged. Others give *emotional* praise—but their *will* and*conscience* do not join heartily in the song; they have good feelings—but lack in *practical obedience*. Some sing *missionary* hymns with zest—but give nothing to missionary work! Or they sing*consecration* hymns—but then live for themselves! The true way to praise God—is to rouse every faculty, energy, power, and affection—to hearty, enthusiastic, practical praise, all that is within us, joining in glad and holy songfulness!

October 13.

"Blessed is the man who makes the LORD his trust." Psalm 40:4

This is not what the world says. It calls the man blessed, or happy—who gets on in business, who prospers and grows rich, or who rises to power. It is along the paths to these places of distinction, that the world throngs. There is no scramble for the honors of *sainthood*. Not many people envy the heroes of Christian faith. Yet as the angels see this world, its highest seats are filled by God's believing ones. If we study the beatitudes, we shall learn who are really "blessed." If we trace the word "blessed " through the Bible—we see who come within the radiant circle.

The man who makes the Lord his trust is blessed. Why? He has been lifted out of the horrible pit. His feet are on a rock which cannot be shaken. He has a joy which nothing ever can break. His trust is one which no storm or flood, no financial panic, no bank failure, no defalcation, no fire, no political defeat—can ever disturb.

Is it not worth while, to have such a secure blessedness? No other trust is absolutely safe, even in this life. Then what about the day of *death*, and the *judgment* that comes after, and the *eternity*? We cannot leave out these stupendous events, when estimating what is best. It is not hard to prove that none are really blessed, except those whose trust is stayed on God. The question, however, is, Where is your trust? Are you among the blessed?

October 14.

"A good name is more desirable than great riches; to be esteemed is better than silver or gold." Proverbs 22:1

We cannot be too careful of our good name. Many things, perhaps not morally wrong in themselves, when seen by other and uncharitable eyes; may yet be construed to mean wrong-doing, and may thus hurt one's good name. There is need, too, of the most delicate moral sense in the regulation of conduct, and the most careful interpretation of duty, lest there be a lowering of tone which shall permit of acts not in accord with the *perfect law of right*. We cannot hold ourselves too strictly to "whatever things are true, whatever things are of good report." A name once tarnished, never can be made altogether bright again.

"The fleece that had been by the dyer stained,
 Never again its native whiteness gained."

October 15.

"If you turn to my reproof—then I will pour out my spirit on you and teach you my words." Proverbs 1:23

After repenting, comes new divine anointing. The Holy Spirit will not enter or stay in a heart that is cherishing sin. But when we turn away from the wrong things—the Spirit will come and live in us.

There is a great deal in the Bible about the conditions on which divine things are revealed. "The secret of the Lord is with those who fear him." These words promise a very sweet confiding—even God tells the secret things of his heart to his children. The condition is, "with those who fear him," that is, reverence, honor, love, and obey him. We have an illustration of this, in God's dealing with Abraham. "The Lord said, Shall I hide from Abraham that which I do? " Abraham was the "friend of God," and the secret of the Lord was confided to him.

In, our Lord's parting words to his disciples, we have the same truth: "No longer do I call you servants: for the servant knows not what his Lord does; but I have called you friends; for all things that I heard from my Father I have made known unto you."

Again we have the condition of this confidence: "You are my friends—IF you do the things which I command you." If we would know divine things—we must submit ourselves to divine guidance.

October 16.

"What do you see?" Zechariah 4:2

The world is full of lovely things which only a few people can see.

Many people have eyes—yet see nothing lovely in all the splendors of earth, or sky, or sea. Well would it be, if an angel walked by the side of everyone, saying continually, at every turn, "What do you see?" The world is full of visions of loveliness, for everyone who can see.

Then in the Bible, too, there are wonderful things on every page. Here, again, we should train ourselves to ask, as our eyes fall on verse after verse, "What do you see?" If we had this habit well formed, we would be ever coming upon new things. Visions of divine loveliness would rise up continually before us, with their heavenly teachings, and their inspirations toward loftier, holier, nobler life!

October 17.

"There is surely a future hope for you, and your hope will not be cut off." Proverbs 23:18

What you see of the brilliance, the delight, and the pleasure of sin—is only a cheat. Wait until the end comes. "Sin, when it is finished, brings forth death!" For a while, a wicked man may seem to prosper in his sin; but there is *a hereafter*, and sin will surely bring its harvest of curse and punishment at last! Indeed, if we could see all, we would find that even day by day, the fruits of a good life are far sweeter than those of sin. No godly young man would envy his mirthful neighbor, if he could follow him from his dissipation and reveling—and see the sickening sequel.

"Sorrow follows wrong,
 As echo follows song."

The *peace* which comes to the heart of him who lives after God's laws, is a thousand times better than the *remorse* which is the portion of the sinner. There would be no envy if a Christian young man could, set the two lives side by side, and see them in fair, honest light.

One young man was placed in unfortunate circumstances. Nearly all the young men he knew drank alcohol. Would he go with them? He took a philosophical look at the older men about him, and saw what drink had done for those who had formed the drinking habit in their youth. Then he looked at the men who had refused to learn to drink. He made his choice. "There is surely a future hope for you, and your hope will not be cut off."

October 18.

"How foolish are those who manufacture idols to be their gods. *Their delectable things shall not profit.*" Isaiah 44:9

"Delectable things," are the things in which they took delight, that is, their idols. They bestowed honor upon them, prayed to them, looked to them as gods. But these *delectable things* could do nothing for them.

We have it all in the old psalm: "For our God is in the heavens, and he does as he wishes. *Their idols* are merely things of silver and gold, shaped by human hands. They cannot talk, though they have mouths, or see, though they have eyes! They cannot hear with their ears, or smell with their noses, or feel with their hands, or walk with their feet, or utter sounds with their throats! And those who make them are just like them, as are all who trust in them." Psalm 115:3-8

These idols could give no comfort in sorrow, no strength in weakness, no deliverance in danger. Suppose you were an idol-worshiper, and had in your house a beautiful 'god of gold'. Then suppose there was death in your family, or some other trouble, in which you needed help that no human friend could give you; what could your idol do for you?

No better than these idols, are other worldly trusts which men have, their money, for instance. Suppose there is sorrow in a home of wealth, filled with works of art and with fine furniture, and without Christ; what comfort can these 'delectable things' give?

October 19.

"Today also my complaint is bitter. His hand is heavy despite my groaning." Job 23:2

Job does not mean that he was rebellious—but that even with his submission to the divine will, he could hardly keep his *pain* from breaking out in *cries*. If we are God's children, we should bear even the greatest sufferings without complaining. It may not always be possible to repress the outcries of anguish; but even if our affliction is too full of pain to be altogether repressed, we should not have in our heart, any rebellious feeling toward God.

An English writer tells of two birds, and how they acted when put into a cage. One bird flew violently against the wires of its prison, in unavailing efforts to escape, only bruising its own wings in the struggle. The other bird perched itself on the bar, and began to pour forth from its little throat, bursts of sweet song. We know well which bird was the wiser, which had learned the best way to meet hard conditions.

Some people are like the foolish bird—when they are in trouble they chafe, cry out, and complain. The result is, they only hurt themselves, make themselves more miserable, and do not in any sense lessen their trouble. It is wiser always, as well as more pleasing to God—for us to bear our trials patiently, singing songs of faith—rather than complaining in rebellion and discontent. Thus we take the bitterness out of trial, making it sweet.

October 20.

"How priceless is Your unfailing love! Men find refuge under the shadow of Your wings!" Psalm 36:7

"He will cover you with His feathers, and *under His wings* you will find refuge." Psalm 91:4

'Under His wings' is a blessed shelter into which to flee—when the world is cold. It is a warm place into which to creep—when the heart is smitten with sorrows. It is when we are troubled—that we find these wings the softest. We call sorrow a shadow, and we talk about the shadow falling upon us and deepening, until sometimes all the light is obscured. Have you ever thought that it is the shadow of God's wings, which makes this darkness? It does not seem *love's* shadow; it seems *unkindness*. But really it is *love*. God is never so close to us—as when we are in deepest sorrow.

As feeble babes that suffer,
Toss and cry and will not rest,
Are the ones the tender mother
Holds the closest, loves the best.

So when we are weak and wretched,
By our sins weighed down, distressed,
Then it is that God's great patience
Holds us closest, loves us best.

October 21.

"Let another praise you—and not your own mouth; someone else—and not your own lips." Proverbs 27:2

We would better not talk about ourselves. People do not want to hear about you—from your own lips. Even though your good deeds, your greatness, or your fine attainments do not become known—what does it matter? God knows about them—and that is enough!

One says wisely, "Think as little as possible about any good in yourself; turn your eyes resolutely from any view of your acquirements, your influence, your plans, your success; above all, speak as little as possible about yourself. The inordinateness of our self-love makes speech about ourselves, very foolish. Nothing but duty should open our lips upon this dangerous theme, except it be in humble confession of our *sinfulness* before God."

October 22.

"If you see oppression of the poor and perversion of justice and righteousness in the province, do not be astonished." Ecclesiastes 5:8

It is a comfort in a world where so many things continually go wrong, to know that God regards His people, and that He will surely in some way bring justice out of injustice, good out of wrong. He is always on the side of the oppressed, of the weak, of those whom the strong would crush.

We naturally pity any person whom we see treated unfairly by others. Our hearts cry out against the injustice—and yet we may be powerless to do anything to set it right. Our comfort, however, is that God sees all this wrong, and not only sees—but cares, and in His own time and way—He will vindicate the cause of those who are made the victims of the cruelty of the strong. We may safely leave the adjustment of the equities, in His hands. The vindication may not come in this world—but the end of events is not here.

The Queen of France once said to her bitter enemy, Cardinal Richelieu, "There is one fact that you seem to have entirely forgotten: God is a sure paymaster. He may not pay at the end of every week or month or year—but I charge you to remember, that He pays in the end!"

One of the strongest arguments for a future life is in this fact: that in the present world, full justice cannot always be had. It takes an after-life, to right earth's wrongs. But we may be sure that they will all be righted in the end!

October 23.

"The people grew discouraged because of the way." Numbers 21:4

There are a great many discouraged people in the world. They have lost heart, and when one has lost heart, life is very hard; the wheels roll heavily.

No doubt there are things in everyone's path, that are discouraging. There are hardships to endure. There are disappointments to suffer. We come up to the very edge of brilliant expectations, when suddenly our path is turned away! There are hostile enemies, too, besetting all the way. No wonder we are discouraged sometimes—if we look no higher than the road at our feet.

Some of the reasons why a Christian should not be discouraged by any hardness in the way are, because it is God's way, and He leads; and because the way leads to heaven; and we should be willing to endure any hardships to reach such blessedness as there waits for us!

October 24.

"Even if my father and mother abandon me—the Lord will hold me close!" Psalm 27:10

We all know how much our father and mother love us. It seems to us there never could be a stronger love than theirs. No matter how wickedly a son may act, the love in his father's and mother's heart, still continues tender and faithful. Though all the world turn him out-of-doors, the 'home door' still stands open for him.

But this verse tells us that even if parental *love* is worn out, and parental *patience* exhausted, and the home door shut in one's face—there is still a place in God's heart and home for the outcast! This is the verse for the man or the woman who has gone down to the lowest depths of shame, until even his mother— if this is possible—has given him up and shut him out of her heart!

God's love outlasts *human* love.

This is also the *orphan's* verse. When God removes father and mother, He Himself takes up the child in special love and care. Very desolate is the world, when both father and mother are gone. Life is never the same again. There is no place to go with the heart's hunger, and with the burden that is too heavy. Yet God remains, and in the loss of the human, there are first revealed, ofttimes, the warmth, tenderness, faithfulness, and help of the divine love.

Cast all your care on God—that anchor holds!

October 25.

"Concerning this salvation, the prophets, who spoke of the grace that was to come to you, searched intently and with the greatest care . . . Even angels long to look into these things!" 1 Peter 1:10-12

Both earth and heaven are intensely interested in the great redeeming work of Christ. There are wise men who are so busy in their researches into little earthly matters, that they cannot get time to study the things of the spiritual kingdom of God. But nothing in this world so merits the thought, study, and research of the wisest beings in the universe—as Christ's work of redemption.

The interest of the *angels* in Christ's suffering as the Redeemer, is very beautiful. There is a picture by Domenichino which represents the scene on Calvary, after the Savior's body had been taken down and laid in the grave. The cross is empty. An angel stands beside the crown of thorns which lies there, feeling with the tip of his finger, one of its sharp points. His face wears a look of wonder. He is trying to find out the meaning of suffering—but he cannot understand it nor fathom its depth.

The artist's thought is, that to this angel the sufferings of Christ were a great mystery which he was trying to comprehend. The same thought is suggested in the words, "even angels long to look into these things!" Surely it is worth while to give thought and attention to the wonderful things of Christ's redemption, since even the *angels* find in them mystery worthy of their deepest study.

October 26.

"*Peace I leave with you. My peace I give to you.* I do not give to you as the world gives. Your heart must not be troubled or fearful." John 14:27

Two artists went out to paint a picture of peace. One painted a silvery lake embosomed deep amid the hills, where no storm could ever touch it—calm, sweet, quiet in its shelter. The other painted a wild sea, swept by tempests, strewn with wrecks—but rising out of the sea a great rock, and in the rock, high up, a cleft, with herbage and flowers amid which, on her nest, a dove was sitting. The latter is the true picture of Christian peace.

Anybody can be confident—when there is nothing to disturb, no danger, no storm. Anybody can be happy—when there is no trouble, nothing to hurt or vex. Anybody can be patient—when there is nothing to make one impatient. Any little lake can be smooth and glassy—when there is no wind to ruffle it, or when it is hidden away within a wall of mountains. But we want a religion which will help us to have peace—when the sorest trials are upon us! How can we get this peace? Only by hiding in Christ!

October 27.

"I have learned to be **content**, whatever the circumstances." Philippians 4:11

Contentment depends upon the person—not upon his circumstances.

One is content, living in the poorest way—with bare necessaries and no luxuries, working hard and enduring many trials.

Another is discontented in a palace—with all the comforts, delicacies, and ease that money can provide.

The difference is in the hearts of the two people.

The former has in himself—all the resources of contentment, and is not affected by changes in his circumstances. The latter depends entirely upon his circumstances for his contentment, and therefore is affected by every vicissitude.

"I know what it is to be in need, and I know what it is to have plenty. I have learned the secret of being content in any and every situation, whether well fed or hungry, whether living in plenty or in poverty." Philippians 4:12

October 28.

"He got up from the table, took off His robe, wrapped a towel around his waist, and poured water into a basin. Then He began to wash the disciples' feet and to wipe them with the towel He had around Him." John 13:4-5

"What I am doing, you do not understand now—but afterwards you will understand." John 13:7

At this time Peter did not know why the Messiah he really needed—was a Messiah with basin and towel. He was thinking of a Messiah with throne and crown and scepter and earthly pomp! He did not understand it—until after the blood of Calvary had been shed. Christ referred to these days by "afterwards."

This saying of Christ, however, may be used in a much wider sense. There are a great many things which He does, which at the time we cannot understand; yet in due time—all of them will become clear. As they appear to us, while we are passing through them, they are unfinished acts; when the work is completed—it will appear beautiful. This is especially true of many mysterious providences in our lives. One time Jacob thought and said, "All these things are against me!" But he lived to see that the very things which he thought were against him—were really all working together for his good.

So it is always, in the providences of God with His own people. "We know that all things work together for good, to those who love God."

The back side of a tapestry appears to be a mystery of tangle and confusion—but there is a beautiful picture on the other side. Just so—we are looking at our lives, largely on the back side. We cannot see the Master's plan—until 'afterwards'.

October 29.

"Three times I pleaded with the Lord to take it away from me! But He said to me—My grace is sufficient for you—for My power is made perfect in your weakness!" 2 Corinthians 12:8

Many prayers which seem to be unanswered—are really answered. The blessing comes—but in a form we do not recognize. Instead of the very thing we sought—something better is given!

The burden is not lifted away—but we are sustained beneath it.

We are not spared the suffering—but in the suffering we are brought nearer to God, and receive more of His grace.

The sorrow is not taken away—but is changed to joy.

Our ignorant prayers are taken into the hands of the great Intercessor, and are answered in ways far wiser than our thought!

Instead of earthly trifles—heavenly riches!

Instead of things which our poor wisdom sought—things God's infinite wisdom chose for us!

Instead of pleasure for a day—gain for eternity!

October 30.

"Therefore, since we have been justified through faith—we have *peace* with God through our Lord Jesus Christ" Romans 5:1

PEACE is a favorite word with Paul. His life was full of suffering, care, toil, and trial; yet his epistles are starred all over with the bright word 'peace'.

He speaks of different kinds of peace. Here it is "peace **with** God." This means the consciousness of *reconciliation* with God. Sin separates us from God. While guilt is in the heart, there is no peace with God. We cannot look into God's face. But when we have repented of our sins, and have confessed them, and received God's forgiveness through Jesus Christ, we have peace with God.

Paul speaks elsewhere of "the peace **of** God." Writing from a prison, he exhorted his friends, "Do not be anxious about anything, but in everything, by prayer and petition, with thanksgiving, present your requests to God. And the peace of God, which transcends all understanding, will guard your hearts and your minds in Christ Jesus." This is a step farther than peace *with* God. It is the peace which holds the heart quiet and still—in the midst of whatever things are hard and trying in this world. It comes from resting in God's love, and leaving all *tangled things* in his hands. Christ promised the same peace when he said, "Peace I leave with you; my peace I give unto you."

Peace is named as one of the fruits of the Spirit. It comes, therefore, through having the Holy Spirit in our heart, and is not an earthly attainment.

October 31.

"May He incline our hearts toward Him—to walk in all His ways and to keep His commands, ordinances, and judgments." 1 Kings 8:58

We must be obedient and faithful—or else we forfeit the divine promises. We are "prone to wander" from God; our hearts are deceitful and incline to lead us away. Hence this prayer is a fit one to be always on our lips—that God may incline our hearts unto him, to walk in all his ways, to keep his commandments.

We are charged to keep our heart with all diligence. The heart is the fountain of all motive and action, and therefore it must be under constant guard. We in our weakness, cannot keep it ourselves, and hence the need of *divine keeping*.

Fenelon's prayer was, "Lord take my heart—for I cannot give it to you; and when you have it, oh, keep it—for I cannot keep it for you; and save me in spite of myself, for Jesus Christ's sake. Amen." This is a good daily prayer for any of us. God will never compel us to be obedient; but he will grant to us the grace of his Holy Spirit, if we ask for it, and will incline us, draw us, help us. We need, therefore, to pray continually to him—to throw over us the mystic influence of his Spirit that we may seek to walk in God's ways.

NOVEMBER

November 1.

"Do not let the sun go down while you are still angry" Ephesians 4:26

It is well for us to have *horizons* which cut off our life for the time, as if it were ended. These *temporary endings* keep us thoughtful and mindful of the *final ending*—after which will come no beginning again in this world. *Evening* puts an end to life's work for a season. We leave the *plough* standing in the furrow, the *hammer* lying by the anvil, the *axe* resting against the root of the tree. We shut the door of the mill or office and go home. Our work is done for the day—and we may never take it up again! Every setting of the sun, should therefore be a testing of life. Everything should be finished—as if it were the ending of all.

Especially should the hour of evening, when we bow at God's feet, be always a time for setting right all that may have gone wrong in us during the day. Then every feeling of bitterness should be cast out of our heart. Life is too critical for us—to venture into any night's darkness and sleep, cherishing anger or envy. "Do not let the sun go down while you are still angry" is a wise counsel.

November 2.

Paul said, "Unless these men stay with the ship—you cannot be saved." Acts 27:31

The sailors were needed to help save the lives of the passengers. Yet Paul had said before, that there should be no loss of life. He had received this assurance from the angel of God. If it was God's purpose that no life should perish—then why did Paul say that unless the seamen stood at their posts and continued to attend to their duties—that the passengers could not be saved? Was God's promise *dependent* on a few heathen sailors?

The divine assurance did not do away with the use of all *proper means* for securing deliverance. We are not to sit down and do nothing, when we find a promise of God; we are rather to do bur whole duty, as if the fulfillment of the promise depended altogether upon us! There is no real conflict between these two truths: that God has a plan which extends to all things; and that men are free moral agents, who are responsible for their acts. *Theology* may find it impossible to harmonize the two—but *common-sense* accepts both, and does not worry about the *harmonizing*. It is clear that the working out of God's purposes depends upon human faithfulness to duty—and that God's purpose of deliverance for us may and will fail unless we do our part. There is no excuse, therefore, for *inaction* in the assurance that God plans for our good; the plan will not be carried out—unless we work it out for ourselves! Every *divine purpose* depends on *human fidelity*.

November 3.

"Cutting loose the anchors, they left them in the sea." Acts 27:40

Anything which hinders our getting to heaven—we should resolutely sacrifice.

An illustration of this is the flight of Cortez, on that fearful night when the Aztecs compelled the invaders to escape for their lives. The vast masses of gold that had been accumulated, were more than could be carried away, as each soldier would have to fight his way through. The men were allowed to take what they would—but the commander warned them against *overloading*. "For," said he, "he travels *safest* in the dark night—who travels *lightest*." The more cautious men heeded the advice so given—but others were less self-restrained. Some bound heavy chains of gold around their neck and shoulders, some filled their pockets with the bulky gold ingots, until they literally staggered under their burden.

The experience of the conflict that ensued, demonstrated the *wisdom* of the advice given by the commander, and the *folly* of those who failed to heed it; for all such became an easy prey to the lances of the Aztecs! To save life—all else had to be abandoned; and that night poverty itself was the greatest riches.

We ought to see whether there is anything keeping us away from Christ or hindering our faithfulness and devotion; and if we find that there is anything, no matter how dear it is to us—we should cut it off or cast it away!

November 4.

"Whoever is faithful in very little—is also faithful in much; and whoever is unrighteous in very little—is also unrighteous in much."
   Luke 16:10

We are apt to under-estimate little failures in duty.
It seems to us a small matter:
that we do not keep an engagement,
that we lose our temper,
that we say an impatient or angry word,
that we show an unkind or harsh spirit,
that we speak uncharitably of another,
that we treat someone with discourtesy, or
fail in some other way which appears trivial.

We think that so long as we are honest, faithful, and loving in the larger things—
that it of small importance, that we make 'little slips'.

But we never can tell what may be the *consequences* of our failure, in even the most minute duty.

It hurts our own life! It leaves us a little weaker in our character, a little less able to resist the next temptation that comes at the same point. It breaks our habit of faithfulness, and makes it easier for us to break it a second time. We sin against ourselves, when we relax our diligence or our faithfulness, in even the least thing!

Then, we do not know what the consequences to others will be—when we fail in their presence. An outburst of temper in a Christian, may hinder many others in their Christian life. The failure of a Christian minister to pay a little debt, may destroy the minister's influence over many in his church.

November 5.

"Do not work for food that perishes—but for food that endures to eternal life, which the Son of Man will give you!" John 6:27

We need to be continually reminded of the unsatisfying nature of the things of this world—and exhorted to seek the lasting things in life. We live in a material age, when the quest of people is for money, for power, for things of the earth.

John Bunyan gives a picture of 'a man with a muck-rake', working hard, scraping up the rubbish at his feet—and not seeing the crown which hung above his head. It is a picture of the great majority of the people in this world. They are wearing out their life in gathering rubbish out of the dirt—not thinking of the heavenly treasures, the divine and imperishable gifts, which they might have—with half the toil and care!

We ought not to spend our life in picking up rubbish which we cannot carry beyond the grave! If we are wise, we will seek rather to gather lasting treasures and riches, which we can take with us into eternity!

Whatever we build into our character, we shall possess forever!

Money which we spend in doing good in Christ's name—we lay up as safe and secure treasure in heaven.

All true service for Christ—stores up rewards for us in the future.

What we keep—we lose!

What we give in love—we keep!

November 6.

"I will bless those who bless you; and whoever curses you I will curse." Genesis 12:3

It is wonderful how God makes *common cause* with his people, in this world. They represent him wherever they are, and the things that are done to them—God regards as done to himself. It is a perilous thing to lift a hand against any of God's people, for he who does so, lifts his hand against God! Christ says the same of his relation to his friends. To harm a Christian—is to harm his Master! To neglect a suffering Christian—is the same as if Christ himself were suffering and we neglected him!

We need to beware that we never do injury of any kind to any of *Christ's little ones*. On the other hand, all kindness shown to a friend of Christ—is shown as to Christ himself, and is rewarded accordingly. Even the *giving of a cup of cold water* to a disciple of his, in his name, does not go without reward.

Surely it is worth while to be a Christian, to have such divine friendship, to have God on our side to defend us, and to make common cause with us!

November 7.

Unconfessed sins give bitterness. It is written in the old psalm: "When I refused to confess my sin, my bones wasted away through my groaning all day long. For day and night your hand was heavy upon me; my strength was sapped as in the heat of summer." Psalm 32:3-4

But the moment he made confession, back on the echo of his prayer of penitence came the assurance of pardon, "I acknowledged my sin to you and did not cover up my iniquity. I said, "I will confess my transgressions to the Lord"—and you forgave the guilt of my sin!" Psalm 32:5

That is always the way. God loves to forgive. The instant he hears the voice of *penitence*, he speaks the word of *remission*. So we learn the only way to get clear of our sins—we must put them out of our heart, by sincere and humble confession. Then they will trouble us no more forever.

Some people try to *flee* from their sins—but they can never get away from them. Their sins are a part of themselves. Some people try to hide from God when they have sinned—but this also is a vain effort. Adam and Eve tried this, hiding in the garden after their transgression, when they heard the footsteps of God approaching. The only safe flight from sin and from God—is to God. In his mercy there is secure and eternal refuge.

November 8.

"My son, if your *heart* is wise—my heart will indeed rejoice!" Proverbs 23:15

Every true father is affectionately interested in the lives of his children. His own joy, in later years, depends largely upon the way they live. He is made very happy by seeing them make something noble and worthy of their lives, and living honorably and righteously among men.

Notice here, also, the place of the *heart*—in the making of the *life*. We are never better—than our own heart. If our heart is evil, full of wrong thoughts, dispositions, and tempers—then our character cannot be lovely and winning. "Beautiful thoughts—make a beautiful soul." As we think in our heart—so we are.

There is a thought here for parents. If they would have happiness in seeing their children live beautiful lives, they must do more than give them good and wise counsels. Solomon was splendid at *advising*. His *words* are full of wisdom. If followed faithfully, they will build into a life, whatever things are true, whatever things are pure, whatever things are lovely. But we know how Solomon *lived*. It is little wonder that his son did not turn out well. Other parents need to guard against the same fatal mistake. No matter how well they may *advise*, if they do not themselves*live* godly lives—they will probably draw their children with them to ruin! They cannot by *good advice*, overcome the force of *bad example*.

November 9.

"Do not grumble!" 1 Corinthians 10:10

No spirit is more fruitful of discomfort, than that of habitual complaining. It makes misery in him who indulges it—and in those who suffer from contact with it. The *complaining man* is never happy himself. Indeed, he strives not to be happy, since in whatever circumstances he finds himself—he at once sets about trying to discover something unpleasant. Of course he never seeks in vain; for people find in this world, what they look for. It would not be so bad, if he made only himself miserable—but he succeeds also in imparting more or less of his wretchedness, to all he meets. It is about as poor a use of one's immortal powers, as one can find—to live to *grumble* and thus add to the unhappiness of others!

November 10.

"What more can David say to you? For you know your servant, O Sovereign Lord." 2 Samuel 7:20

Who has not felt in prayer the utter inadequacy of speech—to express his heart's deep longings? We try to tell God of our sorrow for sin, our hunger after righteousness; but we can tell him only the merest fraction of what we feel. *Words* are never large enough for *thought*. No poet ever gets into his lines—the whole of the vision of beauty which floats before his soul. No true orator ever finds sentences majestic enough—to express the sentiments that burn in his breast. Deep, pure love—is never able to put into language its most sacred feelings. It is only the*commonplace* of the inner life—that can be interpreted in words. There is always more, which lies unexpressed, than is uttered in speech.

In one of Paul's epistles, there is a wonderful word which shows how God understands our unexpressed prayers. "Unto him that is able to do exceeding abundantly above all that we ask or think." God is able to answer prayer, not only beyond what we can *express*—but even beyond what we can *think*. He knows our deepest and most sacred feelings. Even the hungers of our heart, the longings of our soul—he understands. We need not fret because we cannot tell God all that we feel or desire. He reads all that is within our heart, and answers not our mere *words*—but our *yearnings*, our *longings*.

November 11.

"But Samuel said—What then is this bleating of sheep in my ears? What is this lowing of cattle that I hear?" 1 Samuel 15:14

Sin is hard to hide! We may think that we have covered up our disobediences, so that detection shall be impossible; but suddenly something tears away the covering, and they are exposed to the gaze of the world! A man carries on a series of dishonesties through a series of years, and covers them up by expert bookkeeping, thinking he is safe. But some morning he is startled to find that the stolen sheep have been bleating, and the purloined cattle have been lowing, and all the world knows of his thefts and embezzlements.

It is the nature of sheep to bleat, and cattle to low, and they have not sense enough to keep quiet when they are expected to. Indeed, they are almost sure to make a noise and reveal their whereabouts, just when they are depended on to keep perfectly still.

It is the same with *sin*. It is a poor friend to a man. It professes well when it is offering its solicitations—but when it has been committed, it is a poor confidant. It cannot keep a secret. It is sure at some time to betray the man who depends upon it for prudent silence.

In most of our lives there are some bleating sheep and lowing cattle—faults, evil habits, blemishes of character, tendencies or idiosyncrasies, which tell the story of the imperfectness of our obedience, things which we would not want even our nearest friend to know.

November 12.

"I delight to do Your will." Psalm 90:8

This is consecration. All ambition should start and end there. Duty is simple obedience. The highest thing possible in this world for any life—is obedience to the will of God.

Nothing is small if it be God's will for us for the moment. Nothing is great, however brilliant in men's eyes, if it is not God's will. Here should be our life motto, "I delight to do Your will." Since Christ himself filled his life with such loving devotion to his Father's will, it should be our highest joy to do the same.

November 13.

"The people soon began to complain to the Lord about their hardships; and when the Lord heard them, His anger blazed against them!" Numbers 11:1

There are people who can speak of little else, but the unpleasant things in their own experience. If you ask them about their health, or even unfortunately put your salutation in the form of "How do you do?" you get as an answer, a description of many ills and infirmities to which they are subject, instead of any cheerful reciprocating of your greeting. All their ordinary conversation is filled with dolorous rehearsals of discouraging things. They have keen eyes for the unpleasant happenings, and never fail to mention them to others.

We all have troubles things in our daily personal life, that are vexing and annoying; sometimes things that are painful and burdensome. But we should not talk about them. We have no right to scatter our briers and thorns about us—so that others' feet may be torn by them. It does us no good, and it does others immeasurable harm!

Silence about ourselves, should be a rule almost without exception. Especially should the rule never to complain, be an absolute one. No matter how poorly we have rested through the night, we need not tell the whole family about it at breakfast. Patient bearing of the portion of life's ills which comes to us—is the characteristic of ideal Christian living.

November 14.

"Immediately Jesus made the disciples get into the boat and go on ahead of him to the other side." Matthew 14:22

Even when Christ sends us out—we may encounter *storms*. It was so here; the disciples were sent out by their Master, even constrained by him to go upon the sea—and yet a terrific storm arose. We must not expect that when we begin to obey Christ—that we shall have all favoring breezes. We must not conclude, whenever we find obstacles or hindrances in anything we have undertaken, that we are not doing right, and that these difficulties are providential indications that we ought not to proceed in the course. They are providential; but they may have a different mission altogether to inspire us to stronger faith and greater endeavor.

Jesus sent his disciples out alone; but in all their life, they had few more profitable experiences, though the night was one of such terror. They knew their *need of Christ* after that experience, better than ever before. Then they had a new revelation of Christ's power and glory, which they never could have had if he had not stayed behind, and then come to them on the waves. We do not see Christ's cross, until we are left in the night of conviction. We can never understand the sweetness of the divine comfort, if we never have sorrow. So it may be a blessing for us sometimes, even to go alone a little way, to learn lessons we could never learn with Christ beside us. We can at least learn our need of him.

November 15.

"To obey is better than sacrifice." 1 Samuel 15:22

Many people set a great deal more stress on religious rituals, than upon practical obedience. They will be faithful in attendance upon church services, devout and reverent in worship—and yet in their daily life, they will disregard the plain commandments of God! They fill the week with selfishness, pride, bitterness, and evil-speaking, and then go to church on Sunday, with great show of devotion, to engage in the worship of God!

But what God desires before our worship can be acceptable, is that we obey what He commands us. He bids us to love one another, to be unselfish, patient, kind, honest, pure, true; and unless we obey these commands, our religious rituals, no matter how conspicuous, how costly, how seemingly devout and reverent, are not acceptable to God!

There are many other phases of the truth. It is exact obedience which God desires, and not something else of our own substituted. When he tells a mother to care for her child, He is not satisfied if she neglects that duty to attend church. When God wants a man to help a poor family in some obscure street, He is not satisfied if instead of that lowly service, the man does some brilliant thing that seems to bring ten times as much honor to the Lord.

The supreme thing in Christian life—is to obey God; without obedience nothing else counts. The obedience must also be exact, just what God commands, not something else. "If you love Me—you will keep My commandments." John 14:15

November 16.

"The dove returned to Noah in the ark. He reached out his hand and took the dove and brought it back to himself in the ark." Genesis 8:9

One night in a home by the sea, the family sat around the evening lamp. Within, all was peace; without, however, the storm was wild. Rain and sleet beat against the windows. During the evening, one of the group heard a strange fluttering outside one of the windows. Making careful examination, it was found that there was a little bird flapping its wings against the pane. It had been caught in the storm, and was unable to find shelter. The light in the window had attracted it, and there it was beating against the glass. Quickly the window was opened, and the little thing flew in, drenched and faint—but happy and safe. Inside it found shelter, light, warmth, and food.

Often there are lives among us, like the bird caught in earth's storms, swept by temptation, by sorrow, or by passion; defeated, weary, with no shelter. For all such, the only refuge is in the heart of God, under the shadow of the wings of divine love. There the weary heart finds all it craves of refuge, love, warmth, joy, and satisfaction. Flying to the window of the divine ark—a strong, gentle hand draws it in.

November 17.

"Hannah did not go. She said to her husband—After the boy is weaned, I will take him and present him before the Lord, and he will live there always." 1 Samuel 1:22

Just at this time, Hannah's religious duties were at home. Her child required her attention, and she believed that she was worshiping God acceptably, in staying at Ramah and mothering her boy. No doubt she was right. A mother's first duties—are to her children. No amount of public religious service, will atone for neglect of her sacred home tasks. She may attend Dorcas meetings and missionary services, do good work among the poor, and carry blessings to many a sorrowful home; but if she fails meanwhile to look after her own children—she has miserably failed to serve God.

A mother's first duty—is to bring up her children for God. Whatever she can do for others after that, will be acceptable to God.

Many things must be crowded out of every earnest life, things that are good and desirable in themselves. No one can do everything that needs to be done, and we must select the things we shall do. But it will be a sad thing if a mother allows the proper care of her own children to be crowded out of her life, by the appeals on behalf of other people's children, the calls for public service however important, or the cries of any other human needs in the world. These outside duties may be hers in some measure—but the duties of the home—are hers and no others!

November 18.

"I am torn between the two: I *desire* to depart and be with Christ, which is better by far; but it is more necessary for you that I remain in the body." Philippians 1:23, 24

Two desires draw upon our hearts—if we are living in this world as citizens of heaven. The *heavenly* life woos us with its visions of bliss, its being with Christ, its tearless joy, its disenthrallment from sin, its realizations of holy hopes. At the same time, *earth* has its strong hold upon us. It is natural to want to live; any other desire in ordinary conditions is unwholesome. Human affections form a network of chains binding us to this life. So we are all "torn between the two desires."

November 19.

"I was not disobedient unto the heavenly vision." Acts 26:19

Doddridge, in his life of Colonel Gardiner, describes the conversion of this soldier. He was waiting near midnight, the hour fixed for a sinful meeting with another, and was carelessly turning over the pages of a religious book, when suddenly he saw before him, vivid and clear, the form of the Redeemer on the cross, and heard him speak: "All this have I done for you; and is this your return?" Like Paul, he was not disobedient to the heavenly vision—but from that moment turned and followed Christ.

That is what everyone of us should do; when we see Christ and hear his voice—we should immediately leave all and go after him. Not only at the beginning—but all the way through life—God sends us visions to guide us. Every time we see in a verse of Scripture, a glimpse of some beautiful thing commended, it is a heavenly vision given to lead us to the beauty it shows.

Every fragment of loveliness we see in a human life—is a heavenly vision sent to woo us upward. Wherever we see beauty which attracts us, and kindles in us desires and aspirations for higher attainments, it is a vision from God, whose mission is to call us to a higher life. We should make sure that we do not prove disobedient to any heavenly vision—but that we follow every one—as an angel sent from heaven to woo us nearer God!

November 20.

"As He was praying, the appearance of His face changed!" Luke 9:29

Artists put a halo around Christ's face in their pictures—but there was no visible halo on the face men saw, as He walked about and did his works of love. Now, however, for a little while the glory broke through his flesh and the disciples saw it. It must have been an experience of great joy to Jesus. That mountain-top reached into heaven that night; and he climbed up out of the mists and shadows—and stood in his native glory for a little while, to be refreshed by the ministry of the heavenly visitants for his dark way of sorrow.

An Alpine traveler tells of climbing one of the mountains in a dense, dripping fog, and standing at last in the clear air, under a cloudless sky. In the valley below him lay the fog, like an ocean of white vapor, and he could hear the chiming of bells, the lowing of cattle, and the sounds of labor coming up from the villages that were hidden beneath. Now and then a bird would dart up out of the mist, fly about a little while in the joyous sunshine, sing a few notes of sweet song, and then fly down again and disappear.

What this brief time of radiance was to the bird, the transfiguration was to our Lord. His earthly life was spent in the valley, beneath the clouds of suffering and sorrow; now for once he climbed up above the mists into the glory of heaven, bathed his soul in its brightness, heard the converse of messengers from his home.

November 21.

"Jesus entered Jericho and was passing through." Luke 19:1

Jesus had never been in Jericho before—and He never went there again! He was now on His last journey, and in a few days He would be dead. Hence this was the only opportunity the people there ever had of receiving blessings from Him. If any sufferers neglected to seek for help just that one day—they never had another opportunity.

Think what that passing hour was, in the history of the old city. Some caught a blessing at Christ's hand as He went by; and they must ever after have remembered with gratitude, the face that shone upon them and the eyes that looked into theirs. But there must have been many who did not seize the opportunity, and were left unblessed.

Christ is ever passing by. He may come again He does continually come again; but he is ever moving, and the blessing we would get from Him at any time—we must get as He passes.

All the days seem alike as they come to us; but each day comes with its own opportunities, its own calls to duty, its own privileges, holding out hands offering us radiant gifts. The day passes—and never comes again. Other days as bright may come—but that day never comes a second time. If we do not take just then the gifts it offers—we shall never have another opportunity to get them, and shall always be poorer for what we have missed. We need to be alert to take quickly from each day, the blessing which it brings.

November 22.

"What good will it be for a man if he gains the whole world—yet forfeits his soul? Or what can a man give in exchange for his soul?" Matthew 16:26

Eternal life is the only thing worth living for. No matter how much pleasure, or how great success, or how high honor, one may gain in this world, if at the end of life, a man passes into eternity unsaved—of what comfort to him will it be to remember his pleasant life on this earth?

A rich man failed in business. He then gathered together the fragments of his wrecked fortune—in all a few thousand dollars. He determined to go to another part of the country to start again. He took all his money, and bought a splendid car, furnishing it in the most luxurious style, and stocking it with provisions for his journey. In this sumptuous car he traveled to his destination. At length he stepped from the door of his *rolling palace*, and only then thought for the first time of his great folly. He had used the last cent of his money in getting in this *magnificent way to his new home*, and had nothing on which to begin life anew!

This illustrates the folly of those who think only of this life, and make no provision for eternity. They use up all their time, their opportunities, their life's strength—in getting to the gate of the grave, and find themselves forced to begin eternity with nothing, no treasure laid up. The only true success—is that which makes a man rich for eternity!

November 23.

"I tell you the truth, unless you change and become *like little children*, you will never enter the kingdom of heaven!" Matthew 18:3

Our great Teacher spoke strong words, when he said that only those who become *like little children*, can enter into the kingdom of heaven. It is of vital importance that we learn just what the words mean. What is it—to become like a little child?

There is a legend of a man whom the angels loved, and wished to have honored in some way. They asked that some remarkable power might be bestowed upon him. They were told to learn what the man would choose. But he would make no choice. Pressed to name some new power which should be given him, he said he would like to do a great deal of good in the world—without even knowing it. So it came about, that whenever his *shadow* fell behind him—it had healing power—but when it fell in front of him—it had not this power.

This is Christlikeness, goodness, power to do good, usefulness, helpfulness, without being *conscious* of the possession of these qualities. Ambition to have distinction, craving for praise, consciousness of being good, bright, useful, or great—all are marks of a worldly spirit. In another place Jesus said that greatness in his kingdom, is the spirit of unselfish serving, desiring "not to be served unto—but to serve." He who serves others the most unselfishly—is the greatest Christian.

November 24.

"The Word of the Lord abides forever!" 1 Peter 1:25

Men often make promises to others, on which the others depend—perhaps staking all their interests and happiness on the promise given to them, only to find at last that the promises have been forgotten. But God's least Word is sure and eternal. When a soul takes any divine promise, and builds a fabric of hope upon it, sooner might the stars fall from heaven, than that God should forget his Word or fail to make it good.

An English nobleman, walking in the country one day, found a little child in distress. She had broken her pitcher, and her family were poor, and the vessel could not be replaced. The good man put his hand in his pocket to find some money to give the child—but had not a penny. Then he bade her meet him tomorrow at the same place, at the same hour, promising to bring her money to buy a new pitcher. The child ran away very happy, reposing perfect confidence in the stranger's word to her.

Tomorrow he was invited to dine with the queen at the very hour of his appointment with the child. But he promptly declined the invitation. He would not fail in his word, even to an unknown child of poverty. She had trusted him, and his promise had made her happy. He would not disappoint her for a thousand dinners with royalty! Will God be less faithful to his Word? No Word he has spoken shall ever be broken!

November 25.

"It has been granted to you on behalf of Christ, not only to believe on him, but also to suffer for him." Philippians 1:29

We cannot know in what way we can best glorify God. It may be in *hard work*; it may be in *quiet waiting*; it may be in *painful suffering*. It is better, therefore, that we let *God* choose the way in which he would have us serve and honor him.

The *bird* glorifies God—by singing its sweet song; the flower glorifies God—by pouring out its fragrance. Mary praised Christ—by sitting at his feet, Martha—by serving him. If we simply obey his will—that will always be the best.

November 20.

"If he offers it as an expression of thankfulness" Leviticus 7:12

The idea of this offering was, that when there was any special favor shown or blessing received, the heart's gratitude should express itself in this way. If the ship arrived safely through the storm, the passenger, as soon as he reached the shore, hastened to present his thank-offering. If one recovered from a dangerous sickness, his first walk abroad was to the tabernacle with his sacrifice. Should we not bring some new gift to God's altar—after every recovery from sickness, every deliverance from danger, every new kindness enjoyed?

There is a story of a Scotch mother whose child was stolen away by an eagle. Almost crazed, she saw the bird soar away to its eyrie far up the cliff. No one could scale the crag. The mother went to her room and prayed. An old sailor climbed the cliff, and crept down with the child. As the mother was still praying, with outstretched hands and shut eyes—he softly laid the babe on her arms and vanished. Rising in silence, she did not even kiss her little one, until she had carried it to the church and solemnly given it to God. Should not every life given back again, every joy plucked from death and restored, as well as every new blessing granted, be given to God in solemn dedication before it is put to any other use?

November 27

"In everything I did, I showed you that by this kind of hard work we must help the weak, remembering the words the Lord Jesus himself said: 'It is more blessed to give than to receive.' " Acts 20:35

All Christians are brethren. When one suffers—the others should share the pain. Fortunate people should not forget the unfortunate people. There are some of God's other children who are sick—while you are well; some who are hungry or cold—while you have plenty of bread and are warmly clad; some who are in sorrow—while you have joy; some who are orphaned and homeless—while you have home and friends. You, in your comfort and gladness, should not forget those who are in adversity. Keep your heart open toward them. Watch for opportunities to do good to them.

Remember what Jesus said about the judgment day—that the places on his right hand will be for those who have fed the hungry, given drink to the thirsty, clothed the naked, visited the sick, the perishing, and the suffering, and that to these he will say, "Inasmuch as you have done it unto one of the least of these my brethren—you have done it unto me!"

November 28.

"For we are to God the aroma of Christ among those who are being saved and those who are perishing. To the one we are the smell of death; to the other, the fragrance of life! And who is equal to such a task?" 2 Corinthians 2:15-16

The consciousness that others trust us—is one of the strongest possible motives to faithfulness. We dare not fail, when we feel the pressure of other lives upon us; for if we faint, or falter, or prove untrue—we shall draw them down with us. When a man has lived in such a way as to win the confidence and become the guide of others—he bears a responsibility which he can meet only by unalterable fidelity. Every **word** of his is believed and rested upon. What if he speaks an untrue word, a word which misrepresents the divine teaching!

His **example**, too, is of infinite importance. Others believe in him so unquestionably, that anything they know him to do—they will regard as right and will feel at liberty to do themselves. But what if it is not right?

It is a weighty burden which a man bears—who has become trusted teacher, guide, and friend of others. If he is not faithful to his sacred obligation, he misrepresents Christ, and hurts the lives that lean upon him. To know that one stands for God to certain human souls, and is set to do God's work, to be the very *hand of God* to lead, or hold up, or lift up struggling, fainting souls—is enough to crush the strongest, bravest heart, if God is not real to it in his love, power, and presence.

November 29.

"But we have this treasure in earthen vessels, that the exceeding greatness of the power may be of God, and not from ourselves!" 2 Corinthians 4:7

Earthly success is not the test of spiritual life. Sometimes *failure* is better than *success!* God can do more with our weakness—than with our strength. Paul learned that when he was weak in himself—then he was strong, because then the strength of Christ rested on him in fuller measure. Sometimes we do more effective work, when we seem to fail—than when we appear to get through victoriously. Many a preacher has learned that his best sermons are not those he thinks the best. Ofttimes when he has failed in making his discourse, it has accomplished more than any of his finer sermons on which he prided himself.

It has been said that some of the greatest treasures in heaven—will be the *blunders* which God's children have made, when trying to show their love. A mother said that the most sacred treasure in her home was a puckered handkerchief which her little girl, now in heaven, had tried to hem for her.

November 30.

"All the widows stood around him, crying and showing him the robes and other clothing that Dorcas had made while she was still with them." Acts 9:39

A good many people have to die—to be appreciated. They go through the world living quietly, devoted to the interests of those who are dear to them, seeking no recognition. They are merely commonplace people, and so are allowed to love and serve without appreciation.

But one day they are missed from their accustomed place—their work on earth is done—and they are gone! Then the *empty place* reveals the value of the blessing they have been. In their absence, people learn for the first time the value of the services they had been accustomed to receive from them.

DECEMBER

December 1.

"Therefore do not worry about tomorrow, for tomorrow will bring its own worries. Today's trouble is enough for today." Matthew 6:34

One reason our Lord gives for not worrying about the future—is that we have nothing to do with it. Each day has its own duties, its own needs, its own trials and temptations; and God always gives us strength enough 'for the day'. We must not drag in tomorrow's cares, and add them to today's—for our strength will not be enough, for God will not add to the day's portion of strength, just to humor our whims of anxiety.

So the lesson is, that we should keep the days fenced off, each one by itself. Do today's duty, fight today's temptation, and do not weaken and distract yourself by looking forward to things which you cannot see, and could not understand if you saw them. When tomorrow comes—it will bring its own strength. "As your days—so shall your strength be." Deuteronomy 33:25

December 2.

"Go away for now. When it is more convenient, I will call for you again." Acts 24:25

This the way men are continually acting. They *hear* the truth and *feel* its power—but put off *action*. Felix was not true to his own best interests. He was not honest with himself. He saw the wrong in his own life; he had a glimpse of the judgment; he was terrified; he knew what he ought to do—yet he put the matter off. He did not doubt the truth of what Paul said, he did not actually reject the Savior Paul offered; he merely *postponed action*. Some other time, he would find it more convenient to adjust his life to the requisite condition.

This is a well-trodden highway, and there always are thousands upon it. They believe the Word of God, and are terrified when they think of the solemn facts of eternity. They mean to turn and be saved—but they put it off. There will be a more convenient season by and by. It is a terribly mistaken way to go. The best time to repent and be saved—is always NOW. A more convenient season will never come. Countless thousands have been lost by saying *tomorrow* when they should have said *today*.

December 3.

"This is the man who teaches against our people and tells everybody to disobey the Jewish laws. He speaks against the Temple—and he even defiles it by bringing Gentiles in!" Acts 21:28

This was a case of gross misrepresentation. Paul had never uttered a word against either the Jewish people, the law, or the temple. They had perverted and distorted his words—into meanings he never thought of. Many people thus take the words of others, give a wrong sense to them, and then repeat them!

Misrepresentation is a grievous sin. Many a calumny that destroys a fair name, grows from a mere misstatement, an inexact reporting of something said or done. We should be scrupulously careful, if we must repeat what others say, that we state the precise truth. No fault of speech is more common—than lack of accuracy in quoting. Most people's ears seem to hear with a bias in favor of their own prejudices; then in reporting what they have heard, the bias is too apt to show its influence a second time in *emphasizing the distortion*.

Besides, when a story travels as far as from Ephesus to Jerusalem, and passes through a number of ears and tongues, it is scarcely to be expected that it will arrive just the same as it started. It is proverbial, that stories grow in frequent repetition. Paul is not the only person who has not recognized at all his own words after they had gone the rounds. Let us learn the virtue of *accuracy*. Inaccuracy is lying!

December 4.

"Having loved *His own* who were in the world—He loved them unto the end!" John 13:1

His own! How sweet the words are! They tell of a close and most sacred relation. His own! We belong to him, not simply as property—but in the ownership of love. "You are not your own, for you are bought with a price." The prints of the nails— tell of the cost of our redemption. We are "His own" because the Father gave us to Him. "They were Yours—and You gave them to Me!" Then we are "His own" because we have voluntarily given ourselves to Him. That is what you did when you became a Christian. You accepted the love that claimed you.

The relation is like that between two friends. The world cannot intermeddle. It is a close, personal relation. All believers are Christ's own—but there is a sense in which each one has all of Christ for himself. We all sit down at the same communion table and the banner of love is over all; yet each one has a whole communion of his own. The sun shines upon the broad field and bathes all the million grass-blades and flowers in his beams. But each blade and each flower can say, "The sun is mine; he shines for me!" Christ's love is for all his church; but the smallest of his little ones can say, "He is my Friend, my Savior, my Master!" "We are Christ's own." All of Christ is ours—all of his love and all of his grace.

December 5.

"Blessed is the man whose transgressions are forgiven, whose sins are covered!" Psalm 32:1

True blessedness can ever come to anyone—until forgiveness has come. Unforgiven sin lies as a heavy curse upon a life. No other favor or prosperity is of any avail while sin remains uncancelled. But with forgiveness, comes all the blessedness of life and glory. When we are forgiven, we become at once God's children, heirs of God, and joint heirs with Christ to all the rich inheritance of eternal life. All the blessings of salvation are in this one.

We may study also with profit the word "cover." There is one way of covering sin which brings no blessing. We must not try to cover our own sin. "He who covers his sins shall not prosper; but whoever confesses and forsakes them shall have mercy." Sins that *we* cover—are not put away. They are like the quiet fires in the volcano, ready to burst out any moment in all their terribleness. But when *God* covers our sins they are put out of sight forever out of our sight, the world's sight, God's sight.

In one place God says he will remember our sins against us no more. The covering is complete and final. The sins are covered by the atonement of Christ. "All we like sheep have gone astray; and the Lord has laid on him the iniquities of us all." If our sins were laid on Jesus Christ—they are covered forever, and will never rise up against us.

December 6.

"He got up from the meal, took off his outer clothing, and wrapped a towel around his waist. After that, he poured water into a basin and began to wash his disciples' feet, drying them with the towel that was wrapped around him." John 13:4-5

There are many pictures of Jesus the Holy Child in the manger, the Redeemer on the cross, the Conqueror with the keys—but none of them surpasses that of the *servant with the towel and basin*. We get the lesson of *service*. Jesus did not think his holy hands too fine for the washing of the feet of the twelve men who sat around the table. Many of us think we are too fine in the texture of our being, or too high in our rank among men, to stoop to lowly service like this! This picture of the Christ is a New Testament answer to all such pride and pretension.

Our service should be personal. Christ washed the feet of his disciples with his own hands. Too many like to do all their serving by proxy. They believe in washing feet—but they get some other person to do it for them. They will pay something to a missionary to visit and relieve the poor or the sick—but will not do the work with their own hands. This is not what Christ's example teaches us. We would better do the serving ourselves.

December 7.

Jesus replied, "You do not realize now what I am doing, but later you will understand." John 13:7

It is never wise for us to pass judgment on any of *God's providences*, while we can read but a part of their meaning. No work can be fairly judged, while it is only in progress. We must wait until it is completed. As the end must sometimes lie far out of sight, whether it be in future years of earthly life, or in the unrevealed life beyond earth's horizon—we need to train ourselves to trust the goodness and the love of God, believing that he will do only what is right—and what is best also for us. It is faith alone can give us peace.

December 8.

"Everyone should be quick to listen, *slow to speak* and slow to become angry" James 1:19

We ought to think twice before we speak. Sometimes we are advised if we are feeling unkindly, to count ten before we open our mouth. Yet hasty words ofttimes fly from our lips in the moment of excited feeling; and before we have time to think twice, or count half of ten, the harm is done, the sharp word has flashed like a dart into some gentle heart.

These hasty words are spoken, too, most frequently between those who love each other. We control our speech fairly well when it is with strangers, or ordinary acquaintances we are speaking; but with those we love best—we are less careful. We let our worry or our weariness make us irritable, and then we utter the hasty words which five minutes afterward, we would give all we have to recall. But such words never can be recalled. They may be forgiven, for love forgives until seventy times seven times; but the wounds, the scars, remain.

December 9.

"So God said to him, "Since you have asked for this and not for long life or wealth for yourself, nor have asked for the death of your enemies but for discernment in administering justice—I will do what you have asked. I will give you a wise and discerning heart." 1 Kings 3:11-12

The Lord approved the choice Solomon had made. It was an *unselfish* choice. He was thinking of his people, and wanted to be a good king. It was a *spiritual* choice—not gold, power, victory, and fame—but wisdom to qualify him for duty, to fit him for fulfilling well his mission. Such a choice always pleases God. He loves to have us choose the *best* things.

James says that the reason men ask and receive not—is because they ask that they may consume God's gifts on their lusts. The prayer of *selfishness* is never pleasing to God; but he is pleased when we ask for things to be used in blessing others. The prayer for mere earthly things, may really be for a curse upon our life. Midas desired the power to change whatever he touched into gold. His request was granted; and the fruits he plucked, and the food he would put into his mouth—all turned to gold, until in the agonies of starvation he was compelled to cry for the withdrawal of the power. It was a curse, not a blessing to him.

So it is with those who live only for wealth; they get it, but their souls are starving! Solomon asked for wisdom only, and left all other matters to God's own choice. Jesus said, "Seek first the kingdom of God and his righteousness, and all these things shall be added unto you."

December 10

"I had it in my heart to build a house for the Name of the LORD my God. But this word of the LORD came to me: You are not to build a house for my Name." 1 Chronicles 22:7-8

God was pleased with David's *desire*, but it was not David's work to build a temple. His part was to conquer the country, and gather materials for the house. Sometimes the things we purpose to do—we are not permitted to accomplish. They belong to some other worker who is to come after us, and are not part of our mission at all.

There are many people called to do *preparatory* work. A man goes to the West, and clears off a piece of ground, building a crude log hut. His son succeeds him, and in the midst of broad, rich acres erects a palatial home. The father's work was just as important in its place, though not so conspicuous, as the son's. One set of men make the excavations for a building, and then put in the foundations. For weeks they toil underground; and then another set of men come, the walls rise up, and the magnificent building attracts all eyes. The *foundation* work is buried out of sight, but who will say that it is less important than the splendid walls that tower above the street?

But for what David did, Solomon never could have built the temple. It is the same in all life. To each one God allots a place and a part; and if we do that which God gives us to do, he asks nothing more.

December 11.

"This is what the LORD Almighty says: 'If you will walk in my ways and keep my requirements, then you will govern my house and have charge of my courts, and I will give you a place among these standing here." Zechariah 3:7

The way to rise to higher places—is to be faithful where we are. Unless we do well, the smaller things which God gives us to do—he will not entrust greater things to us. The man who was faithful and diligent in the use of his two talents, saw the two become four, and found himself put in trust also with new responsibilities. The promise here was, that *if* this good priest would walk in God's ways, and keep his charge—he would have influence and power in God's house, and should stand among angels.

This latter is a remarkable promise. It seems to mean that even on the earth, those who are faithful in holy things, shall have fellowship with angels. They may not be conscious of the companionship amid which they stand, but really they are working alongside spiritual beings continually while they wait upon God.

Then, those who serve God faithfully and diligently in holy things in this world will be received into the good fellowship of angels in the other world. The lesson, however, is that faithfulness in the common duties of the passing days is the one thing of life with us. If we live thus, God will lead us step by step, even into larger service and greater usefulness, as he may find us ready. We need not worry about our promotion; the only real promotion is that which comes through fidelity.

December 12.

"The entire Israelite community *grumbled* against Moses and Aaron in the wilderness!" Exodus 16:2

As soon as the people of Israel got away from the visible means of sustenance, they lost heart. It is strange, we say, that so soon they could have forgotten all God's wonderful deliverances in the past.

But are *we* any more trustful? We sing and are joyful while things go well; and then when affliction or need come—away go the song and the joy! There is a great deal of *murmuring* still done—when *pleasant Elims* have to be left for *wilderness wanderings*. How much happier we would be, if we had learned to walk by faith rather than by sight! A promise of God really is a great deal better security for provision in life, than any quantity of food in store, or any amount of money in the bank. Nothing in this world is so real—as are the invisible things of God's love. If we are his children—we may trust him absolutely, no matter how dreary the desert may be!

December 13.

"Moses alone shall come near unto the Lord. The others must not come near. And the people may not come up with him." Exodus 24:2

There are always some who are admitted to closer intimacy with Christ than others. In his first disciple family, John came nearest. The way is open, however, for all to come as near as they will. Yet it is not height on earth's hills, that takes us closest to him. Those are greatest in the kingdom of heaven—so the Master said—who are most like children; also those who serve the most sweetly and unselfishly. In the Psalm, too, when the question is asked, "Who shall ascend into the hill of the Lord?" the answer is, "He who has clean hands and a pure heart."

Getting up in the world—may not be getting up toward God; yet we may rise toward God, and that surely is infinitely the worthiest aspiration of an immortal soul. Moses was called up near to God that he might get blessings to carry down to the people. Those who get closer to God than others—are always privileged to become blessings to the world. God fills their hands with gifts that they are to distribute, and reveals to them precious things that they are to communicate to others.

December 14.

"All of you, clothe yourselves with humility toward one another, because, "God opposes the proud but gives grace to the humble." 1 Peter 5:5

What is humility? It is not thinking lowly of one's self. It is not a voluntary humbling of one's self for any particular purpose. It is the spirit which is ready always to use its best powers and its richest gifts—in the lowliest service of love. Love is at the heart of it. When we truly love others—we are interested in them, and will do them any service they need, however hard or costly or lowly it may be, not considering ourselves too fine to serve them, nor any possession of ours too good to be used in their behalf.

It is not the lowly place in which one lives and works which makes one humble. One may be proud, and move in a very obscure sphere. Humility is in the spirit, not in the station.

December 15.

"My little children, we must not love in word or speech—but in deed and truth!" 1 John 3:18

More and more are Christian people learning that true religion must have adequate and fitting expression in the life. A *sound creed* and activity in Christian work, are not the best tests of Christlikeness. It is in Christian character, and in the exercise of the spiritual graces in life's contacts—that Christian culture finds its finest expression.

To put it more simply, love is the true measure of Christian life. Becoming a Christian is simply letting the love of God into the heart. This love is something which cannot be hidden. If the love of God is in the heart—it will work its way out in the life! So it always does. The love of God dwells not in a man—who does not love his neighbor. The nearer we come to the heart of Christ, the deeper and tenderer becomes our interest in our brothers and sisters.

December 16.

"Buy the truth—and do not sell it; get wisdom, discipline and understanding." Proverbs 23:23

It is not with money that we buy the truth; the price we must pay is our self-will, our pride, our self-confidence. We ought, however, to yield ourselves utterly to the truth, and should do it promptly. He who will not pay any price, however great, to be true—is losing where he seems to be saving.

There is a legend of King Tarquin and the sibyl. The old woman came into the king's presence with *nine* large books, containing prophecies and counsels concerning Rome. She offered them for sale, but asked a price so high, that the king hesitated to buy them. "Wait until tomorrow," said the king. Next day she came again, but with only *six* books, having destroyed three; and for the six she asked twice as much as she had asked for the nine. Tarquin again declined to purchase, and the woman again withdrew. Once more she came, this time with only *three* of the volumes, and asking a yet higher price! Tarquin dared delay no longer, and purchased the books at the cost of half his treasure, for they were of great value to him.

Likewise, the truth is offered to us, but at a high price. If we delay, less and less is offered to us, and it ever costs us more to buy. The best time to begin to buy God's truth—is in gentle youth. We *buy* it when we *live* it, no matter at what sacrifice.

December 17.

"He was despised and rejected by men." Isaiah 53:3

The saddest thing about the life of Christ—was the rejection he met among those he had come to bless. He came with a great love in his heart. He wanted to do them good, to draw them away from their sins, to make them love God, to lead them to heaven. "He came unto his own—and his own received him not." He went to their doors and knocked, and they kept their doors shut upon him; and he had to go away with his gifts and blessings unbestowed, leaving "his own" in their sin and sorrow.

It is the same yet. Christ comes with treasures of life and glory, which he offers to all; but men and women pay no heed to his knocking and his calls, and he has to pass on. "He is despised and rejected." He never forces his blessings on any. He knocks, but we must open the door. He will never open it himself.

In Holman Hunt's picture, "The Light of the World," the door has no knob on the outside; it can be opened only from within. You can keep the omnipotent Christ outside your heart if you will; you do keep him out by simply not rising to open to him. It does not need dishonoring sins, nor any violent rejection of the Savior, to make one a lost sinner; the mildest and gentlest *indifference* to his knocking and call—will do it just as effectually.

December 18.

"Boldly and without hindrance he preached the kingdom of God and taught about the Lord Jesus Christ." Acts 28:31

This is the last glimpse the book of Acts gives us of Paul. The glorious apostle appears as a prisoner, though keeping open house and receiving all who came to him. No doubt many came to him with their questions, their burdens, their sorrows. Men with gentle spirit and deep and wide sympathies become a blessing to many people in the world. Those whose hearts are hungry, or who are under the shadow of grief or of sin, turn to them with eagerness, as thirsty animals turn to springs of water. That was the kind of man Paul was, and no doubt many came to him with their needs. He had something they had not. He listened to them patiently, and sympathized with them tenderly.

But notice also, the kind of help he gave to those who came. He preached the kingdom of God and taught about the Lord Jesus Christ. He fed their hunger with the bread of heaven. He pointed them to the only source of comfort. He presented Christ to them as the only One who could help them and bless them. We have nothing in ourselves to give to those who come seeking help or comfort. We can only point them to the Savior!

These prison days of Paul were among the most fruitful of his whole ministry. Likewise, we may make our *shut-in days* full of good for the world.

December 19.

"He went on his way rejoicing!" Acts 8:39

He did not give up his journey and decide to go back among the other Christians, because he was now a believer. He went on his way to his own country and to his own business; but he had a new secret of joy in his heart. Part of the duty of this new convert was to carry the knowledge of Christ back to the people among whom he had been living. He had found something which they needed, and which would bless them as it had blessed him.

We learn that a new-born Christian is not to give up his work. Of course, if he is engaged in any sinful occupation he must give it up. But if his occupation is right, he is usually to stick to it, and carry Christ with him into it. A carpenter when converted, is to continue a carpenter—with Christ.

To be a Christian, makes one happy. This man went on his way rejoicing. His heart was full of song. The Christian goes on in his work day by day; but while he works his heart sings, and the songs make the way shorter and the burdens lighter for him, while at the same time they give cheer to others on whose ears they fall.

December 20.

"The Spirit and the bride say, "Come!" And let him who hears say, "Come!" Whoever is thirsty, let him come; and whoever wishes, let him take the free gift of the water of life!" Revelation 22:17

A great novelist tells of a child that had run away from her home. Every night when it grew dark, a candle was set in the window, to show to the lost one, if ever she crept back repentant, that love's place was kept for her within. The Bible seems to me like a great palace standing in the center of a dark world. It has a thousand windows; and in everyone of them a bright light shines, to tell earth's lost ones of a home where they will find a welcome if they but come to its door.

December 21

"He who is righteous—let him do righteousness still." Revelation 22:11

The life in the eternal world—will not be different from the life here. The same good things we have learned to do here—we shall continue to do there. Those who have learned here to do righteousness shall continue, in the other life, to do righteousness. We shall still obey God there, and do his will; only we shall be more obedient than we have been here, and shall do his will better—perfectly! We shall love God there with all our heart, and love each other as ourselves; our life there shall be a perfect brotherhood, and heaven shall be a perfect home. It will still be more blessed there to give than to receive. They will still be chief there, who shall serve. Love, joy, peace, long-suffering, meekness, gentleness, goodness, truth—will still be fruits of the Spirit there—as they are here.

Life in heaven will not be so strange to us as we think, if we have learned to do God's will in this world. The everlasting life begins the moment we believe on Christ. While we remain on this earthly sphere, it is hindered and hampered by the limitations of earth, but in all true Christian experiences there are intimations of what the full blessedness will be. When we reach heaven the life begun here will go on, only without hindrance, limitation, or imperfection, forever. We are taught to pray that the will of God may be done on earth—as it is in heaven. Thus we are to get ready here for heaven.

December 22.

"It is more blessed to give than to receive." Acts 20:35

We shall have a happier Christmas for ourselves, if we have helped to make a little joy for some others. We give presents to our friends—and that is right; but if we would get the richest blessing from our giving, we must remember also some one who really needs our gift: feeding some hungry one, or sending clothing to one who is shivering in the cold. This is the giving that is more blessed than receiving.

December 23.

"Silver or gold I do not have—but what I have I give you." Acts 3:6

Someone once said, "It's very hard to know how to help people—when you can't send them blankets, or coal, or needed food." With many people this is very true. They know not how to help others, except in such ways. Yet the needs which these material things satisfy, are the *smallest* needs of human lives. There are better ways of helping: with sympathy, hope, cheer, courage, inspiration, comfort. These are the blessings which most people need, far more than they need blankets or coal or food.

So far as we know, Jesus gave no money. He did not have it to give. Yet there never was in this world another such dispenser of true charity as he was. He gave encouragement, instruction, love. He told people of higher things.

None of us are too poor to give help in the same way. We may not have silver and gold to bestow, but out of a warm heart we can give *coins of love* which will mean far more than money! We should always keep a gentle heart—and then we can be a blessing to many.

December 24.

"I bring you good news of great joy that will be for all the people!" Luke 2:10

If we are sitting in peace and joy, our hearts filled with sweet Christmas thoughts, we should remember those whose homes will be dark and sad tomorrow, when all over the land the bells will be ringing. Perhaps we can do little to give them comfort; but we can *pray* for them, and thus call down blessings upon them. For, after all, the best way to send blessings to people—is through God. He has thousands of messengers, and he can always send the blessings of his love, where we can send a kindly wish.

December 25.

"On coming to the house, they saw the child with his mother Mary, and they bowed down and worshiped him. Then they opened their treasures and presented him with gifts of gold and of incense and of myrrh." Matthew 2:11

They were not content merely to worship the King, showing him homage in word or in posture; but they also laid their gifts at his feet. It is not enough for us to sing our songs of praise to Christ, to bow before him in reverent worship, and to speak our heart's homage in words. We should bring our gifts too, the pledges of our love, to lay at his feet.

There is a great deal of mere *sentimentality* in the consecration of many people. It is sentiment only; and when there is call for gifts or sacrifices, or for real services—the sentiment instantly vanishes. People sing missionary hymns with great warmth, and when the collection-plate comes to them—they sing on but allow the plate to pass by. They make prayers that God would send laborers into his vineyard, but they do not themselves respond to God's call for laborers and errand-runners. We need to learn the lesson: that our *singing* and *praying* can never go beyond our*living*.

Not only did these magi bring gifts, but they brought rich and costly gifts; we should bring our best—our gold, incense, and myrrh—the alabaster box of our heart's deepest love, and the best of all our life and service. Too often we give Christ only what is *left over* after we have taken all we desire for self-indulgence, or for the promotion of our own ambitions. We should always let him have the best!

December 26.

"And he will send his angels and gather his *elect* from the four winds, from the ends of the earth to the ends of the heavens." Mark 13:27

There is no danger that in the last day, that anyone will be overlooked or forgotten who has been a true follower of Christ. The obscurest Christian, hidden away in the lowliest or most neglected spot, will not be missed by the angels, when they come to gather in Christ's little ones. On nearly every battle-field where the slain are buried, there are graves marked by the sad word "Unknown." But if among these, there are those who belonged to Christ, the angels will not fail to find them and bring them.

A ship went down on the British coast, and all on board perished. None of the bodies of those who had been lost were found, except the little body of an infant that was washed ashore among the wreckage. The kindly people of the place who picked it up buried the body, and having no clew to its name, put on the little stone simply, "God knows." When the angels come they will know whose body it is, and will not overlook it.

There is only one thing about which we need to concern ourselves, that we are indeed of those who have accepted Christ and have been faithful to him in this life.

It will not matter in that day whether we have been rich or poor, famous among men or unknown; the determining element will be, whether or not we have belonged to Christ.

December 27.

"That all of them may be one, Father, just as you are in me and I am in you. May they also be in us so that the world may believe that you have sent me." John 17:21

The nearer we get to God, and the more of the spirit of Christ there is in us, the less will we, too, think of the things that divide, and the more of the things that bind us together. When we get home to heaven—we shall see how trivial were the things that divided us here, ofttimes keeping us far apart, and what possibilities of fellowship we missed as we journeyed heavenward.

December 28.

"Returning the third time, he said to them, Are you still sleeping and resting? Enough! The hour has come. Look, the Son of Man is betrayed into the hands of sinners!" Mark 14:41

We need to learn the importance of *timeliness in duty*. There are many things which if done today, will prove untold blessings—but which tomorrow, it will not be worth while to do. It is today the sick neighbor needs your visit, your help; tomorrow he may be well, or others shall have ministered to him, or he may be dead. It is today that the tempted one needs your cheer; tomorrow he may be defeated, lying in the dust of shame. *Tomorrow* is a fatal word; countless thousands of hopes have been wrecked on it.

December 29.

"Teach us to number our days aright, that we may gain a heart of wisdom." Psalm 90:12

There are several ways of numbering our days. One way is merely to count them off as we tear off the daily leaves of our calendar. Each evening a man has one day less to live. But that is not true numbering. Another, way is merely to count the days into the aggregate of life. A man is one day older, but that is all. He is no better. He has left no worthy record on the day's page. The true numbering, is that which fills the days as they pass—with records of godly and beautiful living, and with lines of growth in character.

Just now we are looking back over the story of a closing year. What have we given the days to keep for us? What lessons of wisdom have we learned from them, as one by one they have passed? There is little good in worrying over the failures of the year—but we ought to learn from our past. He is the wise man, not who makes no mistakes—but who does not repeat his mistakes.

December 30.

"Jesus Christ is the same yesterday and today and forever!" Hebrews 13:8

We leave many things behind us, as we go on. We can never go back again over the closing year. We never go over any life-path a second time. We never pass a second time through any experience. We have infancy once, childhood once, youth once, manhood and womanhood once, old age once, and we die once. We are forever *leaving* things, places, conditions, and experiences behind us. But through all these, we have the same Christ, unchanged, unchanging.

The Christ of childhood and of youth remains the Christ of manhood and of old age. Whatever changes the years bring to us—we must ever keep our eyes on the living Christ. He will always be all we need. There will never be a path which he cannot find for us and show us. There will never be a dark valley which he cannot light up for us. There will never be a battle which he cannot fight for us. There will never be an experience through which he cannot safely take us. We are leaving the old year behind, but we are not leaving Christ in the dead year. We need not be afraid, therefore, to go forward, if we go with him. We have not passed this new way before, and it is all strange to our inexperience; but Christ knows and he will guide us, and all will be well—if we put our hand in his.

December 31.

"One thing I do: Forgetting what is behind and straining toward what is ahead, I press on." Philippians 3:13-14

There is a proper use of past experiences. We should remember our past lost condition—to keep our hearts ever humble. We should remember the lessons learned from past experience so as to profit by our mistakes. The true science of living—is not to make no mistakes, which is impossible—but not to commit the same mistakes a second time.

We should remember past mercies and blessings. If we do, our past will shine down upon us like a sky full of stars. Such remembering of the past will keep the gratitude ever fresh in our heart, and the incense of praise ever burning on the altar. Such a *house of memory* becomes a refuge to which we may flee in trouble. When sorrows gather thickly; when trials come on like the waves of the sea; when the sun goes down and every star is quenched, and there seems nothing bright in all the present—then the memory of a past full of goodness, a past in which God never once failed us, becomes a holy refuge for us, a refuge gemmed and lighted by the lamps of other and brighter days. Thus there are *right uses* of the past.

But there is a sense in which we should altogether forget our past. It is unwise to live looking back. We should keep our eyes ever turned forward to new hopes, new attainments, new achievements!

Made in the USA
Lexington, KY
19 July 2016